Happy 5th anniver

Love, Hilary + Jeff, Kenny, Morgan

"She was a dear friend, a remarkable politician, and a compassionate humanitarian. Many of us benefitted from her counsel, and our communities and our world have been enriched by her compassion."
David Johnston, former governor general of Canada

"[Flora MacDonald was] a great Canadian whose leadership and compassion will be sorely missed."
Justin Trudeau, prime minister of Canada

"For a single woman from North Sydney to accomplish what she did in the highly competitive male-oriented world in those days is remarkable and she did it on her own."
Brian Mulroney, former prime minister of Canada

"Flora was a contagious example of how much good an active, committed individual can accomplish and inspire."
Joe Clark, former prime minister of Canada

"Flora was the real McCoy – warm, spontaneous, and gutsy. She loved the world in all its diversity, and yet strived to make it more just. She was a gem."
Ed Broadbent, former leader of the New Democratic Party

"Canada has lost a great humanitarian, exemplary parliamentarian, and wonderful leader."
Elizabeth May, former leader of the Green Party

"[Flora] demonstrated that any career was possible – even for a girl from Whitney Pier. She cleared our path and I am grateful."
Lisa Raitt, former deputy leader of the opposition

"Flora was the true, essential trailblazer for the women of her era."
Senator Donna Dasko, co-founder of Equal Voice

"Fighting for justice and fairness were her vocation. She would work for the rights of every person who had been denied them, whether they be in small town Canada or in war zones around our troubled world."
Maureen McTeer, Ottawa Citizen

"Flora was inspirational, a force of nature, one of those people who changed the course of history."

Daniel Taylor, founder of Future Generations International

"Minister MacDonald was instrumental in saving tens of thousands of South Vietnamese by developing a federal matching program to sponsor and rescue 'boat people' from inhumane refugee camps.
We are forever grateful."

Phat Nguyen, president, Toronto Vietnamese Association

"Flora [MacDonald] travelled to Bamyan many times at great personal risk to develop schools for girls, and promote women's local leadership ... Her efforts are the embodiment of Canada's commitment to the rights of women and girls."

Statement from the Embassy of Canada to Afghanistan

"When it came to doing God's work on earth, Flora walked the talk."

Senator (retired) Lowell Murray

FLORA!

The 1979 Progressive Conservative Cabinet at Rideau Hall – Canada's youngest prime minister (Joe Clark), first Black minister (Lincoln Alexander), first female foreign minister (Flora MacDonald).

From left, front row: John C. Crosbie, Erik Nielsen, Flora MacDonald, Martial Asselin, Joe Clark, Governor General Edward Schreyer, Jacques Flynn, Walter Baker, James A. McGrath, Allan F. Lawrence, David S.H. MacDonald
Back row: Ronald Huntington, Ronald Atkey, Jacob Epp, John A. Fraser, John Wise, W. Heward Grafftey, J. Robert Howie, Roch La Salle, Lincoln Alexander, Donald Mazankowski, Steven Paproski, William Jarvis, Allan McKinnon, Elmer MacKay, Perrin Beatty, Sinclair Stevens, Robert de Cotret, David Crombie, Ramon Hnatyshyn, Michael H. Wilson. *Library and Archives Canada/Ted Grant fonds/e010764784. Credit: Ted Grant.*

Flora!

A Woman in a Man's World

FLORA MACDONALD

AND GEOFFREY STEVENS

McGill-Queen's University Press

Montreal & Kingston • London • Chicago

ISBN 978-0-2280-0862-0 (cloth)
ISBN 978-0-2280-0900-9 (ePDF)
ISBN 978-0-2280-0989-4 (ePUB)

Legal deposit fourth quarter 2021
Bibliothèque nationale du Québec

Printed in Canada on acid-free paper that is 100% ancient forest free
(100% post-consumer recycled), processed chlorine free

Funded by the   Financé par le
Government   gouvernement
of Canada   du Canada

Canada Council   Conseil des arts
for the Arts   du Canada

We acknowledge the support of the Canada Council for the Arts.
Nous remercions le Conseil des arts du Canada de son soutien.

Library and Archives Canada Cataloguing in Publication

Title: Flora! : a woman in a man's world / Flora MacDonald and Geoffrey Stevens.
Names: MacDonald, Flora, 1926–2015, author. | Stevens, Geoffrey, 1940– author.
Description: Includes bibliographical references and index.
Identifiers: Canadiana (print) 20210226757 | Canadiana (ebook) 20210226935
| ISBN 9780228008620 (hardcover) | ISBN 9780228009009 (PDF) | ISBN
9780228009894 (ePUB)
Subjects: LCSH: MacDonald, Flora, 1926-2015. | LCSH: Women politicians—
Canada—Biography. | LCSH: Politicians—Canada—Biography. | LCSH:
Women legislators—Canada—Biography. | LCSH: Legislators—Canada—
Biography. | LCSH: Women human rights workers—Canada—Biography. |
LCSH: Human rights workers—Canada—Biography. | LCSH: Canada—
Politics and government—20th century. | LCGFT: Autobiographies.
Classification: LCC FC626.M32 A3 2021 | DDC 971.064/4092—dc23

This book was typeset in 10.5/13 Sabon.

For my father Fred MacDonald who taught me that girls are as good as boys and, given opportunity, there is nothing a woman cannot accomplish in a world controlled by men. – F.M.

For my wife Lin Clarkson Stevens who lived through the telling of this tale, but not long enough to see it published. – G.S.

Contents

FLORA!

Introduction

Flora Isabel MacDonald – adventurer, politician, humanitarian – known across Canada and beyond simply as "Flora," died on 26 July 2015 at the age of eighty-nine.

Hers was an amazing ride. It was a journey that took Flora from secretarial school in Cape Breton to the inner sanctum of the Tory party in Ottawa, to the federal cabinet as Canada's minister of Foreign Affairs, to Mount Everest (which she attempted climb when she was sixty-eight), and, ultimately, to personal fulfillment as an unpaid volunteer teaching life skills to impoverished villagers in the mountain valleys of Afghanistan. It was a journey driven by Flora's lifelong conviction that girls are as good as boys, and, given opportunity, there is nothing a woman cannot achieve in a world controlled by men.

She inspired a generation of Canadian women by pursuing that conviction in everything she did – whether it was carving a path for women in the House of Commons, running for the leadership of her party, exposing the inhumane treatment of inmates at Kingston's notorious Prison for Women, working with AIDS victims and survivors in Africa, or calling the Soviet Union to account at the United Nations over its backstage role in causing the refugee crisis in Southeast Asia after the Vietnam War. (She was undaunted when the Soviet delegation walked to protest her speech or when the UN secretary general reprimanded her for causing such a fuss.)

"Flora was daring," says political scientist John Meisel, her friend and mentor at Queen's University. "She tackled things other people didn't have the guts to try." The American humanitarian Daniel Taylor called her "a force of nature, one of those people who changed the course of history." Her friend and cabinet colleague Lowell Murray put it this way: "When it came to doing God's work on earth, Flora walked the talk." Not everyone agreed. Her nemesis John Diefenbaker dismissed her as "the finest woman to ever walk the streets of Kingston." But if the old "Chief" thought the insult would devastate her, he did not know Flora. She was delighted and amused, and she used the line to warm up crowds in her election campaigns in Kingston and The Islands.

This book is Flora's account of her life's journey, told in her own words.

Let me explain. I had known Flora since the mid-1960s, when I was a young reporter in the Parliamentary Press Gallery and she was about to be fired by Diefenbaker from her job at Conservative national headquarters. I covered her dramatic campaign for the party leadership, and I was there when she, the world's only female foreign minister, travelled across Africa with Prime Minister Joe Clark in 1979.

When Flora and I began talking about telling her story, the premise was that I would write a biography. The more we talked about it, however, the more it seemed to us that the tale would be more compelling if I wrote it in Flora's own words. Hence the memoir format.

I would drive to Ottawa, interview Flora for a couple of days, take the tape home, write a chapter or two, send them to Flora, and repeat the process whenever she was available. Some chapters went through seven drafts before she was satisfied. Life intruded, as it is wont to do, and the process ground to a halt several times – permanently, it seemed, when Flora died with the manuscript about two-thirds completed.

It took the perseverance of Linda Grearson, Flora's niece and executor of her estate, to revive the project. Linda was determined that her aunt's story be told. She supplied encouragement, dug up forgotten facts, researched details of Flora's life, found photographs, and carefully read every word of the manuscript three times. I went back to the interview transcripts, culled Flora's speeches and correspondence, and interviewed a number of her friends, colleagues and advisers, asking each, "Please tell me exactly what Flora said when ..." The object was to fill gaps in my knowledge and to make sure Flora's voice continued to be heard.

I think it works. I think Flora would recognize her own voice. And I believe she would take pleasure from this retelling of her journey. I hope readers will find similar pleasure in the book.

Geoffrey Stevens
Cambridge, Ontario
January 2021

I

Ambushed on the Road from Kabul to Bamyan

∾

25 May 2005
*It was getting dark, and I knew we were in trouble when our
Toyota truck came around a curve on the isolated road in Bamyan
province in the foothills of the Hindu Kush west of Kabul. As we
started downhill toward a small gully, I could see two vans the
size of minibuses blocking the narrow road at the bottom. Their
passengers, including perhaps a dozen children, were standing
or sitting by the side of the road. Our driver, Abdullah Barat, an
Afghan Canadian, manoeuvred the Toyota around the first van,
but could not get past the second. He stopped, and within seconds
six masked men, four of them armed with Kalashnikov AK-47
assault rifles, the weapon of choice among paramilitary brigands
in post-Taliban Afghanistan, surrounded our vehicle. Ordering
Abdullah to turn off the lights and get out of the truck, they proceeded to beat him. Then one of them approached the passenger
side of the vehicle where I was sitting. He began to smash the
window next to my head with the butt of his AK-47.*

∾

Afghanistan was a perilous place that spring, and it has become
even more dangerous since then. The deaths of so many members of
the armed forces have made the Canadian public acutely aware of
the dangers. The Taliban might have been driven from office and its
supporters forced into the hills, but they were not defeated or sup-
pressed. They fought on, waging guerrilla warfare against Canadian
and other Coalition soldiers, and preying on residents and travellers

in parts of the country where law and order was an abstraction, a myth. In this climate of violent conflict, dozens of non-governmental organizations, such as the ones I was involved with, worked quietly behind the scenes to help villagers to help themselves – to mobilize their efforts to build safe and secure futures for their families. What happened that evening to me and my companions from Future Generations International, a US-based NGO that I chaired, will seem tame compared to the experiences of our soldiers – but we were terrified.

I should have known better. After all, that was my fifth trip to Afghanistan, and I had only myself to blame for putting our small group – three passengers in addition to Abdullah and myself – in danger.

In the years after I left politics – or perhaps it would be more accurate to say politics left me when I lost my seat in the election of 1988 – I travelled widely. I went to at least one hundred countries, visiting some of the most exotic places in the world, and working in others that were horribly impoverished, torn apart by war, and extremely dangerous. In my post-politics years, I returned to countries where, in the days when I was a member of the Canadian cabinet, I was received as an honoured guest.

Now – and I am over eighty years old as I write this – I pay my own way when I travel. I am a volunteer. I do not check into five-star hotels; even modest hotels are beyond my budget. I am fortunate to have a parliamentary pension, but my financial means are limited. I eat where the locals eat. I travel with a backpack and a sleeping bag. I sleep in tents, in hostels, occasionally in monasteries or military barracks, or on the floors of villagers' homes. Failing all else, I bed down in the open – as I have done on the banks of the Brahmaputra River in northeast India – and pray that marauding animals, or humans, do not stumble across me before morning.

Most of my travel these days is in the developing world. I have been to South Africa and Namibia with OXFAM, to India with the Shastri Indo-Canadian Institute, to Kenya and Ethiopia with HelpAge International, to Afghanistan with CARE Canada, and to Nepal, Tibet, and other countries with Future Generations.

Future Generations is a teaching institute. In my time, we worked with villagers in high-altitude regions of the world, including Tibet, Afghanistan, northern India, and Peru. Our goal was to help the local people to mobilize human energy and support them as they developed the skills to build schools, train teachers, combat disease and malnutrition, find safe drinking water, grow their own food, and safeguard their environment. In Afghanistan, we persuaded village councils, known as shuras, to tear out crops of poppies, from which opium is produced, and to plant less lucrative, but less lethal, cash crops in their place. Abdullah Barat, our country manager for Afghanistan, had considerable success in this kind of work in the Shahidan valley in central Afghanistan.

I have always felt a special affinity for Afghanistan. This was through my father's eldest brother, Alexander MacDonald, who graduated from Dalhousie University in Halifax when he was just sixteen years old, studied law, then became a newspaperman in Boston, New York, and London. He was in England when the Boer War began in 1899. He went to Edinburgh to enlist in the Second Battalion of the celebrated Black Watch Royal Highlanders and was immediately sent to South Africa where he distinguished himself in battle. When the war ended in 1902, his regiment was posted to India where he completed his term of service.

At home in North Sydney on Cape Breton Island, Alex's family followed his adventures through the letters he sent regularly to his parents. While he was stationed on the northwest frontier of India (now part of Pakistan), he wrote from the fabled Khyber Pass.

∽

Peshawar 29 March 2005

Peshawar where we are now stationed is the frontier of India. The neutral ground dividing us from Afghanistan is right in front of our bungalow. It is a station where you have to keep your eyes open both day and night, especially night, as the surrounding country is infested with roving bands of robbers, all well armed, who are continually trying to surprise you and capture your rifles, the one thing precious above all others to a Pathan or Afghan. They are a very powerful native, nothing to be compared with the down country wretches who are famine- and plague-stricken. The Pathan is a fighter, a good one, and nothing else. We are only two miles from the Khyber Pass where the Russians say they will come some day.

∽

Discharged in Calcutta, he worked for a time in the Dock Commissioner's office there. Over the years, he developed an interest in Indian mysticism. Moving on to Burma, he operated a tea plantation before going to China where he stayed until the First World War began. His career satisfied both his spirit of adventure and his yen for travel, two family characteristics that I inherited. They have been an enormous influence in my life.

With the outbreak of the Great War, Uncle Alex left China and travelled via India to Scotland where he re-enlisted in the Black Watch and joined the campaign in France. He was made a corporal, the rank he had held when he was discharged in India, but he was soon promoted to sergeant of scouts. Twice wounded in action, he received his regiment's medal for "conspicuous gallantry," was nominated for a Distinguished Conduct Medal and recommended for a commission as a lieutenant in the Black Watch.

My gallant uncle kept writing home, and I have treasured his letters for years. Our final letter, dated 29 January 1916, was from the padre of his battalion, extending his condolences to the family on the death of Scout Sergeant MacDonald in the Mesopotamia Campaign of 1914–18. Turkey had allied itself with Germany, and Uncle Alex and his men actually walked across present-day Iraq to attack the Turks from the rear. He was killed in a hail of bullets at the Battle of the Hanna on 21 January 1916. With 2,700 soldiers killed or wounded, that battle was said at the time to have been the British Army's worst defeat since Crimea. An account of my uncle's role in the disastrous engagement was described in a book on the history of the Black Watch.

> As in their capture of, and attempt to hold the Turkish trenches, so in their retirement, they (the men of the Black Watch) fought fiercely and with discipline, making for an advance trench fifty yards nearer the Turks than the main line from which they had advanced. Here fell Sgt. MacDonald, most skilful and gallant of Scouts and most cheery-hearted of men, keeping back the advancing enemy while the last of his men got back into safety.

My thoughts flashed to Uncle Alex when the six bandits – were they murderers, kidnappers, or merely robbers? – surrounded our vehicle in the Hindu Kush. I believe Afghanistan is as dangerous now as it was when he was stationed on the India-Afghan border a century ago and wrote home about those "roving bands of robbers, all well armed." Perhaps it is more dangerous today.

When I was there, the Taliban had not been crushed. Its supporters were simply driven into the mountains of Afghanistan and neighbouring Pakistan. Warlords still controlled large regions of the country. Everyone knew that if the Americans were to leave, the pro-Western regime in Kabul would soon collapse. Thousands of young men in their twenties, who had been kidnapped from their villages as teenagers and forced to join the warlords' militias during the civil war of the 1990s, have been demobilized and left to return, with their weapons, to the valleys and villages from which they came. They have no education, no training, no jobs, and no prospect of legal employment. They have only one skill: they know how to fire an assault rifle. For want of options, they become modern-day highwaymen, utilizing four-wheel drive vehicles and high-powered automatic weapons as they terrorize and rob passing motorists and unwary outsiders.

Our little group from Future Generations fell into the unwary-outsider category on that cool evening in May 2005. We were careless. Anyone who knows Afghanistan as well as I do knows the rules of survival. Those who do not learn the rules do not survive for long in this beautiful but largely lawless land. One of the key rules is to stay off the roads after dark.

Even though I knew better, we broke the rule that May. At my insistence, we took an unacceptable risk. I had been in Kabul, discussing Future Generations projects. We were headed for Bamyan province where Abdullah Barat and I had been developing an exciting idea: to create a national park at Band-e-Amir Lakes in the central mountains of Afghanistan. This is the area where two giant statues of Buddha were carved into a mountainside two thousand years ago. They were among the country's great tourist attractions until they were destroyed, blown up, by the Taliban in 2001. The site of the proposed park is absolutely spectacular, six gorgeous blue lakes in a setting about forty-five miles long by twenty-five miles wide. The core of the park would be protected from development, with rings around the core for hiking trails, farms and settlements. The park would create employment in one of the poorest parts of Afghanistan, and it would bring visitors back to Bamyan to help revive a tourism industry that had been destroyed during the twenty-five years of fighting that followed the Soviet invasion of 1979.

I hoped we could do for Afghanistan what my namesake and political inspiration (but not relation), Sir John A. Macdonald did for Canada in 1870 when his government introduced the National Parks Act. The act set aside land around Banff and Jasper to create our first two national parks. Band-e-Amir Lakes was bound to be a slow process, but I believed Canada, with our experience in creating national parks, could make it happen by sending experts to Afghanistan to train the local people to develop their own parks system.

Our original plan that day was for me to fly to Bamyan with Dr Shukria Hassan, a local doctor employed by Future Generations, and Fauzia Assifi, an Afghan American woman from California who wanted to learn more about the work of Future Generations. We went to Kabul airport about 10 a.m. for the daily flight to Bamyan; it was supposed to depart at noon. The flight, however, was delayed because of bad weather. At 3 p.m., they announced it had been cancelled.

The prudent course would have been to wait for the next day's flight. But I did not want to upset the schedule already lined up for me for the following day in Yakawlang, a village where intense research was underway with women's groups to determine why this area of Afghanistan has the second highest rate of infant and maternal mortality in the country. The women there had changed the time of their regular meeting to accommodate Dr Shukria and me. I hate to disappoint people who have put themselves out to meet with me, and this is especially true in Afghanistan, where communications are difficult and travel is slow on treacherous roads. I did not know how long it might be before Abdullah would be able to assemble the group again.

Even though it was late, I insisted we drive to Bamyan that day. I rationalized that because there had been no serious trouble on the road between Kabul and Bamyan for about a year, we would be reasonably safe. My plan might have worked if we had left Kabul at three o'clock. But we were delayed by traffic and it was not until 4:30 p.m. that we actually got out of Kabul.

We stopped around 7:30 for something to eat at a samawat, as roadside restaurants or inns are known in the Dhari language.[1] Anyone who has not tried a restaurant in the Afghan countryside would find it is quite an experience. These places typically consist of one long room. Diners sit on a large Afghan carpet, and oilcloth is rolled out on top of the carpet to serve as a tablecloth. The menu never changes – shish kabobs with either rice or noodles, but not both.

It was getting dark when we started out again. I rode in the front seat with Abdullah while the others sat in the rear seat. The back part of the truck was open. By this time, the mountain air was growing cold and the road had deteriorated to not much more than a track. We went up a rise, around a curve, and down the hill towards the gully. We could see little children sitting on side of the hill and some adults milling around the two stopped vans. Our suspicion that something unpleasant was taking place was confirmed when the six masked attackers surrounded our vehicle.

They had already robbed the passengers in the vans. As Abdullah stopped, they told him to turn off the truck's lights. Then they ordered him out of the vehicle. Abdullah is a good actor. Even as they beat him, he resolutely insisted that he was just a poor hired driver for a party of innocuous tourists. The thugs kept circling the truck, smashing the windows, and slashing the tires. They ordered us to keep our heads down and to turn over all our money, cameras, and satellite phones. Everyone did, except me. When I saw the vans blocking the road, I had hurriedly stuffed my money belt and passport under the seat. I carry my cameras in a small backpack, and I tucked it out of sight between the back of my legs and the seat.

In those days, there was no functioning bank system in Afghanistan. There were no bank machines and no place to cash travellers' cheques. So we always travelled with US currency, the only useful medium of exchange in the country. I had only about $350 hidden under the seat, but the others surrendered approximately $8,000, much of which had been intended for staff salaries and supplies.

Our captors were speaking Dhari, but their message required no translation: if we did not do precisely as they ordered, they would shoot us on the spot. As these threats were being delivered, two other vehicles, a car and a truck, came along, blocking the road behind us. Their occupants were beaten and robbed, too. Soon there were about thirty of us, victims waiting for whatever fate lay in store for us. I knew we might all be murdered. The gunmen, or so it seemed to me, had nothing to lose by killing us and perhaps something to gain by eliminating witnesses.

How, I wondered, would my family find out? Would I be shot and left to die in the gully? Would I be abducted and carried off into the mountains? Would ransom be demanded or paid? Would my body be discovered? Or would I simply be another unlucky foreigner who disappeared and was presumed dead in one of the world's danger spots?

In the close confines of the vehicle, the tension was unbearable. I suggested we relieve it by singing, a suggestion that was roundly rejected by my companions. The woman from California became quite panicky and irritating, as, for an hour, she chanted prayers to the prophets to rescue us. She kept insisting that I cover my head, as Muslim women do, to show respect and deference to our captors. I can be quite stubborn; I felt no respect at all, no deference, for these thugs; and I kept my head defiantly uncovered. But I also kept my hands tightly clasped so our captors would not see how badly they were shaking.

Our ordeal continued for several hours. While we waited for our captors to decide what to do with us, memories of earlier tight situations in which I had found myself flashed through my mind. My thoughts went back a half-century, to a hitchhiking trip I had made through Europe, in days long before it was fashionable or even socially acceptable for "young ladies" (as we were styled then) to take off for foreign places with little more than a roadmap and a backpack. For the first (and, as it would turn out, only) time in my life, I had to arm myself with a hatpin to defend my honour when a couple of lusty, but quite drunk, truck drivers accosted me and my friend Dorothy Chisholm on the road between Seville and Malaga in southern Spain.

A week later, forced to flee the amorous attentions of two Portuguese men in a hotel in Barcelona, we hitched a ride in a large black Cadillac, only to be stopped at the French border where we learned that the Caddy had been stolen from an embassy in Madrid. The driver was marched off. Dorothy and I were thrown into a cell, then released and left to walk into France – a four-mile trek at night over a mountain road where a British diplomat and his family had been slaughtered by bandits a year earlier.

I remembered some of the tense moments I had experienced in Africa in the tumult of the 1990s. One of the things I did in my early post-politics years was to travel the world for VisionTV with a video crew, taping programs in some of the globe's hottest hot spots. A VisionTV assignment took me to the civil war in Somalia in 1992. We had a particularly scary flight by Hercules aircraft to a refugee camp operated by the International Red Cross and Red Crescent at Baidoa. Driving into the centre of Baidoa, we passed through gangs of armed vigilantes, many of them high on khat, the hallucinogen of choice in much of eastern Africa. We met a woman who told us her harrowing tale of running away from the vigilantes. She had two small children and a baby. The baby was quite sick, but she knew if she stopped to care for it, the vigilantes would catch them. So she abandoned the baby and fled with her other children to the refugee camp where we found them.

A year later, I was in South Africa, in Bophuthatswana, one of the notorious Black "homelands" or bantustans in the apartheid era. I was on a mission for OXFAM, as well as recording VisionTV interviews with Black militants who were defying the white supremacist regime that ruled South Africa until the election of Nelson Mandela as president in 1994. When we finished our interviews, our producer and cameraman, Leo Rampan, went on ahead while I lingered behind in the village with several workers from OXFAM. But we had attracted the unwanted attention of the South African military police. As we left the village, we noticed a white armoured vehicle, known as a Kaspir – it looked like a modified small tank – following us.

It speeded up, narrowing the distance between us as we went down a long hill. It pulled even with our vehicle. When I saw the policemen, their weapons drawn, I shouted, "Get down!" to my companions from OXFAM. We flattened ourselves on the floor. At this point, the road started to climb again. Leo was positioned at the top of the hill, recording the scene on the road. It may have been the sight of the camera – I do not know – but the police vehicle dropped back, then turned around and returned to the village. Leo found the chase so exciting that he wanted to ask the military police to restage it so he could capture the entire drama for television. I vehemently vetoed that idea.

In 1994, I went to Rwanda for CARE and for VisionTV toward the end of the genocide there. After a day spent working in a large refugee camp north of Goma in Zaire (now the Democratic Republic of the Congo), across the border from Rwanda, we were returning to Goma for the night when we encountered a band of militant Hutus, known as the Interahamwe. They had blockaded the road with boulders and were robbing and killing travellers. I wanted to run the blockade, but cooler heads in our group prevailed and we took refuge for the night in a special camp set up to house Swedish road-construction workers. (The Swedes know how to look after their own. That camp had a makeshift spa, a sauna, and enough food to stock a dozen delicatessens in Stockholm.)

I had been frightened on each of these occasions. I was frightened again when, on a subsequent trip to South Africa, I found myself alone and stranded in Soweto, the teeming Black ghetto. And I suppose I was frightened on the night in 1998 when I had to manage without a tent on Mount Kailash in Tibet. But the fear I had felt in those situations did not approach the terror of that night on the road in Afghanistan.

Other memories paraded through my mind as we waited for our captors to decide what to do with us. I thought about my stubbornly independent father, who was my inspiration and role model. I relived the excitement I had felt when I, a proud Scot, made my first visit to Scotland in 1952. I grew nostalgic when I recalled the decade I had spent working at Progressive Conservative party headquarters in Ottawa, until John Diefenbaker had me fired for suspicion of disloyalty. I remembered the heady times I spent plotting and strategizing with Dalton Camp and his supporters to rid the party of Diefenbaker and to replace him with my fellow Nova Scotian, Bob Stanfield. I thought how odd it had seemed when I was elected to Parliament in 1972 and found myself the only woman in a caucus of 107 Tories. I certainly recalled my bitter disappointment when I failed to win the Conservative leadership in 1976 – and the frustration I felt three years later when, stranded in Brussels at a NATO conference, I could not get back to Ottawa in time for the budget vote that brought down our Tory government.

But I also reflected on the fun, the challenges and the satisfaction I had experienced while serving in three different cabinet portfolios in the administrations of Joe Clark and Brian Mulroney. For sheer cloak-and-dagger drama and excitement, nothing in my life could top the saga of Canada's "houseguests," as we called them, in Tehran. I was minister of External Affairs in 1979 when Iranian students overran the United States embassy and compound. Six Americans took shelter in the homes of Ambassador Ken Taylor and John Sheardown, our chief immigration officer. They hid them for twelve weeks until we could spirit them out of Iran with false identities. It came to be called the "Canadian Caper," and I was right in the middle of it, worrying for every minute of the twelve weeks that something would go wrong, that our secret would be discovered, with terrible implications for both the houseguests and their brave hosts.

I thought about the serendipitous circumstances of my first trip to Tibet, truly the country of my dreams; about the time I tried to climb Mount Everest; and about the 2,400-mile backpacking trip I organized in 1998 for six women friends. We went from Lhasa in Tibet to Kashgar in Xinjiang province in Western China, down the Karakorum Highway to Peshawar in Pakistan (the place where Uncle Alex had been stationed nearly a century earlier) and on to the Khyber Pass. We called ourselves the "Silk Road Seven." We had a blast!

Not least, I thought about some of the vitally important issues in international development that began to occupy my time and attention even before I accepted the chair of Canada's International Development Research Centre in the 1990s. These issues encompass the role of women in Third World countries; protection of the environment; relief of refugees and internally displaced persons; assistance to seniors; and conflict resolution (an interest whetted by my work with the Carnegie Commission on Preventing Deadly Conflict from 1994–99).

All my life I have been interested in people. Where do they come from? What do they do? What kind of lives do they lead? Growing up in Cape Breton during the depression years, we knew poverty. We could see it in the children of the unemployed, in the way they dressed, in their homes. At school, some children left class each morning to go to the "teachers' room" where they were given a bowl of bread and milk. In my naiveté, I thought that must be an especially exotic meal because we never had it at home. Quite often, children who had to walk several miles to school each morning would come home with my sisters and me at noon for a substantial mid-day meal. We learned the virtue of sharing while we were still schoolgirls.

That sense of being aware of the people around me, of their problems and their dreams, combined with my longing for travel and adventure, fed an insatiable curiosity that may have made my life seem unorthodox by conventional standards, yet it has been a deeply satisfying life.

It is hard for anyone to assess his or her own accomplishments. I knew I had made a contribution, and I hoped I had made a difference in some of the causes I took on. Yet huge problems still face society. We need to find the resources to improve the lives of millions in the Third World. We must persuade the leaders of affluent countries to share our concerns and our commitment. The poor countries cannot help themselves, the financial resources of our NGOs are sorely limited, and it seems almost impossible to motivate the government bureaucracies that could help the most.

We did not talk much in the Toyota that night. We wondered, worried, and waited. As time passed and nothing happened, the tension began to ease slightly. Apparently concluding that no other vehicles would be coming along the road that night, our captors drifted silently away some time before midnight. I managed to take a photo as they left. Although I was scared that the flash might bring them back, they either did not notice or care.

We spent the next hour repairing the tires of our truck. Abdullah, a man of ingenuity and foresight, had thought to go to Canadian Tire before he left Canada. He purchased a tire-repair kit with a little pump that plugged into the cigarette lighter. He fixed the holes, re-inflated the tires, and we resumed our trip to Bamyan, pulling in at a truck stop that included a hostel of sorts. It was one long room where we could roll out our sleeping bags on mats on the floor. None of us got much sleep, but it was safer than being on the road at night.

We went on to Yakawlang in the morning and met the women's groups. After visiting Band-e-Amir Lakes, we returned as quickly as possible to Kabul. I was anxious to notify the Canadian embassy about what had happened to us so that they could alert the authorities in Kabul and Ottawa that a Canadian privy councillor had nearly come to an embarrassing, and messy, end on the road to Bamyan.

2

The Original Boat People

When we talk of "boat people" these days, we usually think of the flood of refugees from Southeast Asia in the wake of the Vietnam War. I will come to that period later in my story, but for the moment I will simply say that I am particularly proud of my role in persuading the Government of Canada to accept as many of those refugees as it did from Vietnam, Laos, and Cambodia. In 1979, when Joe Clark was sworn in as prime minister, and I as his foreign minister, we and other nations faced a human crisis of unprecedented proportions: what to do about the millions of desperate people – homeless, destitute civilians, their families shattered by war – who were fleeing their homelands in the hope of finding a safe refuge in the West. Thousands perished on the voyage.

It was clear that Canada, like other wealthy countries, had a moral obligation to help. The issue was how wide to open our doors. The previous administration, Pierre Trudeau's Liberal government, had agreed to accept eight thousand Southeast Asian refugees – a paltry and inadequate response to a humanitarian crisis of such staggering proportions. One of my first acts as foreign minister was to persuade my cabinet colleagues that we should accept fifty thousand boat people. We issued a humanitarian challenge to the Canadian people. The government would sponsor one refugee for every one that Canadian organizations or individuals would commit to supporting for a year. We were overwhelmed by the way Canadians responded to the challenge. The total number of boat people accepted in Canada soon rose to sixty thousand and ultimately to one hundred thousand. In relation to the size of our domestic population, Canada was the most receptive country in the world to the Asian refugees.

I did not feel the slightest hesitation when the issue of the boat people came to my desk in Ottawa. Innocent people, collateral victims of vicious warfare were dying, literally, to get to a haven like Canada. They risked everything in their effort to get here. Of course, we had to help them! And we did. It was a national commitment and a national effort – and it was recognized in 1986 when "the people of Canada" were awarded the prestigious Nansen Medal by the United Nations High Commissioner for Refugees. Awarded annually for outstanding service to the cause of refugees, the Nansen Medal customarily goes to individuals or organizations. It was the first time that the honour had gone to an entire nation.

My sympathy for the boat people surely had its roots in my family's history. I have always regarded Scottish Highlanders – my forebears – as the first boat people. At the Battle of Culloden in 1746, the army of Bonnie Prince Charlie (Charles Edward Stuart, the Jacobite claimant to the thrones of England, Scotland, and Ireland) was routed, and his followers were systematically slaughtered, by "Butcher Cumberland" (as Scots still call the Duke of Cumberland, commander of the English forces and younger son of King George II). With their clan organization and leadership effectively destroyed by the debacle at Culloden, the brave Highlanders were subjected to an early version of ethnic cleansing in a two-generations-long process of pacification and resettlement that came to be known, infamously, as the Highland Clearances. Abetted by some of our own Scottish chieftains, the victorious English drove Highland farmers, most of whom raised cattle on land leased from absentee landlords, from their farms by force or by imposing huge rent increases. The land was then leased to Lowland Scots and to farmers from England who turned the Scottish economy on its ear by introducing sheep to replace the cattle that had been the traditional mainstay of the economy of the Highlands. The sheep's wool was shipped south to supply the wool market in Manchester, which in those days was fighting competition from imported silks.

My ancestors had few options. They could resettle on barren plots along the Scottish coast and try to eke out a living by fishing, kelping (harvesting seaweed) or growing potatoes, or they could take their chances with the North Atlantic. They could set sail in one of the dozens of small ships that left from Scottish ports, crammed with impoverished Highlanders bound for the New World where they hoped that enterprise and hard work would produce a better life for themselves and their families.

Tens of thousands of Highland Scots took the gamble on the New World. They dispersed along the Atlantic seaboard of North America. Some ended up as far south as Georgia and the Carolinas where they soon found themselves caught up in the American War of Independence. When they went to British North America (which then encompassed the northern states plus present-day Canada), the Scots, like other settlers, were required to take an oath of loyalty to the British crown. A Scotsman's word is his bond, and when the war began they supported the British cause almost to a man. They set up their own unit, the Royal Highland Emigrant Regiment.

Thousands upon thousands of Highlanders settled in what are now Nova Scotia, New Brunswick and Prince Edward Island and parts of Quebec. No place on this side of the Atlantic was more profoundly affected by the influx of Highlanders than my native Cape Breton Island, where more than twenty-five thousand Highlanders put down roots between 1780 and 1820. The culture they brought with them still thrives. Today, Cape Breton – along with Brittany[1] – remains just about the only place in the world outside the British Isles where Gaelic is still spoken.

I should insert a historical footnote. Following the Battle of Culloden, Bonnie Prince Charlie – the son of James II, he was known as King Charles III to his followers and as the Young Pretender to his adversaries – was forced to flee for his life. Had Butcher Cumberland caught up to him, he would have been summarily executed. A young Jacobite sympathizer – and my namesake – Flora Macdonald, living at the time on Benbecula in the Outer Hebrides, helped the Stuart prince to escape. She hid him in a cave, then disguised him as her Irish maid to smuggle him to safety on the Isle of Skye in the Inner Hebrides and, ultimately, to Brittany in France. That dramatic flight is celebrated in the popular folk song (and one of my very favourites), "The Skye Boat Song."

Speed bonnie boat, like a bird on the wing,
Onward, the sailors cry.
Carry the lad that's born to be king
Over the sea to Skye.

Loud the winds howl, loud the waves roar,
Thunder clouds rend the air;
Baffled our foe's stand on the shore,
Follow they will not dare...

Though the waves leap, soft shall ye sleep,
Ocean's a royal bed.
Rocked in the deep, Flora will keep
Watch by your weary head.

The daring rescue of the Highlander who would be king made Flora a national hero in Scotland – and a criminal in the eyes of the English authorities. She was arrested and imprisoned in Dunstaffnage Castle on Scotland's west coast, then transported to London where she was held briefly in the Tower of London until being released as part of a general amnesty. Despite her notoriety, or perhaps because of it, she was regarded in London as a romantic figure, a genuine celebrity. She was introduced to the Prince of Wales and had her portrait painted by some of the fashionable artists of the day. On her return to Skye in 1750, she married a prominent kinsman, her cousin Allan Macdonald of Kingsburgh.

In 1773, Flora and her husband joined the exodus to the Americas as they emigrated to North Carolina where they became successful farmers. When the War of Independence began in 1776, Allan Macdonald was put in command of a royalist regiment. The war was not kind to Flora and her family. Taken prisoner at the battle of Moore's Creek, Allan was jailed in Philadelphia. Flora and at least two of their children followed him there. He was sent to New York, then to Nova Scotia to be exchanged for captured American troops. Flora also followed him to Nova Scotia. They attempted to settle in the Annapolis Valley where they had been promised land by the British crown. Arriving in late autumn, the family was forced to spend its first winter in a tent. They lived for a time in a blockhouse, which still stands, the last remaining building of its type in the province.

When the promised land grant failed to materialize, the little community of expatriate Highlanders agreed that Flora should go to London to see if she could use her earlier connections to prod the British authorities into keeping their promise. She tried for two years, to no avail. By this time, her husband, who had become quite ill, decided to join her. They returned to Scotland and settled in Skye. Flora died in Kingsburgh on Skye in 1790 in, legend has it, the same bed in which Bonnie Prince Charlie had slept during his dramatic escape. She is said to have been buried in a shroud made from the sheets on which the prince had slept.

My father, who was the historian in our family, recounted the story of the famous Flora Macdonald when I was a young child, and, like any youngster with a vivid imagination, I was enthralled by the romantic adventure of the first Flora and the dashing Bonnie Prince Charlie. People ask whether we were related. Well, we have the same name. We came from the same part of Scotland. But are we related? I do not know. I think it is possible, but I really do not know.

The Flora connection made its way into the proceedings of the Canadian House of Commons following my first election to Parliament in the October 1972 general election. As the new member for Kingston and The Islands, I delivered my maiden speech on 11 January 1973 during the debate on the Speech from the Throne. By tradition, maiden speeches are an occasion for a new member to sing the praises of their constituency and to extol the accomplishment of their predecessors as its representatives. In my case, I was pleased to note that 1973 marked the three hundredth anniversary of the founding of Kingston and, what was more, that 11 January was the birthdate of Sir John A. Macdonald, Kingston's first member of Parliament and Canada's first prime minister. I was pleased to describe the virtues of Kingston and delighted to recite Sir John A.'s many great accomplishments.

When Allan MacEachen, the government house leader and a powerful figure in the Trudeau cabinet, joined the Throne Speech debate a few days later, he made a particular point of commending me for my speech. I should explain something. Although Allan is a Liberal and I was, in those pre-Stephen Harper days, a Progressive Conservative, we were both to the left of centre in our parties. We had a shared history. We were both proud Highlanders (although his Gaelic was better than mine). Our ancestors arrived in Cape Breton in the same group in 1807. Our families settled a few miles apart. We liked each other. We were friends. We might even be related, although I am not sure about that either. What I am sure of is that there are situations, at least among Highland Scots, when blood and tradition are thicker than politics and partisanship.

This was one of those times. "The honourable member for Kingston and The Islands," Allan told the Commons, "bears the name of a Scottish heroine whose memory still lives because of her bravery in several historic episodes, but especially for her ingenuity in planning the escape from the English searchers of Prince Charles Edward Stuart, known in history as Bonnie Prince Charlie." Allan related the story of how Samuel Johnson, the eighteenth-century English writer and critic, had toured Scotland in 1772. Johnson found nothing to praise in Scotland, except Flora Macdonald, whom he met in the Hebrides. Dr Johnson was impressed. "Flora Macdonald," he wrote, "is a name that will be mentioned in history, and if courage and fidelity be virtues, mentioned with honour."[2] To which Allan added: "May I make a prediction today, Mr Speaker, à la Samuel Johnson? My prediction is that the honourable member for Kingston and The Islands, the modern, perceptive Flora MacDonald, will bring in our day added lustre to the old name and the old clan, and will deserve a secure place in our political history."

That was a heady compliment for a rookie parliamentarian coming from one of the giants across the aisle.

The Flora connection aside, I guess I was born with the spirit of adventure that infused generations of my clanspeople – I have already mentioned the wartime adventures of my uncle Alexander MacDonald with the Black Watch regiment – or I may have absorbed my adventurous spirit from the MacDonald family lore that my father would tell and retell to entertain his young children. It is quite a story. The MacDonalds trace their origins to the most powerful of the Highland clans, Clan Donald, which takes its name from Donald, known as "Red Hand," who was the grandson of Somerled, King of the Isles. Believed to have been born in 1113, Somerled was instrumental in driving the Norsemen from the Western Isles of Scotland in the twelfth century. He was killed at the Battle of Renfrew in 1164. Our branch of the clan, the Tulloch MacDonalds, is descended from Angus, the second son of Black John of Bohuntin, who, if I have the generations straight, was the great-great-great-great-great-grandson of the patriarch Donald.

Even my father, G. Fred MacDonald, who usually managed to keep everything straight in his life and ours, admitted that the various branches of the Clan Donald were so interwoven that it was difficult to disentangle them. It was probably impossible for anyone outside the clan to follow our lineage. MacDonald men married MacDonald women and they produced MacDonald children who, more often than not, married other MacDonald offspring. Their given names were drawn from a small pool of Christian names. Margaret was the preferred name for the girls while most of the boys seemed to be John, Alexander (Sandy), Angus, Donald or Ronald. Just to confuse matters, there are variations on the spelling of our surname.

A MacDonald, for example, might be related to a McDonald or a Macdonell, but not necessarily to a Macdonald – or vice versa.

"Mac" in Gaelic means "son of," so MacDonald is son of Donald. Therefore, Donald should properly start with a capital "D." In my view, "Mc" is used by people who are too lazy to take the time to write out "Mac" in full, so they make it McDonald rather than MacDonald. Not that it really matters. What does matter, to devotees of Gaelic, is the capitalization of "Mac." My grandfather, for instance, was a purist. He insisted on using a small "m," spelling his name "macDonald."

Many of the Tulloch MacDonalds, or macDonalds, in Cape Breton are descended from Captain Angus Tulloch MacDonald who was decorated by the British government for gallantry during the capture of Louisbourg in 1758. Captain MacDonald's eldest daughter, Margaret, married my great-great grandfather, Donald MacDonald of Bohuntin, Scotland. They had five sons and four daughters. Margaret and Donald with Angus, their infant first child, left the Highlands in 1807. They landed at Pictou in Cape Breton. After a few months there, they moved to a place called River Inhabitants in Richmond County before finally settling in Inverness County at Mabou Coal Mines, where the last seven of their nine children were born. That is where my great-grandfather, Alexander MacDonald, was born in 1813. Like many of his clansmen, he looked to the sea for his living. And like so many of the men from the coastal villages of Cape Breton, he perished at sea – drowned in 1851 when *Red Wing*, the fishing schooner of which he was owner and captain, went down after leaving St George, Newfoundland, for the run home to Cape Breton. He was just thirty-eight.

Alexander MacDonald had married Sarah Beaton, a pioneering nurse in Inverness Country. My grandfather, Ronald Alexander MacDonald, born in 1844, was their oldest child. He went to sea when he was twelve years old and spent most of his working life sailing the high seas in clipper ships. He went anywhere he could get a cargo. I do not know all the places he went, but I do know he sailed to China in the tea trade and to Chile to pick up cargoes of nitrate and carry them around Cape Horn and across the Atlantic to ports in Germany. He returned to Cape Breton in August 1873 and stayed long enough to marry my grandmother, Eliza Roberts, from nearby Ingonish, at the Baptist parsonage in Upper North Sydney. After the wedding, they sailed away together and my grandmother spent many years at sea with her husband.

She gave birth to three sons during these voyages. I do not know where the first two, Alexander (my gallant uncle Alex) and William (known as Will), were born. The third, Lorne, took his name from the barque, *Marquis of Lorne*, on which he was born, somewhere off the coast of Newfoundland. Their fourth son, and final child, my father Fred, was born on dry land, in Cape Breton, after his mother retired from seafaring life and settled down in North Sydney to raise her brood.[3]

Theirs was not a typical family life. By the time he was nineteen, my father had met his father only twice; one of those occasions came was when he was about ten and his mother took him to New York where his father's ship was being overhauled. Later, when my grandfather was in his sixties, he joined his wife and family in Cape Breton where, being a staunch Tory, he secured a patronage appointment, harbour master in Sydney, from the Robert Borden government in Ottawa. He monitored the comings and goings of ships through the harbour during the First World War.

Ronald Alexander MacDonald lived to be seventy-five. One day in 1919, he simply keeled over and died while climbing a ladder up to a ship dry-docked in the harbour. His wife, Eliza, died two years later. Of their four sons, my Uncle Alex went on to his illustrious career with the Black Watch regiment in South Africa, India, and Mesopotamia. Uncle Will became a banker in Pennsylvania. The third son, Lorne, came to a tragic end when, as a young man of eighteen or nineteen, he was working with a photographer in North Sydney, and he got fatal blood poisoning from some chemical they used in developing films.

My father Fred was very bright and exceptionally well-read. In province-wide high school testing one year, he recorded the highest marks in Nova Scotia, but he failed geometry and had to repeat his year. He finished grade eleven, but there was no way he could go beyond that since the family could not afford to keep him in school. So Fred went to work for Western Union as a telegraph operator. He was a foreman of the telegraphic floor when he retired in 1939 and was immediately hired by the federal government as a wartime censor, responsible for decoding Morse code messages as they arrived in North Sydney by transatlantic cable from London and relaying them to New York. The work was top-secret – it included messages between British Prime Minister Winston Churchill and American President Franklin Roosevelt – and our father would not talk about it at home, no matter how hard we tried to pry information from him. Although he received a commendation from the government after the war, he did not regard his work as all that significant. He thought his volunteer service as chairman of the local war bonds campaign contributed more to the war effort.

After my grandfather, Ronald Alexander MacDonald, retired from sailing and settled in North Sydney, he would recount to my father his tales of adventure on the high seas and in exotic foreign lands. I wish I had known my grandfather; I would have loved to hear his stories directly. But both he and my grandmother died before I was born. As a child, I remember listening raptly as my father told our family about his father's exciting life. During the years she sailed with her husband, my grandmother would send postcards home from the ports they visited. I never tired of examining and re-examining those old postcards. Dad's library was filled with books about travel, and I devoured the works of the great American adventure travel writer, Richard Halliburton – *The Royal Road to Romance, The Glorious Adventure, New Worlds to Conquer, The Flying Carpet, Seven League Boots*. What a man! Halliburton had adventures that I, a young girl in Cape Breton, could only dream about. He enlisted in the French Foreign Legion and was marooned on the very Caribbean island where the fictional Robinson Crusoe was supposed to have been cast away[4]; he climbed Japan's Mount Fuji in winter, followed the path of Ulysses, and swam the length of the Panama Canal. I was thrilled by the glamour of his life. Of all the children in our home, I was by far the most intrigued by the excitement of travel and the romance of adventure in far-off places.

I am still like that today. I will travel anywhere any time. There is no place I will not go and nothing, or almost nothing, I will not attempt. Although I have never been marooned on Treasure Island or swum the Panama Canal, I have searched for the grave of Moses in the Middle East and gone hang-gliding in the Pyrenees. I suppose I collect countries the way other people collect art. In 2005, I finally made it to Mongolia. It was my one hundredth country, and I was not done yet. Not by a long shot.

3

A Man's World

If ever there were a man's world, it was in Cape Breton in the years during and after the Second World War when I was growing up in North Sydney. I knew that no matter how hard I worked in school – and I worked extremely hard – and no matter how well I did – and I usually finished first in my class – I would never go to university. I was not alone in this. Girls, unless they were from well-to-do families, were expected to be "realistic" in their academic ambitions. They were encouraged to finish grade eleven, which is where school ended in our town, then choose one of three options: go into nursing; become a schoolteacher; or go to secretarial school. Then they were expected to get a job until some suitable young man came along to marry them. In those days, men had careers. Women raised families. Although I was the top student in my high school graduating class, the principal told my parents not to worry about university: "She'll be married before you know it."[1]

No, that was not to be the way my life would unfold.

I took the secretarial-school route – one year at Empire Business College in Sydney, a fifteen-mile bus ride from our home in North Sydney. I took shorthand, typing, and bookkeeping, all subjects for which I had no great love. I learned them, although they were less than stimulating intellectually. Until then, I had loved school. I loved English and history, and geography, and Latin and French, although I hated math and geometry.

I wanted desperately to go to university, but I knew it could never happen. It was not just male chauvinism. The Great Depression had been hard on Cape Breton, as it had been on other parts of the Maritimes, and our economic recovery had been painfully slow.

People had large families. If they could scrape up enough money to send a child to university, they would spend it on a son. Education for a daughter was regarded as an expense; for a son it was an investment. With a university degree, a son could have a career and earn enough to afford a home and family.

It was like that in our family. Although I was free to express my longing for university, I knew we could not afford it. During the depression, Western Union had laid off my father, a forty-year employee, along with other employees whom it deemed to be "too old." Dad was always resourceful and for the rest of his life he managed to support the family with an assortment of part-time jobs – bookkeeping and things like that. The only time he had full-time work after being laid off was during the war when he was called back for a high-security job handling secret cable traffic between Britain and North America. But we did not think of ourselves as being poor. We had a comfortable home and plenty to eat. We had money for necessities, if not many luxuries. Higher education for daughters was a luxury. There was one boy in the family, my younger brother Ronald, and he went to university, supporting himself working summers on the DEW line in the Canadian North. There were five girls in the family. None of us went on to university. When I finished business college, I got a clerical job in a bank, and I knew I was fortunate to have it.

I was delighted that Ronald went to university. I just wish his sisters had had the same opportunity. I am not complaining. If I had gone to university, I might well have become trapped in a dead-end "career," like so many frustrated people I see around me today. Having only a business college diploma and my secretarial skills to fall back on, I knew I would have to make my own way in the world. I would have to aim higher and work harder – and that is what I did. It is what I have I been doing for the past sixty-odd years. The fact that I am a woman without a great deal of formal education no longer matters. I have been free to do what I want. I have led a wonderful, productive, and rewarding life, and I would not trade it for anyone else's. I have had opportunities to serve my political party, my country, and the international community. During sixteen years as a member of Parliament, I held three important cabinet portfolios. My decades since politics, devoted to work in international development, have been the most stimulating and satisfying period of my life. I have advised governments and helped run agencies that do vitally important humanitarian work. I have been accorded many honours, including honorary doctorates from nearly twenty universities.

My mother, the former Mollie Royle, was born in St John's, Newfoundland. When she was six years old, she came to North Sydney with her mother who took a job as a live-in housekeeper for a widower with several children. Although her employer subsequently remarried, my grandmother and her lively daughter continued to live in his home for a number of years.

My mother was twenty-one years old, eighteen years younger than my father, when she and Fred MacDonald were married at the Methodist Parsonage in North Sydney in 1922. Mum spent many of the ensuing years pregnant. She gave birth to eight children. Her first, a boy named Lorne, died of scarlet fever when he was three. My sister Jean was next and I came third, a year-and-a-half after Jean. Helen, who died of an aneurysm in 1971, was a year-and-a-half younger than I. Then came our little sister Ruth who died suddenly when she was three. The cause was a ruptured appendix that the doctors at the local hospital inexplicably failed to diagnose. Dad was furious, but there was nothing he could do. I remember he took us all to the hospital to say goodbye to Ruth. Sheila, the next sister, is five years younger than I am. Ronald is eight years younger and Lorna, the baby of the family, is fifteen years younger than I. Of the five surviving girls, Helen and Sheila went into nursing while Jean, Lorna, and I became secretaries.

Our family was more fortunate than many. My father's parents had died not long before he and my mother were married. With my father's three brothers all out of the picture – Uncle Alex killed in the First World War, Uncle Will in banking in Pennsylvania, and Uncle Lorne dead of blood poisoning at a young age – Dad inherited our grandparents' home. Located next door to the parsonage, it was spacious, as it needed to be to accommodate a family of six rambunctious children. Downstairs, we had a living room which was turned into the children's playroom, a den that served as the parlour, a dining room, and a kitchen. On the second floor, there were three bedrooms, plus Mum's sewing room, where Dad kept his old upright typewriter. Then there was the attic, which was full of intriguing items to fire a curious child's imagination, including our grandfather's sea chest and his old telescope through which we watched ships in the harbour. Reminders of his thrilling life at sea surrounded us. His ship's glass, or barometer, had a position of pride in the den.

Our mother, Mollie MacDonald, was a traditional wife. She never had as much influence on me as my father did. Raising the children consumed her life and, if truth be known, I think she preferred it that way. By the time they married, Dad had travelled widely in Canada, the United States, and Bermuda, and he had developed wide interests, from reading the classics and listening to opera to sports such as tennis and curling. And he had a lifelong passion for international news. Our mother never ventured very far from home. Although she liked to read women's magazines and books written for women readers, she had little interest in the literary classics in her husband's library. Some nights he would read to her while she sewed. I remember him reading *Gone with the Wind* and some of the biblical novels by Lloyd C. Douglas, including *Magnificent Obsession, The Robe, Disputed Passage*, and *The Big Fisherman.*

It was only later, when her children were older, that Mum got a chance to see the world. Her father (my maternal grandfather) had originally immigrated to Newfoundland from Manchester, England. He disappeared from the family's life when she was a small child, and they lost track of him. At the outset of the Second World War, Mum heard that members of her father's family in Altrincham, near Manchester, were trying to trace descendants in Newfoundland. When we learned that the family in Altrincham had two young daughters, Dad immediately wrote, inviting the girls to stay with us in North Sydney until the war was over. Later, Mum was notified that she stood to collect a small legacy following her father's death. It was something like $5,000. Because money could not be sent out of England during the war and for a number of years afterward, she decided to go to England to meet her new-found relatives and spend the money by travelling through the United Kingdom and shopping there.

I was about ten when Dad was laid off by Western Union. Suddenly, he had no job and no pension; he fought for years to secure small pensions for himself and others who had been let go. He was our mentor and inspiration. There was never an evening, except lodge nights, when he did not hear our lessons after supper. As soon as we finished the lessons, Dad would read to us. We would sit around the kitchen stove with Mum darning or sewing at one end while Dad at the other end would read from the great classics of childhood and drill us on spelling and other subjects. He was the Pied Piper of our neighbourhood, forever leading the children off on adventures. And because he did not have a regular job, he was home much of the day, so he would take us skating or swimming or teach us the history of Cape Breton as we rambled around the region.

But he was also a strict disciplinarian. He had high expectations for his children, and we held Dad in awe. He was stern. We knew we had to follow his rules. He was unyielding when my sister Sheila started dating a Catholic boy. "That's going to end," he told her. Sheila did not like that order one bit, but she ended the relationship. Jean, the eldest, felt the most restricted. When she was nineteen, she left North Sydney for the bright lights and personal freedom of Montreal.

I was closer to our father than my siblings were. I was only a few months old when our brother Lorne died, and Dad seemed to transfer to me the attention he had hoped to give to his son. He sensed that I shared his interests and his spirit of adventure more than the others. If he could not have a son – and it would be eight years before Ronald was born – he wanted the next best thing. I was it. Of his five daughters, I was the one who was not afraid to try to match his expectations. I became the son he did not yet have.

Cape Breton teemed with servicemen during the Second War World; in addition to sailors passing though the harbour, we had five hundred airmen stationed at the seaplane base in North Sydney. It was a great time for young women like Jean, who loved going to dances in Sydney, New Waterford, or Glace Bay. However, dating and dances never appealed much to me. My focus was on school and homework, church and Sunday school, sports (skating in winter, softball and swimming in summer), and long hikes with my father at any time of the year. On one occasion, we walked fifty miles from Ingonish to North Sydney. As I got older, he took me to political meetings – Tory meetings, naturally.

I was a tomboy. I was far too serious, too intense, and too driven to succeed in school and after-school activities to worry about catching the eye of boys. I knew I was just as good as they were, if not better, but I also knew I had to keep proving it. In school one year, a boy got higher marks than I did. I will never forget his name: Frank Kelly. I was genuinely upset. So I studied harder than ever and beat him the next year. On reflection, I realize I intimidated boys my own age to the point of scaring them off.

In truth, I have always been attracted to older men, preferably married men. Their unavailability protects my independence. People are forever asking why I never married. On more than one occasion I could have married a "good man" and "settled down," but I passed on those opportunities. Although I adore other people's kids, married bliss is not for me. I value my independence too highly. I enjoy travelling with men so long as I can send them home when the trip is done. I could not imagine living with one of them. Among my close friends, I count as many men as women – maybe more men. I like it that way.

Growing up, my social life revolved around the United Church, church camp, Canadian Girls in Training (CGIT) and groups like that. In the winter, we would skate on the frozen harbour or walk two miles to Pottle's Lake. My sister Jean remembers how Mum would put a hot baked potato in the toe of each skate to keep it warm. When we got to the lake, we ate the potatoes as we skated.

When I was in grade four, I won a scrapbook competition. While other students made scrapbooks about plants, pets, and things like that, I did one that was an accumulation of my grandmother MacDonald's postcards sent from various parts of the world while she was sailing on my grandfather's ship. I entitled the collection: "People I Want to Meet, and Places I Want to See When I Grow Up." I took first prize. I suppose that scrapbook was a harbinger of the interests that would chart my adult life.

North Sydney in those days was a busy place as cargoes of fish, coal, and steel were shipped through the port. During the Second World War, the harbour was filled with merchant ships from many countries. As a consequence of the Halifax Explosion of 1917 – the greatest man-made explosion the world had seen – ships carrying munitions were no longer allowed in Halifax Harbour. So when the North Atlantic convoys were forming-up in the 1940s, the munitions ships and the convoys' slower ships were assembled in the north and south arms of Sydney Harbour. When I looked out my bedroom window at night, I could see the munitions ships lined up with red warning lights on their foremasts to identify their lethal cargo. None was blown up, although in 1942 a German U-boat sank the SS *Caribou*, a 265-foot passenger ferry in the Gulf of St Lawrence as it steamed from North Sydney toward Port aux Basques, Newfoundland, with 237 servicemen, civilians, and crew aboard.[2]

We felt North Sydney was very much on the front lines of the war. My sisters and I did our studying at night with blackout curtains tightly drawn. Wardens patrolled the streets to make sure no light was showing. We listened to Winston Churchill on the radio and were acutely aware of the heroic struggle Britain was waging.

When my father was called back to work to handle priority war-time messages on the transatlantic cable, he had to have the highest level of security clearance because some of the traffic consisted of messages between British Prime Minister Churchill and United States President Franklin Roosevelt. It seems odd now, but it was the way the undersea cable functioned. Because there was no direct cable connection between London and Washington, Morse code messages would come from England to the western terminus of the cable at Lloyd's Cove, not far from where we lived. The messages would be decoded at the Western Union office, then resent by land cable to Washington or New York. It's the only secure way Churchill and Roosevelt could communicate on a regular basis.

The war aside, I was comfortable with my life in North Sydney. I loved school and sports. And I really loved to win. In grade nine, we had to write an essay about fire protection. I won the prize for best essay in the province. I remember the occasion distinctly because my parents bought me my first pair of silk stockings for the presentation. The engraved cup I won is still on display in the fire hall in North Sydney. From time to time, I entered spelling bees, and I usually won. I remember a competition in Sydney Mines in which we were tested on the meaning of words. I won because I knew the meaning of mirabile dictu.[3] The definition was not all that hard for a girl who loved Latin and who had a father who insisted that she learn the roots and meanings of words.

Our grade nine teacher, Alice Macdonald, set aside Friday afternoons for instruction in public speaking. She gave us a topic the day before so that we could prepare our speeches. When we finished, the class would rank us. That class was the toughest audience I have ever faced. They were completely uninhibited in their criticism. Speaking to large crowds, even to a Conservative convention, was a breeze compared to that grade nine class in North Sydney. My father helped me develop my speaking skills by having me memorize passages from the Bible – one of his favourites was the apostle Paul's defence before King Agrippa from the Book of Acts[4] – and recite them while he critiqued my cadence and pronunciation. Dad would interrupt me, correct me, and insist I do it again: "You're not emphasizing the right words, Flora."

We never had alcohol in the house when I was growing up. Although Dad was a teetotaler, he was not the sort to censure people who did drink. One cold winter night as he was coming home from a lodge meeting, he came across one of the town drunks staggering along the street. Dad knew that if the fellow collapsed, which seemed likely, he would freeze to death before morning. He decided to walk him home. After about a mile, the road crossed a railroad track. The man insisted on sitting down to rest. So the two of them sat down on the tracks. Then the man wanted to sing. They sat there singing hymns at midnight. It must have been quite a sight. Eventually, the man was able to stand, and Dad got him home. My father would do that kind of thing. It made no difference that the poor man was a drunk. He was a fellow human being.

Fred MacDonald was a man of stubborn principle when it came to religion. Although he was not a Catholic, he chaired the fund-raising drive for the Catholic hospital in North Sydney. He was also a fundraiser for the Salvation Army, and he was active in the Methodist church in North Sydney and, after church union, in its successor, St Matthew-Wesley United Church. He became a pillar of that church. Its secretary-treasurer for forty years, he looked after the financial books. He made sure his children attended two services there every Sunday, plus Sunday school. He was involved in choosing new ministers, and if the janitor fell ill, he would clean the church himself. But he absolutely refused to become a member of the church. There is a story to that.

Although Dad's father, Ronald Alexander MacDonald, had been a Catholic, Eliza Roberts, his wife (and my grandmother), was raised a Methodist. There had been a great deal of distrust and tension between Catholics and Protestants in Cape Breton in that era, and it still existed when I was growing up. My grandparents' "mixed marriage" was not much of an issue while they were at sea together, but when my grandmother settled in North Sydney with her four sons, she wanted to join the local Methodist church. She was denied membership. Years later, when Dad was secretary-treasurer, he looked up the old church records. There was his mother, repeatedly applying for membership in the church; the elders would meet to consider her application, and every time the elders had written: "Mrs Captain Ronald MacDonald, application rejected, married to a Catholic." There was no way my father was going to join a church that would not accept his mother.

Despite the rejection, my grandmother raised her sons as Methodists. I have to say the Methodists were not a lot of fun. They were the strictest of the churches. You polished your boots on

Saturday night to have them ready for church, and you even poured water in the drinking glasses on Saturday night, because you did nothing on Sunday that you did not absolutely have to do. Not that the United Church, as my father interpreted its dictates, was appreciably better. We were not allowed to buy ice cream on Sunday, and if we wanted to swim on the Sabbath, he would insist that we go out of town, to Lloyd's Cove or George's River.

When people asked him why he refused to join the church, he would say, "I need no middleman between me and my maker." He believed religion should not raise barriers based on denomination. He believed in tolerance. On Christmas Eve, we would go to mass at the Catholic church. He coached us until we learned every word to "O Come All Ye Faithful" – in Latin. We were the only ones in that whole Catholic church who knew all the Latin verses. Among the other denominations in North Sydney, Dad had a particular aversion to the Church of England. In his mind, that church considered itself better than God, and he could not stand the elitist attitude of its members.

In fact, my father had an aversion to most things English. Scots do nurse grudges, and my father, as a staunch Highland Scot, was not about to forgive the English for the savagery of "Butcher Cumberland" at the Battle of Culloden. I remember very well his reaction when King George VI and Queen Elizabeth came to Canada in 1939. Europe was on the cusp of war. Canada would surely be involved. After the royal couple had toured the country, they came to Halifax, their last stop before sailing home. People gathered from all over the province. The Boy Scouts were there, and the Girl Guides, and all the organizations like that. Everyone was there, except the MacDonald children. There was no way he would allow us to go to Halifax to celebrate the presence of a usurper, a Hanoverian king! Years later, when I went off to Europe on my own, I found a cable from my father waiting for me when my ship docked at Southampton. Get out of England without delay, he warned me; make for the safety of Scotland.

My father's aversion to the English was rivalled only by his distrust of the Campbells. For much of Scottish history, the Campbells had allied themselves with the English against the MacDonalds and most of the other clans. In 1688, the Protestants William and Mary of Orange had deposed the Roman Catholic King, James II, the last in the star-crossed line of Stuart monarchs. The Campbells supported

the Hanoverians, William and Mary, while the MacDonalds were
loyal to James and to his son, Bonnie Prince Charlie. These deep
differences came to a head in 1692 at what became known as the
Massacre of Glencoe, when the Campbells slaughtered virtually all
of the members of a small branch of the MacDonald clan.

That infamous day was captured for posterity in a song, "The
Massacre of Glencoe," which goes, in part:

They came from Fort William with murder in mind
The Campbell had orders King William had signed
"Put all to the sword" these words underlined
"And leave none alive called MacDonald."
[...]
They came in the night when the men were asleep
This band of Argyles, through snow soft and deep
Like murdering foxes amongst helpless sheep
They slaughtered the house of MacDonald.

With history like that, you could hardly blame the MacDonalds for
being paranoid about the Campbells. My father certainly tended that
way. When my brother Ronald was to marry a woman in Montreal,
my father was appalled to discover that a member of the Campbell
clan was going to be in the wedding party. He visualized a gang of
Campbells descending on the ceremony wielding their claymores, as
the Highlanders' double-edged broadswords were known. Dad went
to the wedding anyway, albeit nervously.[5]

I talk more about my father than my mother because he really
was the dominant influence in my early years. He not only inspired
me to be the best I could possibly be, he insisted on it. From him,
I inherited my respect for learning, my passion for reading, my love
of travel and adventure, and my belief in myself – the belief that I can
do anything I set my mind to do, whether it is memorizing passages
of Latin, running for the leadership of the Progressive Conservative
Party of Canada, or building schools in Afghanistan.

He also encouraged me to hitchhike anywhere I wanted to go and
not let my gender prevent me from doing it. By the time I was in
my teens, I would hitchhike to Halifax or anywhere else in Nova
Scotia. I would take the bus to Sydney for business college, then
hitchhike home. One time, a friend and I thumbed our way right
around the south shore of Nova Scotia to Yarmouth, and up through

the Annapolis Valley, just to get to know the province. Another time, I hitchhiked from Cape Breton to Ontario. In years since, I have thumbed my way across Canada, the United States, and Europe. It is a wonderful way to meet people while seeing the world.

The world is a more dangerous place now, of course, but I still pick up people on the highway – always. Because I hitchhiked so much in my younger years, I feel an obligation to give others a lift. Hitchhiking has been the source of some of my most exciting adventures, as I will recount.

4

A Lust for Travel

I was seventeen years old when I graduated from Empire Business College in 1943. With the war raging, the military was hiring secretaries to work at the seaplane base in North Sydney. It was the first job interview I had ever had, and I failed abysmally to make a favourable impression. Needless to say, I did not get the job. So my father said, "Well, I'll speak to someone in the bank," and he must have, because I was invited to the North Sydney branch of the Bank of Nova Scotia where, after a perfunctory interview, I was offered a position. A banking job was not the worst thing in the world by any means. One of the attractions was the opportunity to move around, to secure transfers to branches in interesting places. Although I find it hard to believe now, I actually spent nine years with the Bank of Nova Scotia.

As the most junior person, I was assigned to count pennies on my first day. Now they have machines to count coins, but in those days we had to count and to roll packages of coins by hand. I must have performed the task satisfactorily because they made me a ledger-keeper, at a monthly salary of $36. The bank had huge heavy ledgers in which we recorded deposits, withdrawals, and interest earned for every account; we had to calculate the interest manually. At the end of every month, we had to make the accounts balance. This meant going through these great ledgers, totalling debits and the credits for every customer and reconciling the results with the previous month's balances. If we were out by even ten cents, we had to go back through it all again. I must have been reasonably competent because it was not long before I was promoted to teller, with a raise to $40 a month.

As my banking career progressed, I became the assistant to the assistant manager of the branch; at one point I was even acting assistant manager. If I had persevered, I might eventually have become the manager of the Bank of Nova Scotia in North Sydney, although there were very few female bank managers in Canada in those years. Banking, however, was not in my blood. Travel was. I kept requesting transfers. First, I got myself transferred to Halifax; then my closest friend from North Sydney landed a job in Peterborough, Ontario, and the two of us decided to share an apartment in that city. So I applied for a transfer to Peterborough, and got it.

I was there for a couple of years and had a great time. Then my apartment mate got married, and I figured I might as well ask for a transfer to Toronto where I had friends, the Finlaysons, who had moved there from Cape Breton. I went to work in the bank's personnel department. As I had in Peterborough, I soon had an active life in Toronto; there was a young people's group in Kew Beach in the east end, skating, and great concerts at Massey Hall. But I soon grew restless. Am I going to be here for the rest of my life? I wondered. It was time to move on so I quit and headed for Europe.

The year was 1952. In that era, young people – especially unescorted young females – did not do what became common a generation later: grab a backpack and bedroll and take off to discover Europe on their own. I was anxious to go to Scotland to see where my ancestors had come from. I particularly wanted to learn more about the life of my namesake Flora Macdonald, the heroine of Bonnie Prince Charlie's escape. And I wanted to pursue the exciting saga of Scotland's Stone of Destiny. "Stone of Destiny" is the Scottish name for what the English call the "Stone of Scone." A symbol of Scots nationhood, this is the stone on which all of Scotland's kings had historically been crowned. In 1296, however, the stone was stolen from Scotland by the English King Edward I, who carried it to Westminster Abbey in London where it was installed beneath the seat of the Coronation Chair, the old wooden chair on which English sovereigns are crowned. English monarchs thought that the physical presence of the Stone of Destiny lent legitimacy to their claims to be the rightful rulers of Scotland.

Proud Scots, of course, never accepted that claim – and they wanted their stone back. Although Edward III promised in the Treaty of Northampton in 1328 to return it, he never did, and succeeding English monarchs used every conceivable stratagem to retain custody of the slab of red sandstone. Scots have long memories. They do not forget such indignities.

On Christmas Day 1950, three intrepid Glasgow University students – Ian Hamilton, Gavin Vernon and Kay Matheson – pulled off a daring heist. They hid in Westminster Abbey at closing time, evaded detection by the security guards, and liberated the Stone of Destiny. It was no easy feat. The stone measures twenty-six inches long by sixteen inches wide and ten-and-a-half inches thick and weighs 336 pounds. As they carried it from the abbey through a small side door, the students dropped the stone. It broke into two pieces. No matter. They put the pieces in two cars and, after a series of adventures, got the Stone of Destiny back to Scotland where it belonged.

They hid the pieces in a quarry where a stonemason reattached them. Later, they took the stone to the altar in the ruins of Arbroath Abbey, about seventeen miles from Dundee, where they held a ceremony to mark its return to Scotland. It was an inspired place to stage the ceremony because the abbey – founded in 1178 for the monks of the Tironensian order – is honoured in Scottish history as the site of the Declaration of Arbroath of 1320. The declaration was in the form of a letter addressed to Pope John XXII in which Scotland's nobles declared their independence from England and swore allegiance to the excommunicated Robert the Bruce. The declaration is famous for this phrase: "As long as a hundred of us remain alive, we shall not on any condition be subjected to English rule."

Of course, I went to Arbroath Abbey. Located on the edge of the North Sea, it had been a huge Gothic cathedral. I was able to track down two of the stone's liberators, Hamilton and Matheson. I met their Scots secessionist friends in Glasgow and Edinburgh and listened to their talk – it never amounted to more than talk – about striking a blow for independence by blowing up railway bridges and other foolhardy schemes. They never really intended to keep the Stone of Destiny. Their point made, they informed Scotland Yard where to find it. The stone was returned to Westminster Abbey and it was back in place for the coronation of Queen Elizabeth II in 1953. The leader of the stone-nappers, Ian Hamilton, later wrote a book about their adventure entitled, *No Stone Unturned: The Story of the Stone of Destiny.*[1]

No doubt, if I had been born in Scotland, I would have been a passionate Scots nationalist just like Ian Hamilton. Instead, I am convinced it was my Scottish blood and temperament that made me a passionate Canadian nationalist, an ardent admirer of Sir John A. Macdonald, a Red Tory, and eventually the first executive director of the Committee for an Independent Canada.

I had sailed from Quebec City on the HMS *Scythia* in mid-July 1952 with two companions. One was a woman named Doreen Holroyd, who had worked at the Bank of Nova Scotia in Toronto with me. The other was Ralph Finlayson, the teenaged son of my Cape Breton friends in Toronto. His father had come from the north of Scotland and Ralph intended to look up his family. When the ship landed in Southampton a cable from my father was waiting: "You should get to Scotland and safety as soon as possible."

After a few days in London, the three of us set off, hitchhiking, for Scotland. Along the way we stopped to see Winston Churchill's birthplace at Blenheim Palace; a Shakespeare play at Stratford-on-Avon; Warwick Castle (the home of the Earl of Warwick and still in superb condition); Coventry, and Sherwood Forest (no sign of Robin Hood or his merry band). At Altrincham, outside Manchester, we met my mother who was there visiting her father's relatives. Mum wanted to go with us to see Wales. Hitchhiking was not her style, so we took a bus to Llandudno in North Wales, travelling through some the most beautiful countryside I have ever seen. Then Ralph and I thumbed our way to Scotland – to Glasgow and from there to the Pass of Glencoe, scene of the massacre of the MacDonalds in 1692, and to Skye in the Inner Hebrides. We visited the ruins of the twelfth century Duntulm Castle, which had been the stronghold of the chieftain of Clan Donald, the legendary Lord of the Isles.

In Portree, on Skye, we had the good fortune to encounter a young veterinarian by the name of Mary Smith. New York City–born and Cornell University–educated, Mary took us under her wing, taking us with her as she drove around the island to check on sick animals. Everywhere we stopped, we were served tea, bannock, scones, croudie (a form of cheese), and shortbread. I was struck by two characteristics in the people we met – their fervent religious beliefs and their love of whisky. We met one old woman who made a point of saying grace before she downed her whisky, straight, and an old fellow who confided that he made his porridge with whisky instead of water. I wondered what my teetotaller father would think.

Back on the mainland, we headed for the site of the Battle of Culloden, which ended the Jacobite uprising led by Bonnie Prince Charlie. What a disappointment! Culloden Moor was no more. Reforestation specialists had planted trees everywhere on the historic battlefield. A small clearing containing a burial ground with mounds marking the mass graves and a memorial cairn was the only reminder of the great battle of 16 April 1746. I searched in vain for a MacDonald grave marker. Although 1,150 MacDonalds died at the hands of "Butcher" Cumberland and his men, I could find nothing that recorded their sacrifice. I made a point of climbing the rock from which Cumberland had watched the battle. It was a good quarter mile from the hostilities. As I wrote in a letter to my family back in North Sydney, "That boy was taking no chances with his precious person."[2]

Doreen, who had gone off to visit relatives, rejoined us in Edinburgh. One night we decided to visit a real Scottish pub, a place where the locals go to drink, not one of those tourist establishments that line Princess Street. We found Robbie Burns's favourite bar. We had been naïve, because it was not until then that we realized "decent" women did not go to bars in Scotland. We were the only females in the place, which was packed with evil-looking old characters. We retreated to a table in a corner. My blood ran cold when a sinister fellow leaned over to ask if the brooches we were wearing were sterling silver. Another pointed at a ring on my finger and demanded to know what it meant. We fled from the pub.

Doreen and I hitchhiked back to London, then on to Dover in time to catch the ferry across the English Channel to Calais in France. Our destination: Paris. As we walked out of Calais, we were picked up by a huge oil truck. The driver spoke no English and our French was limited to the few expressions we could find in our English-French dictionaries. Our clothes reeked with the smell of oil (so much for travelling in oil tankers, we declared). When the driver let us off, we found ourselves on the side of a road in the pouring rain, still 150 miles from Paris.

Our luck held, as it did throughout many of my travels. An Egyptian merchant driving a new Jaguar not only gave us a ride all the way to Paris, he bought us a lavish lunch of fresh trout at a superb restaurant along the way. We stayed in a small pension while we explored Paris, then hitchhiked back to London, visiting some of the famous battlefields of two world wars on the way. By this time,

Doreen had had enough of hitchhiking with me. She thought it was dangerous, that I took too many risks.

I did take precautions, staying on well-travelled roads wherever possible, being careful about the rides I accepted, and doing my best not to travel after dark. I will admit to getting into a few scrapes. The next year, while hitchhiking in France with Dorothy Chisholm, a Canadian nurse I had met on the ship on the way over, we were stopped for vagrancy and hauled into a police station by gendarmes who took a dim view of two females begging for rides. In Spain, we were stopped for violating a law barring truckers from picking up passengers. At the Spanish-French border we were detained on suspicion of being accomplices to car theft.

We never – well, almost never – let our drivers talk us into staying overnight in the same hotel they were using. Although I always carried an extremely sharp hatpin – a female hitchhiker's best friend in the pre-Mace era – I needed to employ it only once. That's when Dorothy and I had to fend off the advances of a pair of amorous, and inebriated, Spanish truck drivers when their vehicle broke down in the Sierra Madre mountains.

At the end of the first summer, Ralph returned to school in Canada while Doreen Holroyd went to stay with relatives in Yorkshire. It was time for me to get serious about finding work to support myself – and to indulge my passion for travel. I found a job in short order in London. It was with Selfridges, the world-renowned department store.[3] Selfridges had about 3,500 employees and the company worked hard to keep their morale high by offering them recreational programs – sports, theatre, dances, dinners, and so on. The Selfridge Club, as its sports and social organization was known, was on Woodcock Lane in Wembley, a tube ride from central London. I was hired to be the number two person in the management of the club, although I confess I did not have the faintest idea what I was expected to do. The club ran sporting events non-stop on Saturdays and Sundays – soccer, rugby, field hockey and other games I knew nothing about.

John Hayward, the man I worked for, was an eccentric Englishman who had served in the Indian army. He was a kind person, patient with someone who knew as little as I did, but he had two failings: he was lazy, customarily showing up for work two and a half days a week and going off for long lunches on days when he did come to the office; and he was afflicted with what he said was malaria whenever he drank alcohol. I am afraid I was not terribly kind about my boss in one of my letters home: "As far as I can see, Mr Hayward has no knowledge of finance, writes horrible grammar, and can't spell words over two syllables. However, he is a very nice man."[4]

On my first or second weekend on the job, he suffered an attack of malaria, and I was left to run the sports events on my own. Luckily, I met a man, Jimmy James, from the store's draperies department who came over to see how I was getting along. "What is this?" I asked. "What do I do now?" He helped me through it, but he said, "Look, we're playing host to Harrods this weekend. It's a rugby weekend! Whatever you do, make sure you order enough beer." I thought, all right, I can order beer. I knew nothing about beer, but how difficult could it be? I found a list of breweries and I phoned Whitbread, the first one on the list. Being completely unfamiliar with the different kinds of beer – in fact, I had never tasted it to that point in my life – I had no clue what to order. "How many pins and how many firkins, mum?" the salesman asked.[5] He might have been speaking Greek for all I knew. Anyway, I figured it out, and I think I ordered enough beer to last until Christmas. We had a very successful weekend of games, with a dinner and dance at the end, and lots and lots of beer.

Anxious to get out of the residence where I had been living, I went around to the Canadian High Commission in London to inquire about lodgings. While I was there, a young woman from Winnipeg, Elaine Barber, came in with a similar inquiry. The person at the High Commission said, yes, there was a flat for two people available not far from Lords, the famous cricket ground, in a posh neighbourhood known as St John's Wood. Elaine and I took the flat. It was on the third floor of an old house owned by an elderly Jewish woman, Hilda Brighton, whose family had once been very wealthy, but had lost most of their money during the Depression. Hilda was extremely well-educated. To keep herself going, she had opened one of the early public relations businesses in London. An entrepreneurial go-getter, she would do anything, or get anything, her clients desired. If you wanted an elephant to ride down The Mall, Hilda would get you an elephant.

In her parents' affluent days, the great Italian tenor Enrico Caruso would stay with them when he came to London. Hilda herself became an important figure on the London arts scene. She was the editor or publisher of a number of leading authors, including Daphne du Maurier, the author of *Rebecca, Jamaica Inn,* and

Frenchman's Creek. Hilda had a tradition of hosting literary gatherings twice a month. They were incredible. The editor of *The Times Literary Supplement*, some celebrated writers, and other big names from the arts world would come to her house on Saturday afternoon for tea, sherry, small cakes, and refined conversation. I would sit in the corner listening.

Across the back fence from Hilda there lived a crotchety old man – I guess he was not really as old as I assumed he was – but I would go to talk with him. His name was Beverley Baxter – "Sir" Beverley Baxter, as I soon learned – and he was a prominent journalist, author, broadcaster, and Conservative member of the British Parliament. He may have been crotchety, but I found him fascinating as we talked about the column he wrote for *Maclean's* magazine for many years.[6]

Money was always tight. Our flat was reasonably expensive, costing Elaine and me each three pounds per week. My take-home pay from Selfridges was only £5.15 after deductions, so by the time I paid my share of the rent, laundry, and gas for the stove, I had about £1 left for food for the week. But I found ways to enjoy myself in London without spending much. I moonlighted for a while as a stagehand in the West End, because it gave me access to cheap theatre tickets. When my friend Dorothy Chisholm and I went to other productions – concerts at Albert Hall, ballet and opera at Sadler Wells, Shakespeare at the Old Vic – we would buy standing room tickets. The money saved was ample compensation for the discomfort of standing for a few hours.

Post-war London was an exciting place for a young woman and I soon developed a busy social life. I had Scottish country dance lessons on Monday nights and badminton on Tuesday, and before long I took up squash, too. And on Friday and Saturday there were dances – Scottish dances, as well as formal military dances held by one regiment or another, plus the special-occasion dances that I organized and was expected to attend at the Selfridge Club. My one formal dress – I could not afford a second – was given a real workout that year in London.

I was under no illusions that I was a great beauty. Dorothy was extremely attractive and drew the attention of every male we encountered. I still looked like a tomboy, wearing my red hair in a short boyish bob, and favouring slacks in place of skirts. My appearance produced some amusing incidents of gender confusion. On several

occasions in Scotland, I was denied admission to the women's lava-
tory and instructed to use the men's, instead.

Nevertheless, and without any real encouragement on my part,
I acquired an informal roster of "boys" (as I called them in my letters
home) who escorted me to dances and parties. I remember Jim, Peter,
Alan, Brian, John, George, Lester, and a second Peter, among others, plus two lads from the Royal Canadian Air Force and some
United States Marines who were stationed in the United Kingdom
and who joined Dorothy and me on some of our hitchhiking jaunts,
but whose names, sadly, I cannot recall. At one point, I wrote home
to complain – or perhaps it was to boast – that I had not had a single evening at home in two weeks. It was all great fun and it stayed
fun as long I did not get serious about any of the men who passed
through my life, as long as I kept playing the field. And that is what
I did. I still had no intention of getting "involved" or "settling down."

Dorothy lived in the nurses' residence at St Thomas's Hospital,[7]
but whenever she was free, she and I would take off in search of
new experiences. Not long after arriving in London, I discovered
an amazing man. His name was Maurice Pike and he proved to be
one of the great finds of my life. He made London come alive for
me. I first met him when I went to visit the Parliament Buildings
and this astonishingly well-informed man, whom I took to be an
ordinary tour guide, led a group of us through the buildings. As I
subsequently learned, Maurice was actually employed as a book-
keeper in the City, but he had a hobby – the history of London and
environs. He liked nothing better than to take visitors to historically
significant places or to spots that were simply interesting or out of
the way. Everyone who visits London should have a Maurice Pike.

As I followed him around the Parliament Buildings that day,
I plied him with questions. No one else was saying much, but I have
never been accused of being shy. When we came to Westminster Hall,
I noticed a door leading downstairs. "Is that the door?" I asked. "Is
that where Guy Fawkes hid the gunpowder?" My question launched
Maurice into a long explanation of the gunpowder plot. I asked him
about two or three other things, and when the crowd broke up, he
stopped me and asked why I had raised so many questions. "Well,
I'm just visiting here from Canada, and I'd like to know about all
of these things before I have to go home," I replied. It was about
four o'clock, and Maurice said, "Look, I have another hour or so.
Would you like to come over to Westminster Abbey with me? I'll

show you around the Abbey." I had been in the Abbey a couple of times already, so I thought I knew all about it. But I agreed, and we spent the next hour doing just one little corner of the Abbey – he had so many wonderful stories!

When I told Maurice he was more interesting than any guide I had ever encountered, he made me an offer: "I go off on a walk-around like this on my own every Saturday afternoon. Any time you'd like to join me, you'll be more than welcome." The next weekend Dorothy and I turned up to meet him. Maurice admitted he had extended a similar offer to a number of other people over the years and we were the first to take him up on it. As often as we could during the next year, we rambled around London with Maurice. He had an encyclopaedic memory and we learned more about the pubs, churches, parks, monuments, art galleries, schools, theatres, and other famous buildings – all the great and intriguing things about London – than we could otherwise have absorbed in a lifetime. He had a fascinating story that made every place he took us come alive in our imaginations.

One day he led us down a back street in the City (London's financial district) to a trap door in the middle of the pavement. We climbed down a spiral staircase into the bowels of the earth where Maurice showed us a surviving section of the original Roman wall built by the legions of Julius Caesar. From there he led us to the well-hidden church of St Bartholomew-the-Great. The only surviving section of a twelfth century Norman priory, St Bartholomew's is London's oldest parish church. I came across an ancient marker there. Although the inscription had almost worn away, I could tell that it was in memory of a husband and wife. The inscription ended with these words: "She first deceased, he for a little tried to live without her, liked it not, and died."

Before we left England, we persuaded Maurice to go to the London Polytechnic and propose to the school that he set up and teach a course on historic London, which is, in fact, what happened.[8] We also invited him to visit us in Canada, and he did that, too.

The winter of 1952–53 was long remembered for the great smog that rolled across London, choking the city, reducing visibility to nil, and bringing traffic to a complete standstill. Nothing moved. That is how thick the smog was. It was so bad that I could not see across the living room of our flat. I recall trying to take a trolley home from Selfridges. We got as far as one of the big railway stations where they told us to get off the trolley and start walking. I helped everyone to get off, telling them, "Now, I want you to line up one behind the other, and put your hand on the shoulder of the person in front of you." And we walked and walked and walked. We walked on the sidewalk and, when we could not see it any longer, we walked on the road. As we came to each corner, I would call out the name of the street, until I finally got to my own street, and somebody else had to carry on.

The smog was so thick and filthy that it was impossible to keep our flat or ourselves clean. Five minutes after washing, our faces would be streaked with dirt again. When I woke up each morning, the only white spot on the pillow was where my head had been. The rest of the pillow was disgustingly greasy. Four thousand people died that winter from respiratory diseases as a result of the smog.

Queen Mary, the widow of George V, died that winter. My friend Helen Beveridge, from Truro, Nova Scotia, and I went down at two o'clock in the morning to view the lying-in-state at Westminster Hall. With soldiers in ancient uniforms standing at each corner of the catafalque, the platform on which the casket rested, and with great torches lighting the hall and illuminating the hammerbeam ceiling, it struck me as a scene from a medieval pageant. We found a convenient spot from which to watch the funeral procession and waited for six hours for it to begin. It was well worth the wait. We saw the Queen, her sister Princess Margaret, the Queen Mother, the Archbishop of Canterbury, Winston Churchill, and even the former King Edward VIII, who was living in exile as the Duke of Windsor. Marching ahead of the gun carriage bearing the coffin were the Household Cavalry and the bands of the Scots Guards, Irish Guards, Coldstreams, and Grenadiers. It was a spectacular display. No one does funerals like the Brits.

That spring brought two events that I would not have missed for the world. The first was the Queen's annual garden party, an intimate little affair for seven thousand people on the grounds of Buckingham Palace. Through Canada House, I received an invitation as did Dorothy Chisholm and two other friends. After the Queen had returned to the palace, I dragged Dorothy over the Royal Pavilion to say hello to Canadian Prime Minister Louis St Laurent. He had come over early for the coronation, which was, of course, the second event I would not have missed. All of London was in frenzied preparation for weeks before the great event. Some people set themselves along the route days ahead with sleeping bags and small tents or awnings to protect themselves from heavy rains. The weather was certainly miserable on coronation day. We watched the parade from a section of stands reserved for Canadians. I have never seen anything as magnificent. As the golden coach, in all its glistening glory, moved the length of The Mall, the vast crowd erupted in one long unbroken cheer. When I wrote home, I said, "I felt a lump welling up in my throat from the majesty and grandeur of the whole performance and I felt like shouting to the skies, 'I'm glad I'm a Canadian, part of an Empire that could produce a show like this.'"

With nightfall, we found ourselves in a group of South Africans, English, New Zealanders, and Canadians as the Queen switched on the lights along The Mall. Four huge crowns sprang into twinkling outline. That prompted another prolonged cheer from the crowd that then surged toward the Embankment to witness a spectacular fireworks display over the Thames. An estimated one hundred thousand people gathered and, as they tried to move en masse closer to the fireworks, they pressed in on those of us who were at the front, forcing us toward the river. I was scared. Some spectators were crushed and had to be carried out with broken arms and legs. A woman near us went into screaming hysterics. Eventually, we fought free of the mob and headed for Piccadilly Circus where we joined street dancing into the small hours. Hand in hand with strangers, young and old, of every nationality, we were dancing the okey-cokey (also known as the hokey-cokey or hokey-pokey) as Big Ben struck midnight.[9]

With the arrival of summer 1953, Dorothy and I quit our jobs, planning to spend the rest of the year hitchhiking in the United Kingdom and on the Continent. But first, we headed for Devon and Cornwall for several days of hiking and hosteling, accompanied by two friends, Peter Goodman and George Turner. The highlight of the trip was a visit to Tintagel in Cornwall, which may (or may not) have been the Camelot of Arthurian legend, the site of King Arthur's Castle, the home of the Round Table and the setting for the adventures of Queen Guinevere, Gawain, Lancelot, Tristan, Isolde, and Merlin. As luck would have it, a Hollywood film crew was in Tintagel at the same time, making a movie, *Knights of the Round Table*, starring Ava Gardner, Mel Ferrer, and Robert Taylor. As the four of us came over a ridge, a company of celluloid knights let loose a volley of arrows in the direction of another group of actors who were hidden in the bracken pretending to be Celtic warriors. The arrows at least were real. We gathered a few stray ones as souvenirs before continuing on our way.

Dorothy was a good sport and a wonderful hitchhiking companion. She was always willing to let me make our travel decisions, although she was sometimes nervous about them – as well she might be. I had what I was sure was a brilliant idea: why not spend a month in the summer of 1953 getting to know the agricultural sector of Britain? I suppose "working as farm labourers" would be a more accurate way of phrasing it. Anyway, I went to the Department of Agriculture and signed us both up. I figured we would get to see more of England and earn some money for our travel. Having committed us, I broke the news to Dorothy, who took it quite well.

We spent three weeks in a camp in Salford Priors in Warwickshire, not far from Stratford-on-Avon, with a large complement of foreign students and factory workers, women as well as men, from France, Spain, Italy, Austria, Germany, Denmark, Sweden, Gold Coast, and India, as well as the UK. The farm work did not pay much, but it provided us with a rudimentary place to sleep and plenty of food to eat. Every morning, we were picked up by a truck that took us to the fields we were to work that day, hoeing potatoes or picking peas, or beans, or other vegetables. At the end of the day, Dorothy and I would jump off the truck as it returned through Stratford, take a shower at the YWCA, then buy a standing-room ticket at the Royal Shakespeare Theatre. We would stand through the play, then walk the six or seven miles back to the camp, get a few hours' sleep and be ready to do it all again the next day. I suppose we should have been exhausted, but we were young and resilient.

When we had seen enough of England, we went to Scotland where I was eager to trace my ancestors who had left the Highlands for Cape Breton in 1807. I knew that my great-great grandfather, Donald MacDonald, had come from Bohuntin. All I knew about Bohuntin was that it was in Lochaber, a wild and rugged region of the West Highlands that had inspired the Gaelic lament "Cha Till Mor Mo Bhean (Lochaber No More)." It was the traditional tune of the Black Watch. A thrill ran through my body whenever I heard it played by the great Cape Breton piper and teacher, Sandy Boyd – *Farewell to Lochaber, farewell to my Jean / Where heartsome wi' her I ha'e many days been / For Lochaber no more, Lochaber no more / We'll maybe return to Lochaber no more ....*

The biggest town in Lochaber was Fort William (pop. ten thousand). But where was Bohuntin? We were not at all sure. We did not even know if the place still existed. As fate would have it, we met a woman who ran a tweed and tartan shop in Pitlochry, a picturesque town that bills itself as the gateway to the Highlands. She was married to a man named MacDonald, who, as a regional hydro commissioner, knew the area intimately. We started comparing notes on forbears and, when I mentioned Bohuntin, he made inquiries and quickly located the hamlet. It turned out to be at the end of a dead-end road on the side of a lonely glen. The entire community consisted of a half-dozen crofts all occupied by MacDonalds.

I was excited to meet the patriarch of the family, my family, an arthritic old man named (like my ancestor) Donald MacDonald. He proved to be a walking encyclopaedia of Scottish history and lore. Leaning on two canes, he expounded on the history of the House of Bohuntin. He confirmed that our Donald MacDonald had come from Bohuntin – the ruins of his croft were still there – and that he had been known as the "Tailer Abrach" ("Tailor of Lochaber"). I was delighted to have found my great-great grandfather's home and to have learned these bits of family history, but was saddened to discover that the MacDonald croft had become little more than a pile of unwanted stones.

Dorothy and I started hitchhiking across Europe in September. What wonderful adventures we had! We were walking peacefully through the outskirts of a small village not far from Chartres in France when we were taken into custody as "vagrants" by two gendarmes. Our passports were inspected and our descriptions recorded. We were not released until the local cops had called their superiors in Chartres for permission to permit us to continue on our way. After touring the wine district of Bordeaux, where we tried to act like connoisseurs – or at least not like complete idiots – as we inspected newly harvested grapes and accepted offers to taste rare wines, we hitchhiked to Biarritz on the Bay of Biscay. That was something else! But the only place we could find to sleep on our last night in France was in a chicken coop.

Then Dorothy and I crossed the border into Spain. Our sneakers had given out by the time we reached Madrid, and we set off in search of sandals. The clerk in a women's shoe store took one look at the size of our feet and sent us to a men's store. There we found sandals – and two young men, the shoe salesman and his assistant, who offered to show us the town. They did, and that evening they insisted on buying us a Spanish meal. It tasted fine to me, but Dorothy became quite ill a few hours later. It seemed that fried bull and snails did not agree with her.

Later, in Seville, we made the mistake of going to a bullfight. Neither of us had ever been to one and we were curious. The loud shouting of a large crowd of extremely smelly Spanish men, the choking cloud of marijuana smoke, the blazing sun, and all the blood and gore as the heroes of the bullring slaughtered their bulls was too much for us. Neither was particularly squeamish, but we both threw up. As I wrote home, "Bullfighting is the bloodiest, cruellest excuse for a sport that I ever hope to witness. The bull doesn't stand the slightest chance, and before long I was wishing he would gore the picadors or matadors."

In Spain the law against truck drivers picking up hitchhikers really cramped our style and slowed our progress. More annoying was the Spanish convention that "respectable" women do not travel without a male escort. Naturally, Dorothy and I were taken to be "loose" women and we had to endure the insults of village urchins and the lecherous suggestions of adult males. In one village, we bedded down in a room on the ground floor of a house and, because it was extremely hot, we left the shutters open. We awoke to find a gaggle of curious villagers peering in, watching us sleep.

In Portugal many villagers, seeing our sandals and backpacks, assumed we were pilgrims making our way to the Fatima shrine where the Virgin Mary is said to have appeared to three Portuguese children in 1917. Villagers came out to offer us bread and wine, and we were not too proud to accept. By this time, we were running low on money, so we went to work for a few days in the grape harvest, contributing to the making of 1953 vintage Portuguese wines by enthusiastically crushing grapes with our bare feet.

We had hoped to travel across North Africa, but because of an armed uprising in Spanish Morocco, we could not get beyond Gibraltar. We turned back into Spain and decided to head for the French Riviera. We had a close call in southern Spain. We were hitchhiking toward the Sierra Madre mountains when we were picked up by a lorry. Two lorries, or trucks, were travelling together and the drivers stopped frequently to eat and drink wine, plenty of wine. Heading into the mountains as night fell, we were going up a very steep incline when the truck in front of us overturned and toppled across the road, blocking all traffic. Our driver got out to talk to the other driver, and their conversation turned raunchy as they contemplated the possibilities of spending the night on a mountain road with two unescorted women.

I always travelled with a hat pin, so I said to Dorothy. "Lock the door beside you, and I'll sit in front of you, and I'll have my hat pin." I figured if we kept the door locked, the two men would have to deal with me and my hat pin. Eventually, many vehicles were backed up in both directions and their angry drivers insisted that the truck be righted or hauled off to the side of the road. While that was being decided, we went to the people in the vehicle behind us and said, "Look, we're hitchhikers, and we need to get a ride to Malaga." We got into their truck and everything was fine, except for one thing. They drove like maniacs. I was terrified going around the curves and twists through the mountains, but we got into Malaga about two or three o'clock in the morning and found a place to sleep. Then we kept going around the south of Spain.

Eventually, we ran out of road. In 1953 there were no connecting roads that would let us go all the way around the coast of Spain. We could not get to Barcelona, so we had to go back toward Malaga and take a train to Madrid. We were in Madrid only long enough to go through the city and out the other side, so that we could start hitchhiking northeast. At Zaragoza, the two thousand-year-old capital of Aragon, we were picked up by two young Portuguese fellows. They offered to take us to Barcelona. It was night when we got there, and we had no idea where to stay. But these fellows said they were staying in a hotel, and they would see if they could arrange a room for us, too. They got us a room adjoining theirs. They seemed like very nice gentlemanly chaps. But one of them had taken a great liking to Dorothy, and he kept slipping notes under the connecting door, saying, "Dorothy, won't you come back to Portugal and marry me?" and things like that.

We piled furniture against the door, and went to bed, but got up very early in the morning and fled from the hotel, leaving the bill for the men to pay. We walked to the outskirts of Barcelona where we saw a small food shop. Dorothy could speak some Spanish so she said, "I'll go in there and buy us a couple of buns or something, and you watch for cars." Suddenly, I saw a Cadillac coming. I hadn't seen a Cadillac since leaving Canada, so out of curiosity, I stuck out my thumb. The car stopped. The driver said he was going to the

French frontier. "Dorothy, forget the buns!" I shouted. "We're going to ride in style." And we did. We started for the French border. After a couple of hours, we came to a road that went off to the right. The driver could speak French – he told us he was from Italy, but was working in Belgium, and had a health problem that necessitated a rest holiday in Spain – and I tried my best to understand him. He said he was going to take the coast road, because it was prettier. We should have suspected that he was trying to avoid a major border crossing. But we said the scenic route, through the Costa Brava, was fine with us. When we got to the small border outpost, Dorothy went first and had her passport stamped. Once that is done, you are deemed to have left the country. The driver went next. He handed them his papers, and all hell broke loose. Police officers wearing three-cornered hats come running from everywhere. We learned much later that our "Good Samaritan" had stolen the Cadillac from an embassy in Madrid, and the police all along the border had been alerted to watch for him.

The police assumed all three of us were car thieves. Our driver was taken away, and Dorothy and I were locked in a cell. Dorothy kept saying, "My poor mother, I've got to write to her and tell her I'll never see her again," and stuff like that. Meanwhile, the guard on duty was chatting Dorothy up, saying, "I'd like to have your picture. Here's mine." While this was going on, we were trying to figure out how to get out of this mess. The police and border guards spoke no English and we had no idea what was going on. I grew angrier and angrier. The angrier I got, the more I shouted, and the more I made uncomplimentary comments about the intelligence of petty Spanish officialdom. The police did their best to ignore me, turning their attention to Dorothy as the voice of calm and reason.

Eventually, they sent a message with our passport details to the British Consulate in Barcelona, which represented Canadian interests in that part of Spain. The consulate must have reassured the police. Anyway, they let us go, but by that time it was evening, and we had a dilemma. Because Dorothy's passport had already been stamped, showing she had left Spain, she could not re-enter the country. My passport had not yet been stamped, so that meant I was free to return to the nearest Spanish village and overnight there, without Dorothy. Although it was getting dark, we decided we had no alternative but to keep going, to walk four miles over the mountains to the first village on the French side. We were really scared because we knew that a British diplomat, his wife and their two children had been murdered by bandits on that very stretch of road the year before. But off we set.

The walk seemed endless. Every time we heard a car coming, we thought, "Are these bandits, or are they people who will give us a ride?" We played it safe and walked the whole way. Once we got to the nearest French village, we were able to catch a train to Perpignan where we found a youth hostel that let us stay for several days.

We carried on across France, hitchhiking to Avignon in Provence, then along the French and Italian Rivieras, to Pisa. South of Pisa, two men gave us a lift in their car and they offered to buy us dinner on the way, in Tarquinia (a town made famous by Thomas Babbington Macaulay in his epic poem, *Lays of Ancient Rome*, with brave Horatius, the Captain of the Gate, and all that). I ate a pail of mussels, and they must have been spoiled because I came down with a horrendous bout of food poisoning. I have never been so ill. When we reached Rome, we found accommodation in a convent, and I spent two days in bed wondering if I was going to die. Then we hitchhiked back north to Florence – I instantly fell in love with the city – and Milan. We had trouble with the Italian police as we tried to catch a ride on the toll road between Milan and Como near the Swiss border. Apparently, hitchhiking was not permitted on toll highways. When the police officers made us get off the toll road, we retreated to a position just outside the entrance and put our thumbs to work. Before long, a car stopped, and we waived gaily as we whizzed past the officers.

As any novice travellers would, Dorothy and I made a number of miscalculations in our months in Europe. One of the dumbest was to set out to hike and hitchhike over the Italian Alps into Switzerland while wearing clothes that were more suitable for the beach than for the mountains. Inevitably, we got caught in an early snowstorm as we made our way to the 6,800-foot St Gotthard Pass. We were wearing sandals, skirts, and blazers. We had no closed shoes, not even sneakers, no boots, no mitts, no down-filled parkas. We had one plastic raincoat between us. It was so cold at St Gotthard that it took our breath away. We probably should have frozen to death, but somehow we made it through Switzerland to Germany.

By now it was November, the weather was cold and wet in Germany and Belgium, and we decided it was time to head back to England. We took a train from Brussels to our final destination on the continent, the

Belgian port of Ostend, where, with a gale howling off the North Sea, we proposed to spend the night in a youth hostel before catching the ferry to England in the morning. To our dismay, the hostel was closed for the season, and we could not afford a hotel. We had to scrape up all our loose change to buy the ferry tickets. For a few moments, we were afraid we might spend the last night of our European adventure sleeping on the street. But in another of those strokes of luck that seemed to find us when we most needed it, we encountered a girl we had met on the train from Brussels. She took us home for the night where we discovered her father was the chief harbour pilot in Ostend, and he had served with the British Navy during the war. We passed an extremely enjoyable evening with them.

We arrived back in England, fresh from the adventures of our lives and ready to go home. But we were stone broke. We did not even have enough money to get from London to Liverpool where we would be taking a ship to Canada. I borrowed two pounds from Maurice Pike to tide us over. While Dorothy took a job in a pharmacy, I went to see Hilda Brighton, who offered me work as a typist. I was ecstatic when she said she wanted me to type a manuscript for her client, Daphne du Maurier. The book was a non-fiction work called *Mary Anne*, and it was the true story of du Maurier's great-great-grandmother, Mary Anne Clarke, who was briefly a royal mistress (to the Duke of York) and who went to prison in a scandal involving the sale of favours and promotions in the military. Her life was the model for George Bernard Shaw's *Pygmalion*. When the book was published, du Maurier sent me an autographed copy.

Dorothy and I sailed home to Cape Breton, glad to be back with our families, but already itching for more travel and adventure.

———————————

Soon enough, the two of us, along with a young English nurse, Connie Savage, who had worked with Dorothy at St Thomas's Hospital in London, set out to explore North America. We bought an old Chrysler for $200 and with Dorothy driving – neither Connie nor I had learned how to drive – we piled into "Jemima" (as Connie christened our teal blue vehicle) in the spring of 1955. Our plan was to drive to New York City and Washington, D.C., then head west to Vancouver, stopping in Rochester, Minnesota, where my sister Helen was living, having married a doctor at the Mayo Clinic there.

We soon discovered why Jemima had cost only $200. It would cruise at forty-five miles per hour, could reach fifty on the downhill, but struggled to exceed fifteen on upward slopes. However, we made it to New York where we booked into a YWCA. Like any young people seeing New York for the first time, we were dazzled. We were fascinated by the spectacular new East River headquarters of the United Nations, which that year was marking the tenth anniversary of its founding, and by the Statue of Liberty, Metropolitan Museum of Art, Greenwich Village, Grant's Tomb, The Cloisters, New York Stock Exchange, and our first Broadway show, *The Teahouse of the August Moon*. We went to Brooklyn to see the Dodgers play the Milwaukee Braves in a National League baseball game.[10] The only touristy thing we would not do was to take the elevator to the top of the world's tallest building, the Empire State Building. Tickets cost $1.50 (roughly equivalent to $15 these days), and we judged that our meagre savings would disappear soon enough without that sort of extravagance.

Back on the road, we managed to push Jemima past fifty mph as we "raced" toward Washington. We were so captivated by the American capital that we would happily have lingered for months. What a great favour the British did for the Americans when they burned down the original city so that it could be rebuilt with its wide boulevards and stately public buildings! From Washington we drove to Williamsburg, once the capital of the Commonwealth of Virginia and now meticulously reconstructed as an eighteenth-century colonial village. Heading north again, we stopped in Greensburg, Pennsylvania, to see my father's brother, Uncle Will MacDonald, and his family. Talk about a passion for our Scottish connection! Uncle Will, a banker, showed us a family tree that traced the MacDonald clan back to 125 AD. He claimed he could have traced us to Noah except he ran out of paper.

The brakes on our car gave out in Minnesota. When we got to Rochester, a mechanic gave us the bad news. Jemima's brakes were shot, and the repair would cost us $45. Forty-five dollars! We did not have that kind of money. My sister Helen's husband, Emerson Moffitt, a young doctor originally from New Brunswick, came up with an inspired solution. The Mayo Clinic, where he was interning, would pay $25 per pint for blood donations. If Dorothy, Connie, and I each gave a pint, we would have $75 – enough to pay for the brake job with money left over for the next leg of our adventure. So that is what we did. We continued west, driving through the Badlands of South Dakota to Yellowstone National Park. The Sunday of the Fourth of July weekend, while we were on the Buffalo Bill Cody Scenic Byway, still twenty miles from Yellowstone, was when and where Jemima decided to die.

I hitchhiked back to Cody, Wyoming, where I found an open gas station with an attendant who had a friend who knew something about the entrails of motor vehicles. The friend, a lanky fellow with a plug of tobacco in his cheek, drove me back to where Dorothy, Connie, and Jemima were waiting. As we drove along, he confided to me that his favourite form of recreation was getting drunk, that he got that way regularly and had, in fact, done so the previous evening. He towed our car back to Cody where he and his pal, the gas station attendant, spent most of the afternoon working on the starter. They got it fixed and charged us only $14. Theirs was typical of the kindness and generosity we experienced many times in our encounters with ordinary Americans. I grew more impressed every day with the country and the people. I fell in love with the West, telling my parents in a letter home that I would not mind living in a place like Wyoming, if only they could move the ocean closer.

I also concluded that while automobile travel has its attractions, I much preferred hitchhiking. Car travel cannot match the thrill that comes from not knowing whom we might meet along the way, what experiences we might have, or where we would end up spending the night. I have always found it more interesting to travel with people I do not know and to hear about their lives than it is to be cooped up in a car for weeks with the same people, rehashing familiar subjects.

But we would be stuck with the car a little longer. We drove through Montana and into Alberta in time to attend the Calgary Stampede. The excitement of the Stampede crowds reminded me of the streets of London during the coronation two years earlier. From Calgary, we went to Banff (where the car's starter failed), then through the Rocky Mountains to Vancouver where we sold the jalopy for $250 – fifty dollars more than we had paid for it in Montreal – and were glad to be rid of it.

We found an apartment in Vancouver for $60 a month for all three of us, and we managed to earn enough money to cover most of the first month's rent by picking raspberries in the Fraser Valley for a week. True, we had to sleep in a barn with cattle and had only a cold water tap for bathing – and it also poured rain every day – but we made just enough money to see us through.

Vancouver was beautiful, and I was thrilled to be able to swim in the ocean again, but I was still not ready to settle down. After about nine months, Connie and I set off on a six thousand-mile hitchhiking odyssey across the United States. As we came down from spectacular Crater Lake National Park in the high Cascades Mountains of south-central Oregon, we came across Adlai Stevenson, the former governor of Illinois, who was making his second run for the White House in 1956. He was also working his way down the coast, although not by hitchhiking. "This is wonderful," I told Connie. "We'll just follow him."

I have no clear idea why I wanted to follow the Democratic Party candidate. Although I had long admired Sir John A. Macdonald, my only personal political exposure to this point had been limited to Tory meetings with my father in Cape Breton when I was growing up. Yet for some reason I was fascinated by Stevenson, the man who became known as the "conscience of American politics." I respected his intellect, his liberalism, and his idealism – qualities that I would later discover and admire in a Canadian political leader, Robert Stanfield, the man they came to call "the best prime minister Canada never had." I can still remember some of Stevenson's speeches in 1956. "A free society is one where it is safe to be unpopular," he said. And this: "A hungry man is not a free man." As we followed Stevenson, from town to town and from one political rally to the next, something was stirring in my blood. It was a passion for politics, and it would change my life forever.[11]

Connie and I were running out of money again by the time we reached San Francisco, so we decided to do what we had done successfully at the Mayo Clinic in Minnesota – sell our blood. Unfortunately, we goofed. The veterans' clinic we went to in San Francisco did not pay for blood. The people there were pleased to accept our donation, and they thanked us warmly, but the thanks came without cash. We walked sadly off, minus a pint of blood each.

Leaving California, we hitchhiked east to Arizona to see the Grand Canyon. In those days, tourists who wanted to go down into the canyon, which is six thousand feet deep at its deepest point, rented ponies for the trek. As I recall, the rental fee was $5. Because Connie and I did not have ten dollars to spare, we walked. I do not recommend this. It was exhausting going down into the canyon and even worse climbing back out. The ground was covered in a deep dust. Every time a pony passed us, it kicked dust into our mouths, eyes, and ears. By the time we emerged from the canyon our hair was standing straight up, stiff with dust.

From Arizona, we went to Texas and crossed the Rio Grande at El Paso. Juarez on the Mexican side was a frightful place. The streets were lined with gaming parlours, seedy bars, and places advertising dancing girls, or worse – all things that nice Methodist girls were taught to avoid like the plague. We wasted little time getting out of Mexico and resuming our hitchhiking north through Mississippi and Alabama.

It was my first time in the Deep South and my first exposure to the racism that prevailed in so many southern states then. The civil rights movement was in its infancy in the summer of 1956. Two years earlier, the United States Supreme Court had ruled in *Brown v. Board of Education of Topeka, Kansas* that segregation was unconstitutional in public schools – not that the South was in any rush to comply with the ruling. In a celebrated incident in late 1955, a Black woman, Rosa Parks, was arrested in Montgomery, Alabama, for refusing to give up her seat on a bus to a white passenger, an arrest that sparked a year-long boycott by Blacks of the municipal bus system.

In 1957, the year after our trip, President Eisenhower sent federal troops into Little Rock, Arkansas, when Governor Orval Faubus barred nine Black students from entering an all-white high school; they became known as the "Little Rock Nine." And that same year, a young pastor named Martin Luther King, Jr became the first president of a new non-violent civil rights movement, the Southern Christian Leadership Conference. Change was coming to the South.

But it was very much unchanged when Connie and I hitchhiked through the region. We met some true rednecks, some truly objectionable human beings, some appalling racists. Our worst experience occurred in Mississippi when we were picked up by two white men in a car. We were no sooner underway than they started to talk about "dirty Blacks." We could not believe anyone would talk like that about other human beings. One of the fellows had a shotgun and he stopped the car to point to a crow sitting on a telephone pole. "Every time I see one of those black bastards, I just take my gun and shoot it," he said. With that, he picked up his gun and shot the bird. I am seldom speechless, but I was that day.

If we had been in the South a few years later, when the civil rights movement really started to take hold, I would have been right there, marching and protesting alongside all the young people from the US northeast who flocked south to battle institutional racism and help register Black voters. As it was, Connie and I were only too happy to escape from the South. We thumbed our way up the eastern seaboard to Maine where we crossed into New Brunswick, then on to Cape Breton.

That summer, I took a job at the Gaelic College of Celtic Arts and Crafts in St Ann's on Cape Breton, a school devoted to the study and preservation of the Gaelic language. I had a variety of functions – showing visitors around the college, telling them about Scottish lore and the history of Cape Breton, helping to run the college shop, and instructing students in Scottish country dancing. The college had been founded before the Second World War by a Scottish clergyman, Reverend A.W.R. MacKenzie. He and his wife were two of the most unpleasant people I ever encountered. They could not get along with anyone, not even with each other. They fought all the time, in private and in public. MacKenzie was a true martinet so he imposed a curfew and enforced it. Even I, at the age of thirty, had to be back at the school and in bed by 10:30. If I was late, I was locked out.

The breaking point for me was the way MacKenzie and his wife treated his niece. Sandra MacKenzie would have been eighteen or nineteen years old when she came from Scotland, ostensibly to be MacKenzie's assistant and to study at the college. Instead, they turned her into a maid in their house and she spent her days scrubbing, cooking, and cleaning for her aunt and uncle, who subjected her to some of the worst verbal abuse I had ever heard. Unable to stand it any longer, I confronted the MacKenzies and we had a fierce row. One day when they were away from the college, I took Sandra to my parents' home in North Sydney with instructions to keep her well away from the college while I arranged for her to stay with my sister Jean in Montreal. Jean helped her to find a job so that she could earn enough money to pay for her passage back to Scotland. The MacKenzies were furious, and for a while I feared that they might put the police on me for "abducting" their niece.

I moved out of the college, accepting an invitation to stay with friends, a couple who operated tourist cabins and a store in South Gut St Ann's in Victoria county. His name was Leonard Jones and he had been nominated as the Progressive Conservative candidate for the provincial election that would be held on 30 October 1956.[12] I stayed on in the fall to campaign for Len. It was my first exposure to politics, Nova Scotia-style. On election day, voters came to our little headquarters and I quickly learned to spot the ones who wanted more than a brochure. In a custom known as "treating," someone would take them behind a curtain and offer them a drink of rum. They were not given the bottle for fear they might not make it to the polls or, worse, might get there and forget who they were supposed to be voting for. After they had their drink, the bottle was taken back, to be offered to the next supporter who came by looking for an election-day "treat."

We made sure they all got their treats.

Life at Sea – My grandfather, Captain Ronald Alexander MacDonald (in front row, holding the ship's dog) and his "merry" crew. My grandmother sailed the world with him, giving birth on board to their first three (of four) children, all of them sons. (Flora MacDonald Collection)

Grade 11 in North Sydney (1941–42) – I loved school and dreamed of going to university. But times were tough, and university was not an option for girls in wartime Cape Breton. I am the tall one in the centre of the second row. My long-haired sister Jean is on my left. (Flora MacDonald Collection)

The MacDonalds of Bohuntin – In 1953, Dorothy Chisholm and I managed with
some difficulty to discover Bohuntin, the tiny hamlet in the Scottish Highlands that my
great-great grandfather Donald MacDonald and his wife Margaret had left in 1807
for a new life in Cape Breton. The community patriarch, an arthritic old man, also
named Donald (pictured with his wife between us), showed us the ruins of my ancestor's croft. The few remaining crofts were all occupied by families named MacDonald.
(Flora MacDonald Collection)

Dad and Daughter – All dressed up and ready to step out, father Fred and
I strike a pose outside the family home in North Sydney.
(Flora MacDonald Collection)

Thumbs Up! – In the 1950s, young women simply did not go off hitchhiking by themselves across Europe or North America. Connie Savage and I neither needed nor desired any male protection. Here we are, ready to hit the road on our six-thousand-mile hitchhiking odyssey across the United States. We had adventures! (Flora MacDonald Collection)

Selfie Time! – I seldom passed up a chance for a photo in a scenic setting to send to my family in Cape Breton. Here I am taking a break during my European travels. (Flora MacDonald Collection)

5

The Tory Backroom

Len Jones did not win the seat, which did not surprise us because Victoria riding had been a Liberal stronghold for many years. But Bob Stanfield led the provincial Tories to victory in that election, ending twenty-three years of Liberal rule in Nova Scotia.

I had met Stanfield just once. That was in the summer of 1949, seven or eight months after he had won the leadership of the Nova Scotia Progressive Conservatives. He came unannounced to North Sydney one day and, as was his low-key style, he wandered around town talking to anyone who showed an interest in meeting him. My father and I were walking in the downtown area when Stanfield came along. We chatted for a while, and I confess I was not impressed with this slow-speaking young lawyer. Nor was my father impressed. "How long, O Lord?" he asked, once Stanfield was out of earshot. "How long will we wander in this wilderness?"

Stanfield's strength was in political organization, not rhetoric. He painstakingly rebuilt the party. It took three elections, but in 1956 he became premier, winning twenty-four of the Legislature's forty-three seats. After that, he won every election easily, and there are those who maintain that if he had not left provincial politics in 1967 to become the Tories' national leader, he would have kept on getting elected premier until he died (and, it being the Maritimes, probably for one election thereafter). I was involved in all of those elections and in later years Stanfield would tell people how highly he valued my political instincts. "Flora can see around corners," he would say. "She can smell trouble miles away." I suppose he was right. I seemed able to anticipate problems before others could.

As the 1956 Nova Scotia election ended, I started to hunt for paying employment. I heard the new provincial government was looking to fill a vacancy in the New York office of the Nova Scotia Travel Bureau. I was an experienced traveller. What was more, I was a Conservative who had just contributed – in a small way, admittedly – to the election of the new government. To my mind I was a logical person for the job. Unfortunately, the new minister of Trade and Industry did not agree, and the job went to someone else. I started to look further afield.

Perhaps the federal Department of External Affairs (or Foreign Affairs, as it is now) could use my services, I thought. So I went to Ottawa to apply. On the day of my interview at External Affairs, I went downtown a couple of hours early and killed time by strolling along the streets south of Parliament Hill. As I walked along Laurier Avenue, I came upon a funny old building called Bracken House. It was the national headquarters of the Progressive Conservative party and had been named after a former leader of the party, John Bracken. I went in to let them know that another Tory was in town.

I met Kay Kearns, for many years the major-domo of Bracken House. She asked me about myself and Nova Scotia and the provincial election. To my astonishment, she offered me a job. Recognizing a bird in the hand, I accepted on the spot. I was there for nine years. I sometimes wonder how my life would have unfolded if I had gone ahead with my original plan to join the diplomatic service. Might I have ended up as the head of mission somewhere, rather than as minister of Foreign Affairs?

The PC headquarters I joined in March 1957 was in transition. "Transition" is too kind. "Disarray" or "anarchy" would be more accurate. The root problem was that the headquarters existed for three, at times incompatible, purposes: to serve the leader, who appointed the party's national director; to serve the PC "association," that club of tens of thousands of party members who at any given time might or might not be on the same wavelength as the leader; and to serve the parliamentary caucus as the link between MPs and the party grassroots.

In the nine years I worked at national headquarters this dilemma was never resolved. Who did I and the others really work for? Was it for the leader as represented by his national director? Was it for association members whose dues paid our salaries and covered the costs of operating headquarters? Was it for the Conservative MPs whose membership lists we maintained and whose speeches and newsletters we pumped out to constituents?

The party had just gone through a wrenching change of leaders when I arrived on the scene. George Drew, the former Ontario premier who had led the national party to defeat in the elections of 1949 and 1953, had stepped down. Desperate to compete with the Liberals, who had been in power since 1935, the PCs had gambled on a charismatic Prairie lawyer and MP, John George Diefenbaker – he of the blazing eyes, wagging finger, quivering jowls, quavering voice, and simulated outrage. "Dief" had an unrivalled ability to eviscerate Liberals. He was also paranoid. He trusted few people beyond his wife and a small inner circle of loyalists. He saw enemies on all sides. He was convinced that Liberal spies had infiltrated his party's ranks and that his caucus was riddled with "termites" who were ceaselessly conspiring against him.

Diefenbaker had been leader for just a few months when I walked through the doors of Bracken House, and he had not yet established his authority over the headquarters. Bill Rowe, who had been national director under Drew, was gone. Everyone assumed his replacement would be Allister Grosart, a Toronto advertising man who had managed the Tories' disastrous 1953 campaign, in which we had won thirty-three seats in Ontario and only eighteen in all the rest of Canada. Unable to trust entirely anyone who had served his predecessor, Diefenbaker dragged his feet on the Grosart appointment. That meant there was no one formally in charge of a staff of twelve to fifteen people and a budget, which in good years could reach $30,000 a month. Each month, the party's chief fundraiser, Bev Matthews, a Toronto lawyer, would send us a cheque and one of my duties was to bank the money and pay the bills. No one ever told me where the money came from. It just came. In lean periods, the monthly allowance might shrink to $20,000, but we always managed to meet the payroll.

In the absence of a national director, the responsibility fell to Kay Kearns, the office manager who had hired me. Kay had been a constant presence at headquarters for more years than anyone could recall, and Diefenbaker did not trust her at all. He eventually managed to have Kay squeezed out. As for the other veterans at headquarters, in the leader's mind they were either Drew loyalists or supporters of Donald Fleming, a Toronto MP who had opposed Diefenbaker for the leadership.[1] Or, like Don Eldon, our research director, they were perceived to be "intellectuals" – and, if there was anything Diefenbaker despised more than Liberals, it was intellectuals. By the summer of 1958, the only survivor among the staff who had served the party loyally in the difficult times was our receptionist, May Lambert.

After Grosart was confirmed as national director – with me as his secretary (or "executive assistant" as they would call the position today) – he came back from a meeting with the leader and told me that Diefenbaker had started referring to personnel at headquarters as "they." To Diefenbaker, the world was divided into people who were for him and those who were against him – "we" and "they." Now, we had become they.

An election was looming. By the spring of 1957, the Liberals had been in power for twenty-two unbroken years ("Twenty-two years of Liberal misrule," as Diefenbaker would thunder from platforms across the country), the last nine of those years under Prime Minister Louis St Laurent. St Laurent was old and tired, and so was his government. The Liberals had grown arrogant, and they had carelessly displayed their arrogance for the entire country to see during the vicious pipeline debate of 1956. St Laurent should have retired then. Instead, "Uncle Louis" decided to go to the well one more time at the age of seventy-five. He called an election for 10 June, less than three months after I had arrived.

We did not expect to win the election. And why would we? We had lost five consecutive elections. We hoped we could add a few seats, and that was as far as our ambition went. But we won that 1957 election, capturing 113 seats, ten more than the Liberals. "Dief the Chief," as the press called him, formed a minority government. Overnight, Conservatives who had been ambivalent or hostile about his leadership became his acolytes. He was lionized at party gatherings. He was the man who had won the election for the party that could not win.

I have never been happy with that interpretation. Diefenbaker was a factor. His dynamic campaigning drove home the message that Dalton Camp wrote as the campaign slogan: "It's Time for a Diefenbaker Government." Not a "Conservative Government," which would have reminded voters of our bleak past, but a "Diefenbaker Government," to herald a new era, a new leader, a new style.[2]

But the new leader and his style did not resonate everywhere – or with me. I did not mention my reservations to anyone at headquarters, but I suspected that if George Drew had given it one more try, he would have won the 1957 election. I still believe that. After all, the Liberals were ready to defeat themselves, and it was Drew's organization and Drew's people who carried the campaign effort that year – Ontarians like Grosart, Bill Brunt, Harry Willis, and my great pal and supporter, Edwin A. Goodman, the ebullient Toronto lawyer who was known to everyone as "Fast Eddie." Interestingly, Diefenbaker appointed Grosart, Brunt, and Willis to the Senate, but Eddie, who would dearly have loved a seat in the upper house, was left out. Diefenbaker never really trusted Goodman. It may have been Eddie's long, close association with George Hees, who was destined to become one of the leading dissidents in Diefenbaker's caucus. Or it may have been the fact that Eddie, like Dalton Camp, was too much his own man ever to be Diefenbaker's man.

National Headquarters was unprepared for victory. We had made our usual plans for a modest election-night party for staff and volunteers – small, discreet, and done by midnight. By eleven o'clock, however, it seemed as though everyone in Ottawa was storming the doors of Bracken House. They cleaned us out of food and drink in a twinkling. If we had had our wits about us, we would have sent the crowds over to Liberal headquarters where they had their customary victory buffet laid out, and no one came.

The months following the 1957 election were Diefenbaker's best. The government moved decisively to address problems that had been left to fester by the Liberals. Reporters in the Parliamentary Press Gallery said they had never seen a government move with such speed. After initially holding the External Affairs portfolio himself, Diefenbaker reached outside the caucus to recruit Sidney Smith, the president of the University of Toronto, for that prestigious ministry. Smith needed a seat, and in November 1957 he won a by-election in the eastern Ontario riding of Hastings-Frontenac by more than ten thousand votes, a huge margin. Smith's victory added to our momentum.[3] Those were tremendous months. We were so high that we felt we were living on a mountain top.

Everyone was aware there would surely be another election, probably sooner than later – as soon, we suspected, as Diefenbaker could find a pretext for calling one. The Twenty-Third Parliament, opened by the Queen on 14 October 1957, was destined to be short-lived. As the government pushed through legislation, we at headquarters mailed mimeographed progress reports to Conservatives across the country. We were determined to keep our troops in a high state of readiness. In early December, Donald Fleming, the finance minister, presented his first budget; Parliament adjourned a couple of weeks later for Christmas.

Diefenbaker went to Nassau on vacation and after a few days Grosart flew down to discuss the election with him. Although the party was doing no polling of its own, we were aware from the published Gallup polls that the Conservatives were on the upswing. The time was ripe for a new election. The only complication was the Liberal leadership race. St Laurent had resigned and the convention to choose his successor was scheduled for mid-January 1958. Rather than risk a public backlash by calling the election while the Liberals were in the process of changing leaders, Grosart and Diefenbaker decided to wait.

It was a good thing they did. The Liberals held their convention, choosing Lester Pearson, the distinguished former diplomat and external affairs minister. Pearson promptly made a monumental gaffe. Instead of introducing a straightforward motion of non-confidence, as would have been customary, he used a two-day supply debate in the Commons to call on Diefenbaker to resign and return the government to the Liberals – without the benefit of an election. His motion was presumptuous and arrogant, coming from the leader of the party that had been rejected by the electorate only months earlier. Diefenbaker was overjoyed. His speech in the House of Commons that night may have been his best ever. He tore Pearson to shreds. Standing in the government gallery, I was thrilled. Diefenbaker was magnificent. It was the one time that he really lifted me off my feet.

I was up to my elbows in preparations for the Young Progressive Conservatives' convention, to be held in Ottawa on 30 and 31 January. Diefenbaker was scheduled to make a major address. The morning the convention began, Grosart took me aside, swore me to secrecy and said: "Don't say anything, but the prime minister left early this morning to fly to Quebec City to tell the governor general[4] that he's going to dissolve the House. We've got to get his speech ready for tonight, because he's going to speak at the YPC banquet, and it is going to be the opening gun in the campaign." And that is what we did.

The 1958 campaign was very different from the one in 1957. In 1957, Diefenbaker was a happy campaigner. He was funny. He sparkled on the platform. He relished the role of underdog. He took time to talk to waitresses and taxi drivers. The people liked him, and he revelled in their approval. In 1958, he was no longer the underdog. As prime minister, he felt he had to be above the crowds. Consumed by his own importance, he no longer paused to talk to ordinary Canadians. He told Dalton Camp that if he stopped to talk to one person, he would have to talk to all of them.

Diefenbaker was a born opposition politician. His forte was attacking governments. As prime minister, he was incapable of defending his government's performance in any coherent way. He did not have what Camp called "the power of positive speaking." Instead of explaining all the good things his government was doing, he attacked his enemies – "they" and "them" – for having the temerity to criticize his government or to oppose his good works.

I was ambivalent about Diefenbaker in 1958. I should explain that I have always had a fear of failure. It makes me eager to make sure I do things right. And that means I am always trying to overachieve. Growing up, I never wanted to disappoint my father or my teachers. It was the same when I got to Ottawa. I still had this fear of failure. I very seldom joined the men from headquarters for lunch or dinner, but would grab a hamburger and milkshake and stay at my desk to work. Lowell Murray, one of my closest friends and political allies, remembers me saying I wished someone would invent a pill that I could take so I would never have to interrupt work long enough to eat.

When I first met Diefenbaker, he was an overpowering presence to me. He was larger than life. I was desperately afraid of disappointing him. I was in awe, almost fear, of him. My feelings changed during the 1958 election. While the whole country was poised to vote Conservative, I, a party employee, could not make up my mind. I had a terrible struggle with myself. I had grave reservations about leaders who set themselves up as gods. It disturbed me that people would almost literally kneel at Diefenbaker's feet or try to touch his clothing. The atmosphere was repulsive to me.[5]

I was in the office alone very early one morning – it may have been a Saturday or Sunday – when Diefenbaker called. He was in Cornwall, Ontario, where he had made a speech the night before. Apparently, he had been well-received there because, when he went out for a walk the next morning, people stopped him to say how good he had been. Praise was always music to his ears, but there was one problem. There were no copies of his speech to hand to the voters of Cornwall. "My speech isn't down here yet," he demanded. "Why hasn't National Headquarters distributed my speech?" Well, I had known he was going to Cornwall, but he had not favoured headquarters with a copy of his remarks, not that he would have stuck to his text anyway. As far as I knew, the speech had not been recorded. What was I supposed to do? I tried to explain the situation, but he was unreasonable. He blamed me personally, which I thought was unfair, and he said that poor support was what he had come to expect from us – "them" – at National Headquarters.

My reservations about the leader were offset by the pride that I, like other Tory activists, felt about the accomplishments of our government. His early years in office – the minority government period and the first year or two after the 1958 election – were innovative and productive. Diefenbaker kept his promises to increase old age pensions and to extend the right to vote to Indigenous Canadians. He appointed the country's first French Canadian governor general (General Georges Vanier) and the first Indigenous senator (James Gladstone, a Blood Indian from Alberta). He introduced the Canadian Bill of Rights, the precursor of today's Charter of Rights and Freedoms. He brought in the Atlantic Provinces Power Development Act and the Agricultural Stabilization Act. And he joined the Queen and United States President Dwight Eisenhower in Montreal for the official opening of the St Lawrence Seaway.

Yet I was appalled by the way Diefenbaker treated some of his senior ministers. He had found out somehow that two of his cabinet members, Gordon Churchill and George Nowlan, had been romantically involved with secretaries on Parliament Hill. A prude in matters involving sex, Diefenbaker had obtained documents that "proved" to his satisfaction that the two ministers were guilty of extramarital misbehaviour. He kept the files in his desk drawer, pulling them out from time to time and threatening to expose the two if they ever wavered in their loyalty to him.

My relations with some of the others at headquarters were strained at times, given that I had arrived as a novice and within a year had assumed an important role in the operation. Although I was technically Grosart's assistant, I was practically running the place when he was away, which was a good deal of the time. I helped our MPs to deal with problems in their ridings, this being the era before members had constituency offices and assistants. I became the person that the constituency associations would call when they needed something from Ottawa. They found that I was almost always available and always tried to be helpful. I suppose that to some of them I *was* Conservative headquarters. I made many friends in the party – and many contacts that would prove invaluable later when I joined Camp in his campaign to oust Diefenbaker and when I sought support for my own leadership bid. I have been told that nobody before or since knew as many people in the party as I did.

Although Kay Kearns had hired me, she and I never had an entirely comfortable relationship. I think she resented the way Grosart and the caucus came to rely on me. In the end, however, it was Diefenbaker's distrust, not my presence, that prompted her departure. When Diefenbaker made it clear he wanted her gone, Grosart proposed that she be given a pension in recognition of her long service. When Diefenbaker refused, Grosart – and I admire him for this – went secretly to some financial people in Toronto and arranged for an annuity to be set up in a way that would not show on the party's books. He swore me to secrecy. In particular, I promised not to breathe a word to Diefenbaker, who never forgot anything he wanted to remember. Suspicious, he called me in more than once to ask, "Now, about Miss Kearns's pension. How much was it again?" The man was utterly devious. I told him nothing.

Although I was never as close to Grosart as I would be to Camp, we respected each other as he came to rely on me. A cultured, considerate man, he was always good to me. His wife was not well, and Allister would sometimes ask me to go to his home in Rockcliffe Park or his cottage in the Gatineau Hills north of Ottawa to stay overnight with his two young daughters if he had to be away. I was glad to do it.

Grosart was loyal to Diefenbaker, despite the misgivings he would express to me about Dief's behaviour. He spent a great deal of time with the leader, functioning as his principal secretary in everything but name. He was the best speechwriter Diefenbaker ever had, having a rare ability to get inside the leader's head to replicate on paper his emotions, rhetoric, and timing.

Diefenbaker appointed Grosart to the Senate in 1962 and Allister used that opportunity to resign as national director. Once again, there was no one in charge at headquarters. Using Gordon Churchill as an intermediary, which he often did, Diefenbaker proposed that Dalton Camp succeed Grosart as national director. But Camp did not want to have to sever his ties to the advertising agency he owned; nor did he and his wife have any desire to live in Ottawa ("a dismal place," in their view). Eventually, an arrangement was negotiated. The national director's position would be left vacant. Camp would assume a new position, chairman of a national organization committee, reporting to the leader, with a free hand to run the next election campaign as he saw fit. He would not receive a salary, meaning that, as an unpaid volunteer, he could keep his ties to his ad agency and the agency could continue to solicit federal government advertising. And he could live in Toronto, commuting to Ottawa. For all practical purposes, I acted as national director and ran the headquarters.

When Dalton was around, we seldom saw him in daylight hours. When he was in campaign mode, he would start work when the sun went down. Dinner for others was breakfast for him, and he would regularly work through the night on speeches, advertisements, and campaign strategy. When he was not sleeping, he would hide himself away, drinking coffee, reading newspapers, and thinking.

I worked closely with him on several provincial elections when headquarters loaned me to help the provincial parties with organization and candidates while Dalton was the all-purpose guru – planning strategy, writing speeches, and creating advertising. We helped Duff Roblin win in Manitoba in 1958, and in 1960 we were in Nova Scotia for the re-election of Bob Stanfield's government. Each victory was satisfying, but the most memorable campaign was probably a losing one, the "Term Twenty-Nine" election in Newfoundland in 1959. Under the Terms of Union between Newfoundland and Canada, the federal government was obligated to make an annual payment to the government of Newfoundland. The dispute was over the amount of the payment. A provincial royal commission came up with a figure of $15 million; a federal royal commission calculated $8 million. The amounts seem puny today, but the principle loomed large in 1959. Joey Smallwood, the Liberal premier, demanded more money, and Diefenbaker would not budge. Smallwood insisted that "Term Twenty-Nine" required Ottawa to make the payment every year "in perpetuity." Diefenbaker read the term differently, although Smallwood was probably correct.

In an attempt to embarrass Diefenbaker into backing down, Smallwood sent a process server to Ottawa to deliver a subpoena to the prime minister, summoning him to appear in Newfoundland court to defend the federal government's interpretation of "Term

Twenty-Nine." It was hilarious. The man came to Diefenbaker's office on Parliament Hill and demanded, in the name of the law, to see the prime minister. He was shown in. He produced a scroll and, looking at Diefenbaker, he intoned, "Are you Mr John Diefenbaker?"

"Yes."

"Are you Mr John G. Diefenbaker?"

"Yes."

"Are you Mr John George Diefenbaker?"

At this point, Diefenbaker blew up, and someone threw the hapless fellow out of the office.

When Smallwood called an election over Term Twenty-Nine, Dalton and I were dispatched to Newfoundland. We never had a chance! We were the bad guys, the black hats, the ugly feds trampling on the rights of the hardworking people of Newfoundland and Labrador. Setting the federal government up as the enemy is the oldest stratagem in a provincial campaign manual. Smallwood may have been an unscrupulous demagogue, but he was a brilliant political strategist. He had virtue, justice, and outrage on his side. Here he was, Newfoundland's Father of Confederation, standing up for his province's birthright against a callous, uncaring, reneging government in Ottawa. On one level, they were fighting over $7 million, but on a more fundamental level, the issue was one of respect and the honouring of a sacred (as Newfoundlanders saw it) Confederation pact. We were demolished. Smallwood swept the province for the fourth consecutive time, and the Conservatives won just three of the thirty-six seats. It would be another thirteen years and four elections before we would be able to bring Smallwood down.

Although I worked closely with Dalton in many campaigns – and came to admire him enormously – as I observed earlier, I never felt that I was "one of the boys." That recognition was reserved for people like Finlay MacDonald (later a senator), Norman Atkins (Camp's brother-in-law who also became a senator), Roy McMurtry (later Chief Justice of Ontario), Patrick Vernon (a Toronto lawyer who became the national party's chief fundraiser), Donald Guthrie (another Toronto lawyer) and Bill Saunderson (who became an Ontario cabinet minister). Nor was I ever one of the boys who met to eat, drink, plot, and gossip in smoke-filled offices on Parliament Hill or in hotel rooms at the Chateau Laurier Hotel. Politics was still a closed society in those days – closed to anyone who was not of the male persuasion.

For much of my time at national headquarters, I was effectively in charge. I hired Marjory LeBreton to fill a vacant secretarial position. Loyalty to the leader was her prime asset. Brian Mulroney made Marjory a senator in 1993, and in 2006 she became a cabinet minister as government leader in Senate in Stephen Harper's administration.

Although I was running the place, I was never seriously considered for the top job, national director. There were two occasions when I might have been appointed. The first time was following the 8 April 1963 federal election, which the Tories lost, although Diefenbaker fought magnificently. As he had agreed to do, Camp directed that campaign from Ottawa. When it was over, he returned to Toronto, saying, "I've done my duty." A three-member caucus committee, chaired by Gordon Churchill, was created to oversee the operations of headquarters until a national director could be named. During that period, I was in charge, reporting to Churchill who dropped in from time to time to see how I was doing. Diefenbaker eventually chose Dick Thrasher, a former Ontario MP who had been his parliamentary secretary, to be the new national director.

I was not even considered. Furious, I put the keys to headquarters in an envelope for Churchill, telling him, "This is it, I'm off." I went to the United Kingdom, then to the continent, trekking around the Greek islands. I came back to Paris, intending to stay there and study for a year. Somehow Dalton Camp found out where I was. He sent me a message: "Come back to Nova Scotia, we need you." We were into a provincial election there, and I got very involved in that campaign. When it was over in October – Bob Stanfield was re-elected – Churchill asked me to return to headquarters in Ottawa, which I agreed to do.

The second time was when Thrasher left to be a candidate in the 1965 federal election. Diefenbaker surprised everyone by picking Jim Johnston, an economist and small-town newspaper publisher with no background in national politics. Johnston knew little about the party and he had no aptitude for organization. His only known asset was his deep and abiding loyalty to Diefenbaker. When Diefenbaker wanted me fired, Johnston did his master's bidding.

Of course, I knew why I would never be national director: It was because I was a woman. When Dalton was national president, I was his confidant, adviser, and all-purpose assistant. We were a team. We worked together when Camp launched his unprecedented leadership-review campaign in 1966 and again the following year in Stanfield's successful campaign for the national party leadership. Dalton was more enlightened than most men, and I know he valued my knowledge and advice. Yet I was never included in any of the "roasts," birthday parties, and other little galas that he and his male friends loved to arrange. While he would seek out my guidance on matters of strategy and policy, he still expected me to type his speeches. And I did.

6

John Diefenbaker

History has not been kind to John Diefenbaker, Canada's thir-teenth prime minister. In rankings of the nation's leaders, he gener-ally places toward the bottom of the list. Yet his 1957-58 minority government offered real promise, and his 1958 election campaign, with its "Northern Vision" and its promised "Roads to Resources" program, captured the nation's imagination. But the voters did not do Diefenbaker or our party a favour when they gave us 209 of the 265 House of Commons seats on election night, 31 March 1958. The surfeit of seats proved to be more a burden than a gift.[1]

His first government had been nimble, quick on its feet. It had to be to get legislation through a Commons that it could not control by force of numbers. His second government was sluggish. Every vote was a safe one, its outcome preordained. The government was unwieldy. There were too many MPs and too few attractive cabinet and committee assignments to go around. It would have taken a much more adroit manager of people than Diefenbaker to keep 209 pairs of hands busy, productive, and out of trouble. The government soon bogged down, a victim of its size and inertia.

The massive majority created another problem. It inflated Diefenbaker's already healthy ego. He saw himself as the infalli-ble saviour of the party and the country. His paranoia hardened. Every critic became an enemy, an agent of the ever elusive "they" and "them." His lists of perceived enemies broadened to encompass everyone from financiers on Bay Street to journalists to members of his own caucus to employees at party headquarters and, of course, to all Liberals everywhere.

Dalton Camp was beginning to worry. He had assumed an expanded role in the 1958 election. While Allister Grosart directed the overall campaign, Camp took on responsibility for the party's national advertising. He also ran our campaign in the Maritimes, traveling with Diefenbaker and writing his speeches when the leader was in the region. Dalton did not like what he saw and heard. The Diefenbaker of 1958 was not the Diefenbaker of 1957. He was aloof, angry, and out of touch. As Dalton put it, "He was just paranoic. He imagined things that never happened. He didn't want to see people."[2]

Others either did not notice or did not care. They smelled victory. In Ontario, Premier Leslie Frost, who had sat out the 1957 campaign, climbed on the Diefenbaker bandwagon. He traveled everywhere in Ontario with the Chief in 1958. On the Saturday before the Monday election, they worked their way through four Ottawa-area ridings. At the end of the day, the motorcade stopped at national headquarters where we, the staff, waited to make a presentation to Diefenbaker to thank him for all his hard work – although I, personally, thought *he* should be making the presentation to *us*. Grosart made a gracious speech thanking the leader for all his help and co-operation. "And now, Mr Prime Minister ..." he began, holding up a beautiful new fishing rod for Diefenbaker, who was an avid fisherman. But in Ontario in those days the premier also liked to be referred as "prime minister." Frost, assuming he was being thanked for his election support, smiled and stepped forward to accept the gift. What an embarrassing moment! It was painful. The two leaders shuffled back and forth until Frost realized his mistake and backed off.

During the election, I went for a walk with a friend who was working on a degree in social work in Ottawa. I confided to him some of my reservations about Diefenbaker. Then I stopped, thinking, "My God, did anybody overhear me?" There was no way I could mention the little alarm bells in my head to Grosart. He was Diefenbaker's man and was deeply loyal to him. Camp was much more his own man, but Dalton believed first and foremost in the Conservative party. To him, the party was an essential national institution and he would not express any doubts about the leader that might jeopardize the party's prospects. He continued to support Diefenbaker – or at least not actively work against him – long after others had given up on him.

I do not want to create the impression that I was obsessed with Diefenbaker. I was busy, frantically busy, doing my job: keeping the party machinery going; trying to instill a sense of teamwork at the grassroots level; helping our members of Parliament to resolve problems in their ridings; and organizing meetings of the national executive and other party groups. I tried to make sure everyone got along with everyone else. And whenever a federal by-election or a provincial election was called, I was usually involved – assembling an organization, helping with strategy, and working with the candidate.

Although I was putting in fourteen-hour days, six or seven days a week, I knew I was at the heart of the action in Canadian politics, and I loved every minute of it. I did not even mind serving as a typist for Elmer Diefenbaker, the leader's brother. It was one of the little secrets of national headquarters that Dief had his brother on the party payroll from 1958 on. In return for a modest stipend, Elmer, who lived in Saskatchewan, sent in a long biweekly report – usually twelve handwritten foolscap pages that I would decipher, type, and send to the leader's office. I guess the letters were supposed to be assessments of the political mood in Saskatchewan, but they struck me as mostly aimless chitchat about people Elmer knew.

Although I was unsettled by the mood of arrogance that permeated Ottawa following the 1958 landslide, I buried myself in my job. As the years passed and disillusion grew – in the years between the great victory of 1958 and the disastrous election of 1962 (when we lost ninety-three seats and very nearly lost office, too) – the person I felt most comfortable talking to was Richard Hatfield. Hatfield was one of a handful of party activists – Finlay MacDonald, Lowell Murray, and Eddie Goodman were others – whom I considered "kinfolk" because of their passion for politics, love of adventure, good fun, and high spirits. They always managed to come up with a positive outlook on events around them, no matter how dire a situation seemed. Richard was the son of a Tory MP, Heber Hatfield, and I had known him slightly before he arrived in Ottawa in 1957 as chief of staff to Gordon Churchill, whom Diefenbaker had made minister of Trade and Commerce.

Richard and I hit it off beautifully. We had some great times together. A few months after Richard started work in Ottawa, the Liberals held their leadership convention to choose Louis St Laurent's successor. Never ones to pass up a good political battle, Richard and I decided to attend. By sheer happenstance, I was wearing my Nova

Scotia tartan kilt and scarf that day. When we arrived at the convention, somebody grabbed me and said, "Here's another one of us!" They took me, with Richard tagging along, straight to the section reserved for the Nova Scotia delegation. We were seated directly in front of Alistair Fraser Sr, who had just finished his term as lieutenant governor of the province. I had known him back home, and he knew I was anything but a Liberal. "What the hell is that woman doing here?" Fraser asked, loudly. It was very funny. We stayed to hear the speeches, but we did not attempt to vote.

Richard and I were close. We were both night owls, and whenever my phone at home would ring at four o'clock in the morning – as it did fairly often – I would simply answer with two words: "Yes, Richard."[3] He was a happy warrior. He reveled in his time as a member of the New Brunswick legislature, as opposition leader and as premier. Even when the going was extremely tough, as it was in his final years as premier, he remained upbeat. New Brunswick nourished him. He knew every village, every town, the people who lived there, and what they were thinking. And it didn't make any difference to him whether they were rock-ribbed Baptists in the St John River Valley, or French Acadians on the Eastern Shore – he enjoyed them all. And the pleasure he took in politics was contagious.

I understood his quirkiness, and I suppose I knew intuitively from the early days of our friendship that he was gay. In those days, gay politicians stayed in the closest. It was not a subject Richard and I ever talked about. I understood what he was, and he understood that I knew. We did not need to talk about it. It was as irrelevant as the colour of his eyes. He was my friend, he was great company, and we supported each other in our political battles. After I was fired from Conservative headquarters, Richard worked with us in the leadership-review campaign, and then in Bob Stanfield's campaign for the leadership. He came to Kingston to help me when I ran for Parliament in 1972 – not every candidate could claim to have a premier working in their campaign – and when I ran for the PC leadership in 1976, Richard was one of my staunchest supporters. I think he delivered virtually every New Brunswick delegate to me. Politics is all about people and loyalty. I could not have asked for a more loyal friend than Richard.

We did some fun things together. There was a Quebec provincial election in the spring of 1970 – about six months before the New Brunswick election in which Richard was elected premier – and

Richard, who was bewitched by campaigns, wanted to see what was going on. So we went to Montreal for a few days. Richard became intrigued by a young Parti Québécois candidate by the name of Bernard Landry, who was running in Joliette. He was the same Bernard Landry who would become premier many years later, but 1970 was the first election contested by the PQ, and very few people had ever heard of him. "Landry isn't a Quebec name," Richard said. "It's a New Brunswick name. It's an Acadian name."[4] So we went off to Joliette to meet this candidate. We followed Landry around, and he invited us to his home for dinner before an evening campaign rally.

Neither Richard nor I had much facility in French – I struggled with the language throughout my years in Parliament – and we did not follow everything that was said that evening. But we did understand what was expected when the organizers passed a bucket through the audience. Richard put $50 in the pail, but people were also expected to put a card with their name in the bucket with their contribution. As the Tory leader in New Brunswick, Hatfield did not want to be recorded as a financial backer of a separatist party. So he put my name on the card. I have often wondered whether there exists in some RCMP file today a notation that Flora MacDonald was an early contributor to the Parti Québécois.

I think it was Richard's curiosity, his enthusiasm, and his eagerness to meet new people and to explore new ideas that made him the most successful politician in New Brunswick history. In an era when many Conservatives in his province had little sympathy for the French-speaking population – to be blunt, they were bigots – Hatfield had the courage to court the Acadian minority. He attended their festivals in northern New Brunswick, visited their homes, and championed their causes. As premier, he took the risk of alienating his core voters by making New Brunswick Canada's only officially bilingual province. French-speaking New Brunswickers responded. In time, the unilingual Hatfield became as popular – perhaps more popular – in the Acadian north and east as he was in the English-speaking south and west.

It is said that the hardest decision a politician must make is deciding when to get out, when to move on to a new life. It was a decision Richard was incapable of making. In 1982, he was elected to his fourth consecutive term. It was his greatest victory, as the Conservatives won thirty-nine of the fifty-eight seats in the legislature. Although he had been premier for twelve years by then, he was only fifty-one years old – young enough to embark on a new life. He should have moved on, as his friends urged him to do, but there was nothing Richard wanted to be as much as premier of his beloved province. So he hung on. His capricious personal life began to catch up with him. The police charged him with possession of marijuana after a small quantity of cannabis was found in his luggage while he was travelling with the Queen on a royal tour of New Brunswick in 1984. He was acquitted of that charge, but his reputation never recovered. People who had turned a deaf ear to gossip about his homosexuality began to talk openly about it. Knowing his government was doomed, Hatfield waited a full five years before calling a provincial election in October 1987. The result was worse than his worst nightmare. The Tories were wiped out as the Liberals under Frank McKenna won all fifty-eight seats.

My friend Richard never recovered. He was a lost soul. In 1990, Prime Minister Brian Mulroney appointed him to the Senate. Richard was delighted by the appointment, but within months he was diagnosed with an inoperable brain tumour. His funeral in the Anglican cathedral in Fredericton was a deeply moving event, a reflection of Richard's life. Edith Butler, the great Acadian singer, performed some wonderful old melodies, and Alden Nowlan, who was known as the poet laureate of New Brunswick, read some of his poetry. It was a fine send-off for a great Canadian and a dear friend.

The disintegration of the Hatfield government in 1987 was remarkable, but it was by no means unique. Much the same thing happened at the federal level in 1993 when Mulroney, having led the Tories to new depths in the opinion polls, turned the party and the government over to Kim Campbell. The Conservatives won just two seats in the election that fall. The situation was similar in 1962, when the Diefenbaker government lost ninety-three of the 209 seats it had won four years earlier but managed to cling to power with a minority government. There was no single cause for that fall from grace. It was a combination of controversial decisions, policy blunders, a crippling indecision at crucial junctures and, most damaging, a loss of public confidence in Diefenbaker's ability to lead the country.

His February 1959 decision to cancel the Avro Arrow jet interceptor program, while it may have made economic sense, created massive layoffs among highly skilled engineers and other specialists in Canada's aeronautical industry, many of whom left for the United States where they would soon play key roles in the US space

program. The government fought a pitched battle with the Bank of
Canada over monetary policy. The ugly dispute ended in the worst
way possible – with the departure of the ostensibly independent governor of the central bank, James Coyne. On the international front,
Diefenbaker allowed his love for the Commonwealth to cloud his
judgment. In the opinion of many economists and business leaders
in Canada and elsewhere, who were applauding the integration of
European economies, Diefenbaker put his government on the wrong
side of history when he declared his opposition to Britain's entry
into the European Economic Community.

Anti-Americanism was never far beneath the surface with
Diefenbaker. Deliberately or not, he allowed Canada's relationship
with the United States to sour. He convinced himself that the administration, under the Democratic Party President John Kennedy, was
conspiring to bring about the downfall of his government so that
it could be replaced by Lester Pearson's Liberals. There is no doubt
that Kennedy thought Pearson would be a more congenial neigh-
bour than Diefenbaker, but "evidence" that Kennedy was plotting
to bring about a Liberal victory existed in Diefenbaker's mind and
nowhere else.[5]

As the 1962 election approached, Diefenbaker was enraged that
Kennedy had not only invited Pearson, winner of the 1957 Nobel
Peace Prize, to attend a White House dinner for Nobel laureates,
but had used the occasion to spend forty minutes in private conversation with the Liberal leader. Diefenbaker subjected the outgoing
United States Ambassador to Canada, Livingston Merchant, to
a two-hour tirade in which he accused Kennedy of interfering in
the Canadian election. And he very nearly provoked a major diplomatic incident by threatening to go public with a briefing note
that one of Kennedy's advisers, Walt Rostow, had written for the
president when he visited Ottawa the year before. In the memo,
Diefenbaker claimed, Rostow had urged Kennedy to make sure
he "pushed" Canada into joining the Organization of American
States (OAS) and into taking other actions that Washington desired.
Diefenbaker told Merchant the Rostow memo had come to him
through the Department of External Affairs, which had been given
it by some unknown person. Almost certainly, however, the truth
was that Kennedy had inadvertently left the note behind following his meeting with Diefenbaker. Instead of returning it to the
White House, as protocol would dictate, Diefenbaker locked it in

his office safe for possible later use. All of this was reported by Merchant to Kennedy.

Diefenbaker's relations with Kennedy worsened later, in October 1962, four months after the Canadian election, when the Cuban missile crisis brought the world to the brink of nuclear war. Kennedy sent Merchant to brief Diefenbaker and to ask for his support for Washington's plan – to be announced by the president on national television in the United States – to demand that the Soviet Union withdraw its nuclear missiles from Cuba immediately or face a total American military blockade of that island. British Prime Minister Harold Macmillan gave his immediate and unconditional support, as did French President Charles de Gaulle, who was not normally a fan of the United States. But Diefenbaker dithered. His anti-Americanism and distrust of Kennedy were so great that he could not bring himself to offer support. But neither could he bring himself to openly refuse Kennedy's request. Stalling for time, he proposed that an independent commission composed of representatives of eight non-aligned countries be sent to Cuba to verify the presence of the missile bases. That was tantamount to calling Kennedy a liar, and the president was furious. Diefenbaker's defence minister, Douglas Harkness, was appalled. And my friend George Hogan, a national vice-president of the Conservative party – one of those rare Tories who managed to maintain good relations with both Diefenbaker and Camp – made a speech in Toronto denouncing his leader's procrastination. Three days later, Diefenbaker finally offered his support to the Americans, but the damage had been done.

Harkness's disenchantment and Hogan's public dissent were symptoms of the malaise that pervaded the party. Early in 1962, Allister Grosart, as national director, invited Camp and other key Conservatives from across the country, to a secret strategy meeting at the Queen Elizabeth Hotel in Montreal. He went around the room, asking everyone for their views about the next election. He was alarmed by the responses. As Camp summarized them later, "The game was over ... we'd probably lose the next election, or we'd take an awful pounding." They all agreed that Diefenbaker was a liability and they urged Grosart to keep him off television during the campaign. Dalton commissioned a national opinion poll that deepened the insiders' despair. It confirmed the worst fears of the Montreal meeting. The poll found an overwhelming lack of confidence in Diefenbaker. He was dragging the party down. For the first time since he became leader, he was running behind his party. The leader who had achieved the greatest victory in Canadian history had become, four years later, a liability to his candidates.

The 1962 campaign was the worst one, federal or provincial, that I ever had to live through. Nothing went right. The formal opening was scheduled for London, Ontario, the hometown of John Robarts, the new Conservative premier of Ontario. The idea was to signal to voters that Diefenbaker had the support of Robarts, just as he had had the support of Leslie Frost in the 1958 election.[6] Because foggy weather can play havoc with air travel on the east coast in the spring, however, we decided to take advantage of a spell of apparently good weather to send Diefenbaker to Newfoundland before the campaign officially began. Diefenbaker never liked campaigning in Newfoundland, and the experience on that occasion reinforced his dislike. He flew to St John's in his campaign aircraft, only to find the airport was fogged in. Fog also prevented a landing at nearby Torbay. He had to land at the United States air base at Argentia, then drive ninety miles over dirt roads to St John's, where he made a speech that night. In the morning, he had to get up very early to meet some local Tories, then drive back through the fog to his plane at Argentia. Because there had been no place at Argentia to provision the aircraft, there was no food on board. The leader and his entourage headed for Cornerbrook, where he had an event. Landing at Stephenville, they discovered the airport restaurant had been closed. It was a hundred-mile drive to Cornerbrook, but someone remembered there was a restaurant on the highway along the way. When they got there, they found the restaurant had not yet opened for the season. By the time they got to Cornerbrook, it was nearly twelve hours since they had left St John's and no one had had anything to eat. At party headquarters in Ottawa, the phones rang off the hook as everyone blamed everyone else for screwing up the Newfoundland trip.

The confusion threw Diefenbaker off stride. By the time he reached London for the official opener, he was thoroughly stressed. It was a hot night and he spoke for an hour and a half. It was the worst speech of his life. For some reason, he decided to announce the party's entire election platform that night. Not only that, he gave a full review of everything the government had done since 1957. I had to type a transcript of the speech. It was ghastly.

The campaign was barely underway when a monetary crisis caused Donald Fleming, the finance minister, to devalue the dollar. After much discussion and disagreement, Fleming recommended that the dollar be pegged at 92.5 cents. "It will cost us the election," Diefenbaker told him, although he had little choice but to accept Fleming's advice. While devaluation did not – quite – cost us the election, it certainly handed the Liberals some marvellous ammunition. They distributed tens of thousands of play banknotes – dubbed Diefendollars or Diefenbucks, with a stated value of 92.5 cents. For the rest of the campaign, we were on the defensive. The Liberals had no compunction about misleading the voters. A dollar that used to be worth 100 cents was now worth only 92.5 cents, they contended. That was patently false, but when Camp prepared a newspaper advertisement to illustrate that one dollar still bought the same amount of goods as it always had, Diefenbaker vetoed the ad. At least he was decisive about the ad. On most issues, his indecision drove us crazy at headquarters. People kept asking us, "Where are the pamphlets?" We had to tell them the pamphlets were not ready because they had not yet been approved by the leader. Diefenbaker insisted on vetting everything, yet he was incapable of making even simple decisions.

Allister Grosart was running the campaign, but he was not a well man. He had been under tremendous strain for a long time and had developed a serious ulcer. He carried a bottle of white medicine that he would gulp at periodically, hoping it would ease his pain. Both he and Diefenbaker were exhausted, far too tired to make sound decisions. To make matters worse, the campaign was marred by anti-Diefenbaker protests and near riots. One of his appearances, in Vancouver, turned into a mob scene, but Diefenbaker, who was often at his best in the face of hecklers, bravely stood his ground on the platform as others fled. Camp wanted to use the television footage of that scene for a fifteen-minute free-time telecast on CBC, on the theory that the sight of the prime minister being abused by his opponents would earn him sympathy from the voters. But Grosart vetoed the idea, saying "You should never show the prime minister of Canada being heckled." Camp was so discouraged by Diefenbaker, by Grosart, and by the whole campaign that, even though he was in charge of the party's national media, he did not show his face in Ottawa even once in that election.

On 18 June 1962 – coincidentally or ominously, the 147th anniversary of the Battle of Waterloo – we won 116 seats to ninety-eight for the Liberals. Our popular vote dropped by seventeen percentage points from 1958 and we actually won 4,815 fewer votes nationally than the Liberals. The dissent that had been building within the party gathered volume. Diefenbaker's distrust of just about everyone grew. His mood was even blacker because he had broken his ankle and spent several weeks hobbling in considerable pain. Shortly after the election, we had a meeting of the 140-member national executive at the Chateau Laurier. It was a sour meeting. Some members blamed Diefenbaker and his inner circle for a dreadful campaign. Others, the loyalists, blamed the leader's detractors within the party for undermining the campaign by sowing dissension. I was seated at a table with Dalton and Finlay MacDonald. When Diefenbaker addressed the meeting, he delivered a tirade against people who had not given 100 per cent in the campaign. He talked about the "termites" that he believed were infesting his party. When he said "termites" he looked straight at our table. A good many executive members left muttering that they had not come all the way to Ottawa, at their own expense, to be chewed out by the prime minister.

There was a deferred election in Stormont riding in eastern Ontario that summer. The Liberal candidate had died just before the general election and the vote in the constituency was postponed until a new Liberal could be nominated. Diefenbaker planned to go to Cornwall to campaign for our MP, Grant Campbell, who had won the seat in 1958. The local Tories, however, asked that the prime minister stay away, fearing his presence would hurt their campaign. It was an extraordinary request to make. I am not sure how Grosart broke the news to Diefenbaker, but it was agreed that his wife Olive would represent him. My assignment was to get her there.

Contrary to her carefully cultivated image of a sweet and loyal helpmate who preferred the shadows to the spotlight, Olive was a malevolent force in her husband's career. She fed his paranoia. She, too, detected enemies on all sides and was quick to point them out to John. She distrusted French Canadians in particular. The drive to Cornwall was painful. We were in a chauffeur-driven car, and she spent the whole trip complaining about those horrible Quebecers who had voted against her husband and declaring we should never trust French Canadians. She was either oblivious to, or did not care, that our driver, who could hear every word she said, was a French Canadian or that the riding we were about to visit was predominantly French speaking. When the ballots were counted and recounted, the new Liberal candidate, Lucien Lamoureux, won by seventy votes. Lucien went on to become speaker of the House of Commons. I liked him.

While the Cuban missile crisis was building in the fall of 1962, I was out of Ottawa, doing battle in the provinces. Camp and I went to Newfoundland for a provincial election in November. Although it ended up as another loss to Joey Smallwood, I think I had more fun in that campaign than just about any other I was involved in. Our new provincial leader, James Greene, was an impressive young politician, articulate and principled. His party had no money at all, but Dalton and I, with help from Allister Grosart, managed to find $15,000. That is all we had for the entire province-wide campaign. But we got lucky, twice. Don Jamieson, who later became a Liberal cabinet minister in Ottawa, was co-owner of a private television station in St John's. He offered us and the Liberals each a fifteen-minute free-time slot once or twice a week during the election. The deal was that the broadcasts be live with the two parties taking turns going first. That television exposure did much to level the playing field.

Our second stroke of luck came when our candidate in the riding of Ferryland arrived at Conservative campaign headquarters clutching a glossy booklet that the Liberals had produced. The candidate, who was barely literate, did not know what the booklet said, but Dalton and I knew instantly. It was a piece of campaign literature in which Smallwood listed his accomplishments as premier and, on the back cover, set out all of the Liberals' election planks: "We are going to build 1,800 new fishing craft ...," and so on. The booklet had been printed before the election was called and had been sent to postmasters across the province with instructions not to deliver it to residents until a certain date. The postmaster in Ferryland, however, had delivered the booklets prematurely.

Greene took the document to the television studio. It was our turn to go first. Greene announced that a Conservative government would build 1,801 new fishing craft. Camp and I were sitting offstage with Smallwood as he waited to go on air. Joey was beside himself. He spluttered with rage. "They've stolen it," he declared, as Dalton and I doubled over with laughter. Then Greene took another Liberal promise – to provide 1,200 of something else – and pledged that the Tories would provide 1,201 of whatever it was. He did that for approximately fifteen Liberal promises. That campaign was a pure delight. We knew we could not win – no one could have beaten Joey in those days – but we did manage to win seven seats, up from three in 1959. Interestingly, all seven were in urban areas that had access to television. The winds of change were beginning to blow in Newfoundland.

From Newfoundland, Dalton went to Manitoba to help Duff Roblin in his re-election in December. Meanwhile, I moved over to Prince Edward Island where Walter Shaw was seeking a second term as premier. We won in both provinces. By the time I got back to Ottawa, discontent with Diefenbaker's leadership was building. Some of his ministers wondered whether he was headed for a nervous breakdown. His procrastination during the Cuban missile crisis had exposed a rift in the party, and by December the government faced another crisis in Canada-United States relations: the Bomarc missile affair.

Following the controversial cancellation in 1959 of the Avro Arrow, Canada's most ambitious aerospace project, our government had made a commitment to acquire Bomarc-B surface-to-air missiles from the United States. But having agreed to accept the missiles, Diefenbaker was unable to decide whether to allow them to be armed with the nuclear warheads that they were designed to carry. His cabinet was split into two camps. The hawks, led by Defence Minister Douglas Harkness, wanted to accept the warheads without delay. External Affairs Minister Howard Green and the doves were opposed. No one was quite sure what Diefenbaker's position was on any given day.

On my return from Newfoundland and PEI, I was caught up in a flurry of preparations for the party's annual meeting, to be held in Ottawa in January 1963. In preparation for the annual meeting, Eddie Goodman, the chairman of the resolutions committee, convened a meeting to review the policy motions sent in by constituency associations and other groups in the party. "Fast Eddie" had something up his sleeve. He asked Allister Grosart, who was attending in his capacity as the former national director, to leave the meeting while the committee members discussed the resolutions. He did not want Grosart, loyal to the leader who had just appointed him to the Senate, to alert Diefenbaker to what the committee was doing. Specifically, he did not want Diefenbaker to know about a resolution – approved by a large majority of the twenty-one committee members – that called on the government to accept the nuclear warheads.

The only problem was, I was trying to package all the resolutions into a booklet to give to about two thousand delegates and journalists as they arrived for the annual meeting. But we needed Diefenbaker's approval before we could distribute the booklet – and that would mean showing him the controversial nuclear-arms resolution. We had not resolved that dilemma when I received a phone call from a journalist friend who said I might be interested in a speech that Liberal leader Lester Pearson was going to make a few days later in Scarborough, Ontario. Pearson, my informant confided, was going to reverse Liberal policy and call for Canada to acquire the nuclear warheads.

I immediately called Eddie to warn him that his committee was about to be scooped by the Liberals. I told him I thought we should try to pre-empt Pearson by releasing our resolution before he delivered his Scarborough speech. In my view – and I was probably naïve – that would not be an attempt by me or Goodman to embarrass Diefenbaker or to meddle in government policy. I took a purely partisan approach. Once it got its head together, our government was going to accept the warheads – I felt sure of that. Public opinion would make it happen. My concern was to make sure we got there first, before the Liberals.[7]

"Well, fine. I'll release it. I'll phone the prime minister," Eddie said. He called me later to report on the conversation. He had told Diefenbaker what Pearson was planning to announce. He had reminded him that the resolutions committee was composed of party activists from all parts of the country. But then Eddie had gone on to gild the lily. He told him that national headquarters was being "inundated" by resolutions calling on the government to acquire the warheads. Diefenbaker saw through that ploy. "Send me the resolutions," he commanded.

We spent the rest of the night frantically phoning Conservatives across the country, asking them to wire resolutions to us. The next morning, we sent a batch to his office. I do not know whether Diefenbaker read them. I do know they had no effect. He remained as irresolute as ever. However, he did ask Goodman to discuss the nuclear issue with the cabinet the next morning. While I sat at headquarters, staring at my two thousand incomplete booklets, Eddie made his pitch to the cabinet. The ministers were too divided to be able to agree, so Diefenbaker appointed a cabinet committee to continue the discussion. Eventually, the committee came up a watered-down resolution, and Howard Green stomped out in protest. It was like that in the days of the disintegrating Diefenbaker administration.

Around noon, Gordon Churchill, one of the ministers on the committee, phoned me from Parliament Hill and dictated the amended resolution so that I could have it translated into French and printed on a separate sheet, to be inserted in the booklet in time for a press conference that Goodman was holding that afternoon. Not long after, Eddie arrived at headquarters to see me. Our regular switchboard operator was at lunch, so he instructed the relief operator, "I'm going to be in Miss MacDonald's office, and I don't want her or myself to be interrupted." The regular operator would have known better, but the relief operator took him at his word, and when the prime minister called, urgently, to speak to Goodman, she refused to put him through.

It turned out that Green had gone to Diefenbaker and persuaded him to kill the nuclear resolution. By the time we learned this, it was too late. The resolution had been printed, inserted in the resolutions book, and sent to the Press Gallery. I can still see Eddie sitting there, laughing hysterically and thinking it was a huge joke that he had managed to out-fox everyone. About five minutes later, Grosart burst into headquarters. "Where were you?" he demanded. "What's been going on down here? Don't you know the Prime Minister's Office has been trying to get you?" Eddie just sat there, looked at him innocently, and said, "Oh, really? We'd just gone out for a sandwich."

Goodman was not so happy when the resolution came up for debate in a policy session at the annual meeting. Although he arranged the roster of speakers carefully to maximize the appearance of support for the resolution, it never had a chance. The night before Diefenbaker had made an emotional appeal to delegates to defeat the resolution. It was not that he was necessarily opposed to acquiring the warheads. Rather, his plea was, "Don't tie my hands on this. Leave me some flexibility." The delegates gave him the flexibility he sought when they voted down the resolution. But the battle over the resolution had exposed the division in the party for everyone, the press and the public, to see. In turn, public awareness accentuated the split in the cabinet. Within a week or so, Harkness resigned. It was the beginning of the end for John Diefenbaker, although the process took longer than anyone could have predicted.

What happened with Harkness was that Diefenbaker had spoken in the House on Friday to outline the government's position on nuclear arms. Harkness had serious reservations about the prime minister's argument. On Saturday he released his own explanation. That infuriated Diefenbaker who, it was said, reprimanded Harkness severely. The defence minister went to the annual Press Gallery dinner that night and told several people he was "damned well going to resign." He sent his resignation to Diefenbaker on Sunday and the next day he announced it in the House. Monday also happened to be the start of a two-day supply debate, one of the traditional opportunities for non-confidence motions.

The Hill buzzed with gossip, rumour, and clandestine meetings. Several ministers, including George Hees, Davie Fulton, Ernest Halpenny, Richard Bell and Pierre Sévigny, were talking about finding an interim leader to take over from Diefenbaker who, they agreed, was no longer capable of leading. Their preferred choice to head the party pending a leadership convention was Nova Scotia's George Nowlan. The confidence vote was scheduled for Tuesday evening. It was almost surreal. While the dissidents met in Hees's office on Tuesday morning, the press corps was parked outside the door, broadcasting the proceedings to the nation. Meanwhile, Diefenbaker was holed up at 24 Sussex Drive with two cronies, Grosart and Senator David Walker.

There were frantic negotiations with the thirty-one-member Social Credit caucus for the votes the minority government needed to survive the confidence vote. Nobody had a clear idea what was happening. Social Credit leader Robert Thompson had the floor when the House adjourned for dinner on Tuesday night. Before dinner, he sounded as though his party was going to support the government; he quoted approvingly from a *Globe and Mail* editorial that had said an early election would be "a disaster." After dinner, however, he outlined four conditions – including a clear statement of policy on national defence – on which Social Credit would support the government. The Tories, he said, had failed to respond to his party's conditions, and he moved an amendment to the Liberals' non-confidence motion; the amendment incorporated the four conditions. The House adjourned for the night without a vote being taken. Desperate negotiations and backstage manoeuvring – fuelled by copious quantities of Scotch – extended deep into the night. A group of dissident ministers, led by Hees, came up with a plan acceptable to Thompson. It called for Diefenbaker to resign – and perhaps become chief justice of the Supreme Court of Canada – and be replaced as prime minister by Donald Fleming. When Diefenbaker rejected that notion on Wednesday morning, the die was cast. His government – our government – was defeated 142–111. The election was called for 8 April 1963.

7

Leadership Crisis

The fall of the Conservative government in February 1963 inspired a brief display of solidarity in our dissension-wracked caucus. Differences over John Diefenbaker's leadership were put aside as members of Parliament began to prepare for the election on 8 April. As if with one voice, they declared that verily they were united for the electoral battle to come.

The unity lasted for three days – from Wednesday until Saturday, when the party's national organization committee, chaired by Dalton Camp, met for a two-day strategy session at the Bruce MacDonald motor hotel in the west end of Ottawa. I went to headquarters early on Saturday morning to gather supplies for the meeting. I called Dalton at the Chateau Laurier and said I would pick him up at the side door of his hotel. "Don't ask me any questions," he said. "Do just as I tell you. You go out there and get that meeting opened and I'll be along as soon as I possibly can. Something terrible has happened, and I can't tell you anything about it."

I went to the motel and got the meeting started until Dalton got there. When he arrived, he looked absolutely haggard. A young man from headquarters who was guarding the door, beckoned to me, saying there was a long-distance call for Dalton in the lobby. I went to see who it was. It was Eddie Goodman calling from Toronto. He asked, "Well, has the news been announced yet?"

"What news?" I asked.

"Hees and Sévigny are on their way over to the Press Gallery with their resignations." (George Hees was the minister of Trade and Commerce and Pierre Sévigny was the associate minister of National

Defence.) When Eddie said that, I just about dropped the phone. I had barely hung up with Goodman when the woman at the motel desk said, "Miss MacDonald, there's a call for Mr Camp from the prime minister."

I called Dalton out of the meeting. "Look," I said, "the prime minister wants you, and Goodman has just called to say that Hees and Sévigny are resigning. What the hell's this all about?" We went to the lobby together. There he was in the lobby of a motel, talking on the phone to the prime minister of Canada about the collapse of his cabinet while I listened in. One tends to remember moments like that.

I heard Diefenbaker say, "You know, these fellows have resigned?"

"Yes, sir, I've already heard," Camp replied.

"You've heard? How did you hear?"

"Flora told me," Dalton said, "Flora's just been talking to Eddie Goodman."

Goodman was already in Diefenbaker's bad books because he had led the revolt on the nuclear arms issue at the party's annual meeting. Worse, he was a close friend and ally of George Hees. I heard Diefenbaker say to Camp, "Put her on the phone."

"Not me. Not me," I signalled to Camp. He told the leader I had gone back to the meeting but would return his call shortly. When I did, I told Diefenbaker that Goodman had called because he had heard a rumour in Toronto about Hees and Sévigny and wanted to know if it was true. I said I had told Goodman it was news to me. I don't know whether Diefenbaker believed me, but I had the distinct impression that I had joined Goodman on his ever-growing list of enemies. In hindsight, it is amazing that I survived another three years as an employee of the Conservative party.

Back at the committee meeting, everyone knew something big was going on, but no one knew what it was. Dalton decided to tell them and their reaction was astonishing. People who a couple of hours earlier had been critical of the leader suddenly closed ranks behind him. They were jumping up and down, as they denounced Hees and Sévigny and called them "traitors" for running out on the party. Egan Chambers, who had lost his Montreal seat in the 1962 election and was now one of our "Nuke Nuts" (supporters of the warheads), declared, "I'm going to be a candidate for John Diefenbaker!"[1] Everyone applauded. Then my friend Finlay MacDonald, a broadcaster who had been one of Diefenbaker's great critics, made an emotional speech. "I'm going home to find out if there's any way I can be released from my commitments at the television station (in Halifax) to run as a candidate." He did, and he lost.

The organization committee resumed on Sunday. Dalton phoned Diefenbaker that morning to say, "Now look, this committee is behind you 100 per cent." In fact, I could think of only one committee member, Harvey Cole from Newfoundland, who spoke out against the leader. Diefenbaker invited the entire group to come to 24 Sussex Drive that afternoon. He put on a one-man theatrical production, describing with high drama how "these fellows" – Hees and Sévigny – had "crept up to my door." It was a great, great story. In telling it, Diefenbaker implied that the two ministers knew he had something on them, that he had a "hold" over them. He did not explain and none us knew what he was referring to. Only much later did it become clear that he had been alluding to the involvement of Hees and Sévigny with Gerda Munsinger in that sex-and-security affair.

I did not share the rally-behind-the-leader feeling. When I got up every morning, I would say to myself, "O Lord, please let him resign today. I don't want it to be vicious. I don't want it to be mean, but why can't he go?" The nuclear issue did not matter much to me, but I cared about the turmoil in the party. I felt there was something terribly wrong that could only be made right if Diefenbaker were to leave. During one sleepless night, I told myself I would go to Dalton in the morning and say I could not carry on. I had made up my mind. When I went to work the next morning, I found that Dalton's wife Linda had come to headquarters with him. Just as I was steeling myself to tell Dalton, Linda came into my office and said, "Dalton and I had a long talk about this last night, and I know he just wouldn't be able to get through this campaign without you." My resolve melted.

I stayed and threw myself into the campaign. To my great surprise, it was like day and night after the dismal 1962 campaign. Diefenbaker found himself back on familiar and comfortable ground, as the underdog, the little guy battling stronger, meaner opponents. He put up a tremendous fight. He was more relaxed and there was a spring in his step again. In 1962, he had campaigned by aircraft, but Diefenbaker never liked planes. In 1963, Dalton had him use a train, as he had in 1957, and he was much happier. He stopped at every little village in the West. I remember choirs in long blue gowns serenading him from railway platforms. Diefenbaker loved that kind of stuff.

The protests and riots that had marred the 1962 election did not materialize in 1963. The Liberals sent out a "Truth Squad" to monitor the accuracy of Diefenbaker's pronouncements and distributed cartoon colouring books that mocked him. Diefenbaker was in his element. He turned that nonsense to his advantage, mocking the Liberals at every stop. He had his audiences rolling in the aisles.

We did not win the 1963 election. We had too much baggage to carry. But we did better than most of us had expected – better perhaps than we deserved. We held the Liberals to 129 seats, four short of a majority, while winning a respectable ninety-five seats ourselves. In June, two months after the election, Diefenbaker appointed Dick Thrasher as national director. I cleaned out my desk and took off for Europe, determined not to return to Canada or Conservative politics any time soon.

I was happy. My plan was to spend to spend some time in Britain and the continent before going to Paris where I had a cousin who was a Central Intelligence Agency liaison officer at the US Embassy. I hooked up with Ralph Finlayson, the young man with whom I had travelled in the United Kingdom in the summer of 1952. We agreed we would meet at the Trevi Fountain in Rome at an appointed hour on a certain Saturday afternoon. We both turned up on time. We set off for Greece, travelling by train from Rome to Brindisi on Italy's Adriatic coast to catch the overnight ferry to the Greek island of Corfu. At least, that's what we thought we were doing. Getting to Brindisi early, we bought our tickets. I thought they were charging an awful lot, but everyone spoke Italian and my high school Latin did not cut any ice with them. We wandered around for a while, then went back to the docks to board our ship. I do not know how we could have been so stupid! While we were aboard a small ship with our hammocks hung in the bow, suddenly we saw this big, multi-deck ferry sailing out and realized we had purchased the wrong tickets. And we went for a lovely cruise, all along the eastern Adriatic, from Dubrovnik in Yugoslavia, along the coast of Albania, to Corfu. We sailed through the Corinthian Canal, enjoyed superb food and, after a delightful week, we reached Piraeus, the port city of Athens. I was dazzled by the monuments and history of the Greek capital. We explored Athens until Ralph had to return to Canada where he was teaching school.

I took off to see the Greek Islands and spent several weeks going from island to island. I wanted to find the grave of Rupert Brooke, the young English poet who was buried on the little-visited island of Skyros.[2] I found two fishermen who took me three miles down the coast to his gravesite. From Greece, I flew to Austria. At Innsbruck, I took a cable car up a mountain. What I did not realize, or had neglected to check that it was the last car of the day. Oblivious to this, I wandered around happily until I returned to the cable car station and found that I was stranded. I had to walk down the mountain in the cold and dark without proper boots or a flashlight. After falling several times, I made it to the bottom – only to discover that, in my stupidity, I had come down the wrong side of the mountain. I had to walk around the mountain to get back to Innsbruck.

When I finally got to my cousin's place in Paris, I found a telegram from Dalton saying, "The election has just been called in Nova Scotia and we need you." I decided to go back. It was a terrific election. During the day, I worked with Rod Black, Bob Stanfield's organizational genius; at night, I worked with Camp on speeches, posters, and campaign advertising. On election day, Rod and I went to see one old fellow who lived in a basement apartment in Halifax.

"Ah, Mr McNeill, I've come to take you to the poll," Black said.

"I told you, Mr Black, I wouldn't go anywhere until you brought the VON nurse to give me a bath," the old man replied.

Rod responded, "I just happen to have the VON nurse with me."

So I ended up giving this old man a bath. The things I did for my party and my country! And, yes, we got his vote. Bob Stanfield won his third term, and when it was over, Dick Thrasher asked me to return to national headquarters in Ottawa. With misgivings, that is what I did.

Most Conservatives and probably a majority of Canadians assumed Diefenbaker would retire after we lost the 1963 election. However, retirement was the furthest thing from his mind. As the months passed, his resolve hardened. He convinced himself that he, and he alone, could lead the Conservatives back to power.

The year 1964 was pivotal. It was memorable for two events. In February, Dalton Camp was elected national president at the party's annual meeting, which gave him a springboard to challenge Diefenbaker two years later. In September, the party held a "thinkers' conference" in Fredericton, a gathering that dramatized the widening gulf between the party's two solitudes – its pro-Diefenbaker and anti-Diefenbaker factions. The National Conference on Canadian Goals, as Fredericton was officially known, was Camp's inspiration and he wanted it to be held in the capital of his home province. It was a project of the party, its elected officers, and national headquarters, and not of the leader's office or the caucus. Camp was a creative thinker, but never an organizer. He would come up with an idea, then leave the tedious details to others. In the case of Fredericton, he assembled a secretariat. His brother-in-law, Norman Atkins, assisted by Joe Clark, looked after invitations and travel arrangements for delegates. My assignment was to assemble the conference materials, distribute position papers, and prepare verbatim reports of the proceedings. Lowell Murray handled press relations. George Hogan chaired the proceedings one day, Eddie Goodman another day, and so on. We were all people who worked well with Dalton. In Diefenbaker's eyes, I suppose, we were all "termites."

Dalton hoped the conference would distract Tories from the controversy over the leadership, the election defeat, and the internal battles that were tearing the party apart. He wanted to give younger Conservatives some mental stimulation. The conference, he thought, could broaden Tories' thinking by exposing them to informed opinion about French Canada. And he wanted to establish some sort of relationship between his party and at least a few intellectual leaders. The plans for Fredericton reflected his interests, his approach to politics, and his belief that civil discourse should take precedence over partisanship, confrontation, and vitriol.

That, of course, was not Diefenbaker's way. He had always been contemptuous of intellectuals and, having mocked the Liberals when they held a thinkers' conference in Kingston in 1960, he did not relish the prospect of being seen to be consorting with pointy-headed academics. He also suspected (rightly, as it turned out) that Fredericton would turn into a forum for dissent over his leadership. And he feared that the conference would divert attention from what he regarded as more important business – the prolonged flag debate in Parliament in which he and his supporters were fighting a desperate, and increasingly pathetic, rearguard action to prevent the adoption of the red and white maple leaf flag as Canada's national flag – "Pearson's pennant," Diefenbaker sneered.

The roster of speakers confirmed Diefenbaker's worst fears. Camp recruited Marshall McLuhan to be the keynote speaker. McLuhan started by posing a question for the audience: what is purple and hums? An electric grape was the answer. And why does it hum? Because it does not know the words. That led McLuhan into an

extended discussion of communication, language, and the need
to know the words in order to communicate. The reaction of the
audience was mixed, to put it charitably. I thought McLuhan was
brilliant. His lecture was one of the most extraordinary I had ever
heard. Camp declared McLuhan had been "an absolute sensation,"
and Richard Hatfield agreed. But Finlay MacDonald came closer to
capturing the sentiment of the audience. "This is the price we have
to pay for losing the election," he told the conference. And Gene
Rhéaume, the MP for Northwest Territories who had been assigned
to go to the airport to meet Diefenbaker when he finally arrived,
decided not to bother. "Marshall McLuhan taught me I could kiss
[Dief's] ass from here," he said.

The rest of the roster was impressive: historian W.L. Morton;
Eugene Forsey, the great constitutionalist; Claude Ryan, publisher of
Le Devoir; Montreal lawyer Marc Lalonde, a Liberal who had once
worked as an assistant to Diefenbaker's first justice minister, Davie
Fulton; and financier Marcel Faribault. I got another name from
Michael Pitfield, who was then on the staff of the governor general
and would later be the clerk of the Privy Council. The name was
Pierre Elliott Trudeau, who in those days was known as a left-leaning
academic and writer who had broken with the Liberals over nuclear
arms and had dismissed Lester Pearson as the "unfrocked priest of
peace." It would be another year before Trudeau entered politics
(as a Liberal). I arranged for Camp to have dinner with Trudeau in
Montreal so that he could check him out. The dinner was a disaster: the chemistry was terrible and their egos clashed. Camp found
Trudeau superficial and he told me never to ask him to meet that
man again.

Although Diefenbaker wanted no part of Fredericton, he was suspicious. He called me one day to demand, "What's going on down there
today?" In the end, his curiosity overcame his hostility – curiosity plus
concern about what his "enemies" were saying about him behind his
back. He flew in, made an uninspired speech, and left.

The confrontation between the anti- and pro-Diefenbaker factions
heightened after the 1964 Fredericton conference. In November, we
lost – badly – a federal by-election in the New Brunswick riding of
Westmorland. In December, the national executive met in Ottawa.
Ned Murphy, our candidate in the Westmorland by-election,
presented a post-mortem. "The greatest handicap I had in my campaign was John Diefenbaker, and it's about time we got rid of him,"

he said. Most members of the executive were stunned. Many of them had been thinking the same thing. They had been muttering among themselves, as had a growing number of caucus members. But others hoped Diefenbaker would be reasonable, choose his own time, and leave voluntarily. Few seriously expected him, after waging a spirited campaign in a doomed cause in the 1963 election, to hang around to fight another one. How little we knew!

Once Ned Murphy opened that door, several others jumped up to say they agreed with him. The first to register agreement was, significantly, Leon Balcer, Diefenbaker's Quebec lieutenant. Balcer talked about the difficulties the party was having in Quebec because of the leader and about his own lack of rapport with Diefenbaker. He proposed that the executive pass a motion calling on the leader and caucus to abandon the flag filibuster. Although Camp, as chairman, managed to prevent Balcer's proposal from coming to a vote, it was clear the issue was far from dead.[3]

Events moved quickly. A few days after the executive meeting, Balcer rose from his seat next to Diefenbaker's in the House of Commons and, on a question of privilege, attacked his own party's tactics in the flag debate. He asked the Liberals to use closure to cut off the filibuster, causing Gordon Churchill, the Conservative house leader, to declare that Balcer did not speak for the party. Balcer and his group – we had managed to retain eight seats in Quebec in the 1963 election – decided to wait until after the Christmas break to make a move on the leadership.

Meanwhile, Eddie Goodman and George Hogan began to take soundings. Hogan, a Toronto car dealer and Tory vice-president who had broken with Diefenbaker at the time of the Cuban missile crisis, telephoned about one hundred senior Conservatives across the country. He described his concerns, explaining that the party's position was deteriorating under Diefenbaker's leadership. He asked them to write to Dalton, as national president, with their frank opinions on the leadership. About eighty replies came in, of which perhaps seventy-five were critical of the leader. The idea was that Dalton would take the letters to Diefenbaker and advise him that opinion in the party, as he was receiving it, was strongly opposed to Diefenbaker's continued leadership. Hogan hoped Dief would see the light and retire gracefully.

Meanwhile, Senator Wallace McCutcheon, the former big businessman whom Diefenbaker had made minister of Trade and

Commerce after Hees's resignation, was trying to raise money to finance the party's operating costs and build a war chest for the next election. Working with Lowell Murray, his executive assistant, he sent out four thousand "personalized" letters to business people, lawyers, and other professionals asking for $100 contributions.

Only about 10 per cent of the recipients responded – about one-half the normal response rate in our fund-raising campaigns.[4] Some of the four hundred–odd letters that did come in were delightful. "Wally, I would be glad to contribute, but under the circumstances I can't contribute to the Conservative party. If you would please let me know what your favourite charity is, I'll send you a cheque for $100."

McCutcheon replied: "I understand your views. My favourite charity is the Conservative party."

In mid-January, Leon Balcer and his supporters made their move. Meeting in Montreal, they issued what amounted to an ultimatum, calling on Camp, as national president, to convene a meeting of the national executive to discuss Diefenbaker's leadership and the holding of a leadership convention. Claude Ryan wrote an editorial in *Le Devoir* endorsing Balcer's stand, and Marcel Bourbonnais, a Conservative MP from Quebec from 1958 to 1963, sent seven hundred letters to Conservatives in the province asking them to let Camp know what they thought.

Dalton was not amused. I was well aware of his low regard for Balcer. He distrusted his motives and thought his methods were inept. Most of all, he feared that a confrontation would harm the party, cause Diefenbaker to dig in his heels, and do nothing to resolve the crisis. Although the national executive had met only a month earlier, Camp felt an obligation to poll the membership. When a narrow majority opted for another meeting, he set Sunday, 6 February as the date.

Camp knew Diefenbaker would never agree to convening an executive meeting to consider Balcer's demands, so we came up with a strategy. Diefenbaker was away in London, attending the funeral of Sir Winston Churchill. I checked his flight schedule and found his return flight to Canada was due to leave London at midnight Ottawa time. At midnight, I went to the telegraph office and sent wires to all 140 members of the national executive, including provincial premiers, asking them to be in Ottawa for a meeting on 6 February. By the time Diefenbaker landed in Canada, it would be too late to head off the meeting.

Dief was furious. Always resourceful when threatened, he advanced the date of a scheduled meeting of the parliamentary caucus. He rescheduled it for the day before the executive meeting in the belief that a resounding vote of confidence from Conservative MPs would defuse Balcer's challenge when the executive met the next day. Diefenbaker arrived back in Ottawa on a Monday and Dalton arranged to see him on Tuesday. He had a thick pile of letters that had been generated by George Hogan's campaign and he planned to deliver them to the leader. On Monday evening, I made two photocopies of each letter to ensure they could be preserved for posterity. I also typed a memorandum that Dalton had written in which he synthesized the contents of the letters, noting the tributes some of the correspondents had paid Diefenbaker for his service to the party and the country, and making the point that it was now time, in the opinion of the letter-writers, to terminate that service. Dalton's memo was couched in a more-in-sorrow-than-in-anger tone.

It was fairly obvious the memo had been produced at national headquarters because the IBM typewriters we used had a distinctive typeface. Looking back, I can see how Diefenbaker and his supporters would have identified me as one of the conspirators against the leader. Yet I had this ambivalent feeling that I worked just as much for the national association as I did for the leader or his caucus – and Dalton was the elected leader of the national association.

He went in to see Diefenbaker at noon and did not emerge until nearly six o'clock. With the House not sitting, the Press Gallery had nothing better to do than to stake out Diefenbaker's office and to crank up an air of crisis by issuing frequent bulletins about the meeting stretching on and how cucumber sandwiches were being sent in. George Nowlan phoned me frantically. "Flora, do you know what's going on? Have you any idea what is going on?" he asked. "Do you suppose we should try to rescue him? Will you have Dalton phone me as soon as he gets out? I want to know that he's all right."

When I met Dalton for dinner at the Chateau Laurier later, he told me he had gone in with the intention of explaining his memorandum and carrying on from where it left off. But he never got a chance. For the first fifteen minutes, Diefenbaker shouted at him about matters he felt Dalton had crossed him up on or had tried to put over on him. Camp attempted to explain that although he had the leader's position in mind, he had all these letters from Conservatives across the country who felt that he, as their national president, was not going far enough or fast enough to address their concerns about the leadership. At the same time, he was under great criticism from Diefenbaker for being disloyal and treacherous. How, he asked, was a party president expected to walk this lonely line? Diefenbaker never did look at the letters. When Dalton tried to show them to him, Diefenbaker said, "Mail! Wait till I show you my mail!" The rest of the meeting was taken up with a series of Diefenbaker monologues.

I will never forget Dalton's frustration at dinner that night. "The terrible thing about Diefenbaker is that he has the Conservative party by the throat and he's choking the life out of it," he said. Neither of us knew how to make him let go. As we ate, Dalton was called to the phone to speak to Erik Nielsen, the Conservative MP for Yukon and a key Diefenbaker loyalist. Nielsen wanted to meet, and Camp invited him to come to his room in the hotel at 10 p.m. He wanted a witness, so he said to me, "Now look, I'll go up and meet him, but just in case anything's going on, you come up at 10:30 and say that you're here to get me to do some work."

I went to the room as arranged. At the time of this meeting, Nielsen was Diefenbaker's hatchet man in Parliament, and he was leading the Tory attack on the Lucien Rivard affair[5] and some of the other Liberal scandals. But that night he was critical of the leader as he described Diefenbaker's reaction when he first took him information about the drug dealer Rivard. "For the first time in my life, I saw someone who was abnormal, who was in a bad mental condition," Nielsen said. "He literally slathered when I told him about this. He couldn't contain his venom and his anxiety to get at the Liberal cabinet. I realized then that I had come up against something evil."

The phone rang and Dalton went to answer it, but he signalled to me to keep the conversation going. I was stupidly indiscreet. I had been working closely with Erik over the previous month on some of the scandal allegations he was raising in Parliament. I thought we were on a fairly friendly basis. Forgetting where his first loyalty lay, I responded to his comments about Diefenbaker by telling him how I really felt about the leader and his mishandling of the party. I spilled my guts, is the way Lowell Murray described it later. After Nielsen left the hotel room, Dalton looked at me and said, "You know, I think you said things tonight you will be sorry for."

Dalton was right, of course. Erik had not come to exchange confidences about the leader. He had come to see if he could find out what Dalton's next move would be. When he left us, he went straight to

Diefenbaker and reported my disloyalty. Nielsen himself confirmed this a couple of years later, after Diefenbaker had had me fired. Erik invited me for a drink during the 1967 leadership convention in Toronto. He asked me if I remembered the critical things I had said about Diefenbaker in the hotel room in Ottawa. He explained his philosophy this way: "I have a thing about leaders or people I work for, you know, and that is, regardless of what they're like or what wrongs they commit or anything else, as long as that person is my leader, my chief, or commanding officer, or whatever, as long as he is the head of the group I'm in, I'm loyal to him. There's no question – right, wrong, or indifferent. He's going to have my full loyalty."

When the Conservative caucus met on 5 February, the day before the national executive meeting, the ninety-five MPs gave Diefenbaker a rousing vote of confidence. All those who supported the leader were asked to stand. No count was made of those opposed.

Normally, the national executive would meet in a conference room at a hotel. But we were worried about security for our meeting on 6 February, so we changed the venue to the unoccupied fifth floor of a small office building that national headquarters had moved into on Queen Street, two blocks south of Parliament Hill. Headquarters occupied the lower floors and, with only one elevator in the building, we could control access to the meeting floor. The theory was that reporters, photographers, and camera crews would stay on the fourth floor until we were finished. It did not quite work. When some reporters climbed the fire escape to peer in the windows of the fifth floor, we pasted large sheets of brown paper over the windows. Later, I heard a noise coming from the elevator shaft. When I looked I saw two legs. I grabbed the legs, pulled them down and discovered they belonged to a reporter from the *Ottawa Citizen*. He started running down the stairs. I kicked off my shoes and ran after him. He made it as far as the second floor before I tackled him and held on for dear life. Dick Thrasher called the newspaper's owners to complain, but that did not stop them from publishing a full-page story about their "scoop."

Our meeting room was a long, narrow space that ran the length of the building. The 116 members of the executive who showed up were seated along the sides of a U-shaped table with a head table that would seat eleven – Dalton, the eight other principal officers, Diefenbaker, and me. "You stay quite close to me because if I have to ask you any questions about what happened previously, I want you handy," Camp told me. That worked until Diefenbaker arrived, unexpectedly bringing his wife, and Olive took my seat.

The night before, Dalton had met with the other principal officers. They hoped to reduce the likelihood of a messy public confrontation by severely limiting the debate. The idea was to allow Balcer to present his resolution and Diefenbaker to respond, then ask the members of the executive to vote by secret ballot on a questionnaire with two questions: "Should there be a leadership convention?" and "Should the leader resign?"

Meeting Diefenbaker for breakfast before the meeting, Camp had presented the plan. As national president, he would collect the questionnaires and tabulate the results. Only the outcome, not the actual numbers, would be made public. The numbers would be revealed to Diefenbaker alone. He could interpret them as advice from the executive, which he could accept or reject, as he wished. In Camp's view, the leadership convention question would not carry because too many Tories were worried about the minority Liberal government calling a snap election while the Conservatives were preoccupied with changing leaders. He thought the other question, about the leader resigning, would be close, but he told Diefenbaker he thought he would probably win it. Diefenbaker seemed prepared to accept the questionnaire, if Camp would add two questions: "Should the party create a policy advisory committee?" and "Should the party fully accept the new Canadian flag?" Camp agreed. He thought they had a deal when the breakfast ended.

The problem with Diefenbaker was that agreements or understandings would evaporate whenever he had second thoughts. When he arrived for the meeting that day, he not only brought his wife but many of his supporters from the caucus. They lined the sides of the meeting room, an intimidating presence, and a cheering section for the Chief. Balcer made a short, non-confrontational speech. He was trying, I think, to avoid enraging Diefenbaker. If that was his intent, he failed spectacularly.

Diefenbaker spoke for nearly ninety minutes. He was out of control. He was irrational. For the only time in my life, I saw a speaker literally foam at the mouth. I thought he was insane. He resurrected every favourable thing Balcer had ever said about him, then ripped into anyone and everyone who had ever opposed him on anything, any time. He unleashed a furious broadside against the late President John F. Kennedy, accusing him of working personally to undermine the prime minister of Canada. He referred to the Gerda Munsinger scandal and talked about the files on George Hees and Pierre Sévigny that he said he had on his desk – "The day will come when I'll tell what they did to me, and I have the files, and I knew right along what these people were doing."

Everything he said was a personal attack on people he felt had crossed him. I remember that Davie Fulton, who had quit Diefenbaker's cabinet to go into provincial politics in British Columbia at the time of the 1963 cabinet revolt, came in for a special lashing. Speaking without notes, Diefenbaker leaped from subject to subject to subject. His anger shook some of his listeners to their cores. He sent a chill through the room when he reminded the executive that William Ewart Gladstone had been almost eighty-three when he won his last British election. And he rejected the leadership questionnaire out of hand – "I won't accept it. Nope."

I knew Camp had not thought through a strategy. He assumed that Diefenbaker, having agreed to the questionnaire, would let it proceed. When he refused, we had no fallback. I went with Dalton and the other principal officers to Dick Thrasher's office on the third floor to work on the wording of the questions. When we were satisfied, I typed the questionnaire – it ran to two pages – and made copies for everyone at the meeting. Dalton gave Diefenbaker a copy, then tried to read the questions to the meeting. When Diefenbaker started arguing with him – "No, no, I won't agree to this. You've got to stop. I'm not taking part in any ... You're trying to get me again." – Dalton stopped reading in consternation. The acoustics in the long room were terrible. People knew Dalton was trying to read something, but they could not hear what it was. They could see Diefenbaker was arguing, but did not know what he was saying.

A loud babble broke out and I remember Marcel Lambert, an MP from Edmonton and former Commons speaker, calling out: "For God's sake, will you give us some leadership? You people are supposed to get together and do something. Well, tell us what it's all about." Meanwhile, Diefenbaker kept insisting that the second question – "Should the leader resign?" – be deleted; he talked darkly about "termites," and he accused various persons (unnamed but undoubtedly including George Hees and Davie Fulton) of being consumed by ambition.

With everyone talking or shouting at once, we lost control of the meeting. A big part of the problem was Dalton. He had no idea what to do if the meeting did not go as he anticipated. After a half-hour of confusion, the principal officers withdrew again. Dalton seemed to be almost in shock. He thought Diefenbaker had agreed to the questionnaire and was dumbfounded when he attacked it. "I think we should all resign," Dalton said. But Finlay MacDonald was having none of that – "I'll be damned if I'm going to resign. I'm going to fight this out."

While the principal officers were meeting, Bill Macadam, a party vice-president from British Columbia and an ardent Diefenbaker supporter, tried to reason with Dief. Camp and the others, he told Diefenbaker, were trying to proceed in a democratic manner and the leader should not deny the national executive the right to have its say. If Diefenbaker persisted, Bill warned, "I will have to vote against you."

The principal officers, meanwhile, were trying to talk Dalton out of resigning as national president. "I've completely lost everyone's trust, and I don't think I can be effective any more," he said. Partly to show solidarity with Camp, the principal officers agreed to proceed with the questionnaire without any changes. And they reduced the pressure on him by asking Finlay MacDonald to chair the meeting when it resumed. It very quickly turned acrimonious. Eddie Goodman, impatient with Camp's equivocation, moved that the meeting proceed with the questionnaire. His motion produced the donnybrook that Camp had been trying to avoid. While Eddie spoke, Diefenbaker kept up a running commentary until I wished I could take shorthand with both hands. "I knew this was all a Goodman plot," he muttered. "That fellow, I know who his friends are." Erik Nielsen, ever the loyalist, moved that the second question be deleted. He delivered an emotional defence of the leader. That provoked Joe Clark, whom Camp had been endeavouring to restrain, to demand angrily that Diefenbaker resign and that a leadership convention be called.

Nielsen's motion had the effect of forcing a standing confidence vote in Diefenbaker's leadership. There would be no secret ballot to shelter the faint of heart. The loyalists voted with Nielsen to delete the question. Those who wanted a change of leaders voted against it. The vote was close and chaotic. If it had been a secret ballot, the second question would have survived and Diefenbaker might have lost. But some members of the executive, especially the women members, found it unnerving to have to stand and be counted under the baleful eye of Olive Diefenbaker. She glared at them as they voted. When one of the representatives from New Brunswick, Mrs Hugh MacKay, the widow of a former provincial leader, rose to vote, Diefenbaker commented, "That woman hasn't been at a Conservative meeting in fifteen years, and they brought her up especially to vote against me." (Dief had a point. Mrs MacKay almost never came to meetings.)

Provincial premiers are automatically members of the national executive. Three of the Tory premiers at the time, Walter Shaw of PEI, Robarts of Ontario, and Roblin of Manitoba, did not attend that climactic February 1965 meeting. But Bob Stanfield was a faithful attendee at gatherings of the national party. Even when he knew it might be in his political best interests to stay away, he believed he had a duty to be there to speak for Conservatives in Nova Scotia. And Stanfield was a man whose actions were always guided by his sense of duty. He was there that day, and he agonized over what to do. When the time came to vote, he sat in his seat for a long time before slowly rising and casting his vote in favour of Nielsen's motion to delete the second question – in other words, in favour of Diefenbaker's continuing leadership.

Like Dalton Camp, Stanfield was coming to despair of Diefenbaker. Like Camp, he feared Dief would do irreparable damage to the party and hoped he would resign. But like Camp, he was not yet ready to raise his hand against the leader. As Stanfield rose, George Nowlan, one of the principal dissenters in the caucus, rose with him and the rest of the Nova Scotians followed their example. "I probably made a mistake in coming to this meeting," Stanfield told me later. "I'm sorry it happened the way it did." Then he asked me a revealing question: "How much damage do you think this did me with the French Canadian group in the party?" It was the first indication I had that Stanfield might be thinking about seeking the leadership when Diefenbaker was gone.

The votes cast by Stanfield and the Nova Scotia representatives were crucial. They probably tipped the balance. In the noisy confusion – many of the people could not hear when to stand or sit and they kept popping up and down – the count had to be taken several times. In the end, it was clear that the motion to delete had carried by about two votes, probably 55–53 or 53–51. Diefenbaker had beaten back another challenge.[6]

I felt like a drowning person. I felt as though I had been drowning for so long that I did not really expect to be rescued. Diefenbaker's leadership was something I lived with and expected to have to continue to live with. Although there was much about him that I still respected, I knew he was the wrong leader for the party. I knew we would never get the party back on the right course until he left. But I had no great hope that he would ever leave of his own accord. It was not until I witnessed that desperately close vote at the national executive that I realized how many other Conservatives felt that they were drowning, too.

After the meeting, Diefenbaker went on television to lash out at his detractors, implying that he had been the target, not of well-intentioned, democratically inclined fellow Conservatives, but rather of sinister outside interests, whom he did not, of course, identify – because they did not exist. The caucus was irreparably divided. One Quebec MP, Remi Paul, left to sit as an independent. Two months later, Balcer followed. "At first, I thought that Mr Diefenbaker just didn't understand Quebec," he said. "Now, I am convinced that he is genuinely against French Canada and that as a political expedient he is trying to whip up an English Canadian backlash for an election campaign." Even those of us who had little use for Balcer suspected his assessment was painfully close to the mark.

On 15 February 1965, the new Canadian flag – the one Diefenbaker had fought so hard against – was raised for the first time on Parliament Hill. I went with Lowell Murray to watch the ceremony. It was a dramatic and moving moment. Diefenbaker wept as the flag was raised. But his long-time personal secretary, Bunny Pound, applauded as the flag was unfurled on the flagpole atop the Peace Tower. Someone reported this to Diefenbaker, and he did not speak to Bunny for months. She got the cold shoulder in the office, was given nothing to do, and was excluded from office activities.

The Liberals waited until the fall of 1965 to call a general election for 8 November. It was a very different campaign for us. For the first time since I had gone to work at Conservative headquarters nine years earlier, Dalton Camp was not involved in the national campaign. Camp had managed the entire campaign in 1963, but in 1965 he decided to run for Parliament. Some of his friends urged him to seek the nomination in York North riding where he would have faced a weak Liberal incumbent. But I am sure Dalton was already toying with the idea of running for the leadership whenever Diefenbaker left. He decided to run against a powerful Liberal minister, Mitchell Sharp, in Toronto's Eglinton riding, which was

Donald Fleming's old seat. Dalton reasoned that he could do himself more good in terms of recognition and stature by losing to a giant like Sharp than by defeating a non-entity. And if he had knocked off Sharp, he would have been a power in the caucus and a leading leadership contender. Although he did not manage to defeat Sharp, he cut the Liberal plurality to fewer than two thousand votes, polling more votes than any Tory in Toronto.[7]

Our ranks at headquarters in Ottawa were thin. Not only was Camp, the national president of the party, unavailable for the central campaign, we once again had no national director. Dick Thrasher, who had been appointed by Diefenbaker in 1963, resigned to seek election (unsuccessfully, as it turned out) in his former riding of Essex South in Windsor. Diefenbaker was in a quandary. He had to lead a party into an election with no campaign chairman and no one to run national headquarters. He tried to interest several people whom he trusted to chair the campaign, but had no luck. A group of us decided that Eddie Goodman would be our best bet, if he would consider it. I had to persuade Diefenbaker to accept him and Eddie to agree to take on the responsibility. I managed this feat by exaggerating to each the high regard in which they held each other. Dief was certainly not pleased about putting his campaign in the hands of a person he believed to be disloyal. And Eddie was not happy to be running a campaign for a man he believed should no longer be leader. "Why should I leave my law practice and come down and do something for which I'll probably not be thanked?" he asked me. I had to appeal to his sense of excitement and his love of being involved. He had coordinated provincial campaigns in Ontario but never one at the national level. He was intrigued.

In the end, Eddie reluctantly agreed, provided Diefenbaker allowed him the autonomy to manage the campaign as he saw fit. That condition was tested early on. Diefenbaker told Goodman he wanted one of his faithful cronies, Arthur Burns, a Montreal advertising man, to organize his leader's tour. I had never felt comfortable with Burns, and I advised Eddie to keep him away from the campaign. So he told Dief he could not have Burns – "If Arthur Burns comes to headquarters, Flora MacDonald won't stay, and it's more important that I have Flora working with me than Arthur Burns." I had never said I would not work with Burns, but Eddie exaggerated my objections to fortify his hand with Diefenbaker.

Having no realistic alternative, Diefenbaker reluctantly accepted Goodman and his conditions – with the proviso that my friend

Lowell Murray not be allowed to set foot in national headquarters. That did not matter much. Lowell was actively involved throughout the campaign; we simply met with him in other locations. And as the organization came together, I took on the role that the national director would normally play.

A group of us met at the Chateau Laurier to make plans. We struggled to come up with an election slogan, and someone – it may have been Brian Mulroney – came up with a slogan that we could not, alas, use: "Let's give the old bugger another chance."

No one had written an election platform, and, if we wanted to be taken seriously, we needed some policy planks. When I had been in England a couple of years earlier, I had gone to the Labour party meeting in Scarborough where its leader, Harold Wilson, had given a brilliant address on science policy. I brought back a copy and tucked it away. When we decided we needed some policies, I gave it to Eddie, who made a few minor adjustments and had it published in the *Globe and Mail* as the Progressive Conservative science policy. No one twigged to its true origin. People told us, "Gee, you've got some great thinkers."

I think we ran a brilliant campaign. It was two campaigns, actually. While we in Ottawa concerned ourselves with candidates and organization, Diefenbaker was off on his own, travelling the country and haranguing the Liberals over assorted scandals – controversial furniture purchases by cabinet ministers, Lucien Rivard, and the discovery of the bodies of organized crime figures in lime pits in Quebec. The master of innuendo, Diefenbaker made it sound almost as though Prime Minister Pearson had helped Rivard to escape from Bordeaux Jail in Montreal or to push the bodies into the lime pits.

At one point, the leader's tour came to Ottawa, and I realized that all his old paranoia about national headquarters had resurfaced. He called me. "About headquarters," he said, "I know they are not working with me 100 per cent." He went on about how headquarters was not pulling its weight, which infuriated me because I had been working eighteen-hour days, as had everyone else. "I'm telling you I want to see an improvement in twenty-four hours or you'll hear from me again." I thought his criticism was probably directed at Goodman, and I decided not to tell Eddie for fear that he would abandon the campaign and return to his law practice in Toronto. A few days later, however, on a Sunday, Eddie was at headquarters when Diefenbaker called for him. I sat there listening as they talked, and it was apparent they were talking about me. "Well, now, Sir, I know that she's doing her best," Eddie told him. "Yes, Sir, I'm sure she's working. She has no questions about you, Sir."

When they finished, Goodman said to me, "Mr Diefenbaker's very suspicious of your motives." He said it with a laugh, but I was appalled.

"I'm upset, and I can tell you this: you're going to have my resignation right here and right now, and I'm walking out," I said. "I'm going to go to the press and say I resigned because Mr Diefenbaker doesn't trust me."

Eddie tried to cool me down, to talk me out of quitting in mid-campaign. "Don't, please don't," he said. "If you won't do it for Diefenbaker, do it for me. Stay on. I can't get along without you."

We spent the afternoon talking. In the end, I agreed to stay until the end of the campaign. I found it very difficult because I knew Diefenbaker was questioning every move I made. The strain destroyed the fun we had been having. I found I no longer cared what happened in the election. I did not let up in the effort I put into the campaign, but my heart was no longer in it. My earlier conviction that it was important for the country that the Conservatives be elected just melted away.

There were bumps on the campaign road – not that the public noticed. Diefenbaker kept the crowds entertained, and headquarters kept the machine running smoothly. None of us in Ottawa worried too much about what Dief was saying on the hustings, because we all knew he could not win. Or so we thought. Eddie, Lowell, and I made a light-hearted pact. Each of us had a slightly different memory of our agreement, but here is mine. If Diefenbaker won, Goodman would go on television and announce, "My fellow Canadians, I just want to say that this election victory is the greatest practical joke that's ever been perpetrated on the Canadian people." Then the three of us would join hands and jump off the Peace Tower.

We had a scare on election night. Lowell was at CJOH, the CTV affiliate in Ottawa, monitoring the voting in Atlantic Canada. Under the Canada Elections Act, the results could not be published or broadcast in Ontario until the polls had closed in the province. But Lowell could see a trend developing as the Tories began to gain Atlantic seats. It looked as though we might actually eke out a victory. Eddie and I were still waiting for results to be broadcast when Lowell phoned: "I'm coming over there. Get ready to jump!"

That dramatic gesture proved unnecessary. We did not win, but we astonished ourselves by holding the Liberals to a second minority government with 131 seats to our 98. None of us did much celebrating, however. We knew that Diefenbaker's success – we actually won three more seats than we had in 1963 – would only make it more difficult to persuade him to retire. We also knew that the Liberals were in such disarray and disrepute that we would have won the election if we had a different leader.

Following the election, Diefenbaker called a caucus meeting for late November. There was an air almost of celebration as the MPs gathered from across the country. There was a sense that we had achieved victory despite defeat. We had not won in terms of seats, but we had won by preventing the Liberals from securing a majority. Diefenbaker almost never attended caucus meetings, but he was there that day. Someone moved a special vote of thanks to Mrs Diefenbaker, and it was heartily endorsed by the caucus. Then someone moved a vote of thanks to national headquarters, especially to Flora MacDonald for all the support she had given to candidates across the country. Diefenbaker refused to allow that motion to come to a vote. He was as magnanimous as ever, I thought, sourly.

I was exhausted. Not having had a break in a couple of years, I left Ottawa for an extended vacation in the Caribbean. Duff Roblin kindly offered me the use of his house at Ocho Rios in Jamaica, and I stayed there for more than a week before deciding to take a trip by freighter around the Caribbean. I was determined to resign from headquarters. I saw no point in subjecting myself to any more mental torture. I never felt free to say what I was thinking or to laugh about anything without fear of it being misconstrued.

The holiday was good for me. By the time I returned to Ottawa in mid-January 1966, I had made up my mind to go back to headquarters, to keep my head down, and to work as quietly and as efficiently as I could. But Diefenbaker had his eye on me. One day, Lowell Murray and I were having lunch with another Cape Bretoner, Bill MacEachern, who worked at Liberal headquarters. We invited both Eddie Goodman and Keith Davey, who had just resigned as national organizer of the Liberal party, to join us. Eddie was called back to Toronto, and we went ahead without him. When I returned to headquarters, I was informed that Diefenbaker's office had called to ask why I had been having lunch with the Liberal Davey.

Diefenbaker was ready to settle scores. Without consulting Dalton Camp, the national president, he appointed James Johnston as the party's new national director. Johnston had a PhD in economics and a background in publishing newspapers in small communities in Ontario,[8] but his only political experience at the national level had been in the 1965 election when he directed our advertising campaign. Although he had no discernible aptitude for political organization, we got along fairly well. Initially, he left me alone to do the work I had been doing for nine years. However, on a Tuesday in mid-April 1966, not long after his appointment, Johnston walked into my office around 5 p.m. to announce he was making changes at headquarters and my services were no longer required. When I asked for reasons, he said it was not a question of my work. Everyone gave me the highest marks. Why then did he want to get rid of me? "Well," he said, "we can't afford to have you when we have to cut back. We can't afford your salary. You're paid a very high salary for a woman."

"For a woman"? Really! I was making about $8,000 a year at the time. Would that have been deemed "a very high salary" if I had been a man? I doubt it.

What, I asked Johnston, if I could get party members to raise enough money to pay me? But money was clearly not his real reason. "If we got that money, we'd have to use it in other ways," he replied. "Look, the basis of this is that I'm the national director and, as long as you're here, there are two bosses at national headquarters. The place can't have two bosses. I've got to be the only one and you just can't continue."

I was furious. I was absolutely wild. He was terribly uncomfortable, and I was not going to make it easy for him. I knew, of course, that he was acting on Diefenbaker's instructions and that he had no authority to do anything except to fire me. I doubt whether Diefenbaker ordered him to march into headquarters and sack me. It would have been more like Henry II condemning his former friend, Thomas à Becket, the archbishop of Canterbury – "Who will rid me of this troublesome priest?" I could just hear Diefenbaker saying to Johnston, "How on earth are we ever going to get rid of that girl at headquarters?"

But I kept pushing Johnston. "I'm going to tell you right now I think you've made a bad mistake," I said. "You can't treat this headquarters like some corporate office. You're going to find it's very different in politics. You're only going to be able to deal with people on the basis of the confidence that you build up in the party. And you've made the first move in destroying that right now. You're going to regret this."

I stood up, wished him "good luck" and offered to shake his hand. Johnston was dumbfounded. He had obviously been expecting tears, not cold anger, because he said, "Look, I realize this is quite a shock to you, and if you want to cry or yell at me or anything, go right ahead. I'll understand."

Me? Cry? The man did not know me.

"I just want to tell you you're not dealing with one of your children, that's all," I replied.

By this time, it was after 6 p.m. and Johnston said he had to go to dinner. He said he would come back at 8 p.m. to continue the discussion. I had no intention of waiting. I cleaned out my desk and went home. My days at national headquarters were over.

8

Diefenbaker's Demise

I have never been a helpless victim, no matter the circumstances, and I certainly was not one when Jim Johnston fired me. Before leaving party headquarters that night, I scooped up lists of names and addresses of Conservatives whom I had known and worked with over the years.

In the course of the next several weeks, I wrote to about two thousand people. I told them how much I had enjoyed working with them and how greatly I had benefited from my nine years with the party. I made no reference to the reason for my departure; I simply said I was sorry I was no longer there, that it had been a tremendous experience, and I hoped to be able to work with them again in the future. The response was overwhelming. Most of these people considered me to be their friend and ally at party headquarters, and they were dismayed that Johnston, a man they had never heard of, would fire me.

Tories who had never questioned Diefenbaker's actions began to wonder – "To let Flora go ... why?" They asked how long he intended to stay on as leader and where the party was headed. Many of them became supporters of the leadership-review campaign at the party's annual meeting in November 1966, and they helped to elect me national secretary of the party.

All this was in the future. "There ends a political career," I told myself as I headed back to my apartment that night. Lowell Murray was out for dinner, but I tracked him down. "I'll be over in about an hour," he said. We talked about what had happened and what it meant for the party. "Go to bed and get a good night's sleep and don't ask me what I'm going to do," he told me.

He phoned some of our friends in the caucus – Gordon Fairweather, Gordon Aiken, Jed Baldwin, and Heath Macquarrie. He also called Eddie Goodman, who phoned me, sounding shocked, to ask if it were true. Eddie phoned George Hees, who had been re-elected in the 1965 election. George called me to say, "We're not going to let this go by without a fight."

George was as good as his word. The next morning, Wednesday, was the weekly caucus meeting. Diefenbaker was not there, but as the meeting began, Hees rose: "I'd like to bring up a question of real concern." Many of the MPs were stunned when George told them I had been fired.

"Is this your idea of a joke, George? Who in heaven's name fired her?"

"Jim Johnston fired her?"

"Jim Johnston? Who's he?"

"Why would anyone want to get rid of Flora?

"You know who did it. It was Diefenbaker."

It went on for two hours. One MP proposed a motion of non-confidence in Johnston. It probably would have passed if Erik Nielsen, one of Diefenbaker staunchest supporters, had not cooled out the members by telling the caucus that a vote of non-confidence in Johnston was tantamount to a vote of non-confidence in Diefenbaker, a move most MPs were not prepared to make. I think it was Doug Harkness, the former defence minister, who interceded to say that while caucus may discuss any matter MPs wish, it cannot pass formal motions. So instead of a motion of non-confidence, the MPs decided to establish a six-member committee to inquire into my dismissal. Alf Hales, a highly regarded backbencher from Guelph, Ontario, was chosen chairman.

The committee trooped off to interview its first witness, John Diefenbaker. They marched into his office and announced: "We're a committee of inquiry and we want to know if you had anything to do with firing Flora MacDonald." They were tossed out of the office so quickly that their heads are probably still spinning. Although Johnston and I both appeared before the Hales committee, without Diefenbaker's cooperation the inquiry could not accomplish anything – and it did not.

The next day, Thursday, I was scheduled to have lunch with Senator Grattan O'Leary in the Parliamentary Restaurant. A man of letters and a long-time parliamentary correspondent who had become editor, then president of the *Ottawa Journal,* O'Leary was one of the grand old men of the Conservative party. I called Grattan on Thursday morning to say:

"Look, Senator, I want you to know that I've been fired and there's some discussion about this, and I do think that it might cause you some embarrassment to be seen with me."

Grattan was wonderful. "Whatever was the reason for being seen with you before, let me tell you, it's been multiplied. Just come up."

I went to his office in the Senate where he recounted tale after tale of his differences with Diefenbaker. As we went into the restaurant and passed the first alcove on the left, I felt Grattan take my elbow and guide me down the aisle. The place was packed with MPs of all parties, senators, and journalists. All the way along, people were standing, waiting to shake my hand. It was like a royal procession. Suddenly, I realized why Grattan had taken my elbow. The first alcove was where Diefenbaker habitually had his lunch. Olive was with him that day. If looks could kill, Grattan and I would have been struck dead in front of the buffet of cold cuts and poached salmon.

Not everyone was on my side. Some Tories thought I deserved to be fired because they believed, as Diefenbaker clearly did, that I had been a headquarters spy for his enemies, including Dalton Camp. That was not so. I had worked with MPs and party members without regard to their views on the leadership. I believed that the national president, having been elected by the whole party, had a right to be kept informed about what was going on. He was as much my boss as the leader was.

Camp was vacationing on Eleuthera in the Bahamas when his office in Toronto phoned to tell him of my firing. I think Dalton had had an intimation that I was in jeopardy. The fact that he had not been consulted or even informed before Diefenbaker made Johnston the national director was ominous.[1] It was a sign, I think, that Diefenbaker was trying to seize control of headquarters, to bring control of the party machinery into the leader's office and get it away from people like Camp, Eddie Goodman, Lowell Murray, and Flora MacDonald. Camp told historian Jack Granatstein in an oral history interview in December 1967 that before going on vacation he had sent a warning in Diefenbaker's direction – "If Johnston came into headquarters and Flora MacDonald went out, Johnston was dead." Camp also spoke to Johnston, urging him to define responsibilities at headquarters so that the two of us could work together. Two days after Dalton left for Eleuthera, Johnston fired me.

"I took that as a declaration of war," Camp told Granatstein. His anger grew when he heard from a friend that Diefenbaker was spreading a rumour that it had been necessary to let me go because I was involved in a personal relationship with Dalton. "When I heard this, I was absolutely enraged. ... It was so patently untrue," Camp said.

The battle lines were being drawn. Dalton had a deep-seated belief that leaders were properly the servant of their party, that they owed as much loyalty to the party as the party owed to them, and that just as party members had the right to elect a leader, they had a right to change the leader. Diefenbaker's approach to leadership was closer to the divine right of kings: the leader was paramount and loyalty was a one-way street – from the followers to the leader.

As Dalton said later, my firing was one of three events that spring that set him on his course to bring Diefenbaker down. Another was the suicide of our good friend George Hogan; George had always exercised a restraining influence on Dalton, and when he died Camp realized that life was short and he could not wait forever to do things that needed to be done. The third event was a panel discussion on "The Press Looks at the Conservative Party" at a conference of young Tories at McMaster University in Hamilton. The journalists on the panel were brutal in their assessment of our party and leader, and what disturbed Dalton most was that none of the young Tories in the audience protested or defended Diefenbaker. Instead, they laughed and applauded. Dalton told me he had been shocked. "Are they all saying by their acceptance or non-argument that they in fact endorse [the criticism]?"

Camp would soon fire the first salvo in his leadership-review campaign. It came in a brilliant discourse on political loyalty and the responsibilities of leadership that he delivered to an audience of about 120 ranking Tories at a private dinner at the Albany Club in Toronto on 19 May 1966. While he was working on that speech, I was busy settling into my new, post-headquarters life.

I had had job offers from some advertising agencies in Toronto, including Camp's, but that was not what I wanted. My friend Don Jamieson, the Newfoundland broadcaster who had helped us with free television time in the 1962 provincial election, had been nominated as the Liberal candidate for a federal by-election in June 1966, and he suggested that I, being no longer in the Conservative fold, might like to run his campaign. If I had accepted, I suppose I might have become an executive assistant to a Liberal minister in Ottawa, but I demurred.[2]

I decided instead to take a job at Queen's University in Kingston. That came about by fluke, or coincidence, or serendipity, I am not sure which. When I had gone to Jamaica for a rest and holiday at the end of 1965, I took a cruise on one of the two ships – the *Federal Maple* and the *Federal Palm* – that Canada had presented as a gift to the new Federation of the West Indies, a short-lived (1958–62) union of former British colonies. Just before Christmas 1965, I boarded the *Federal Maple* in Kingston harbour. As I stood at the rail watching the cargo being loaded, I turned to chat with a woman standing next to me. She told me she and her husband had boarded the ship the night before, but that she had gone ashore in the morning in search of a pair of comfortable shoes. She was happy because she had been able to find a Bata shoe store. Bata was a Canadian-based company and she and I talked about that. It turned out that she was Alice Corry and her husband was J. Alex Corry, a prominent constitutional scholar and political scientist, who was then the principal of Queen's. She told me there was a political science professor at Queen's whose father had been involved with Bata. I knew who that was. It was John Meisel, whose father had been the export manager of Bata.

When I first met him, John was teaching and working on his doctorate at Queen's. He decided to do his thesis on the 1957 federal election, and he came to Ottawa that fall to gather information. The Conservative national director at the time, Allister Grosart, was impressed by Meisel. "Give him anything he wants on the election," Allister told me. We gave him an office and John conducted his research from our headquarters. He and I became good friends during that period. Thereafter, whenever I was driving from Ottawa to Toronto or somewhere else in southern Ontario, I would stop off in Kingston to see John and Muriel ("Murie") Meisel.

Cruising on the *Federal Maple*, I became good friends with Alice and Alex Corry. We tied up in Barbados for a couple of days over Christmas where two other Canadians whom I knew well from Ottawa, Wallace McCutcheon and Richard Bell, both former Diefenbaker ministers, were vacationing with their wives. They invited the Corrys and me to join them for Christmas dinner at their hotel in Bridgetown, the capital. We had a great celebration, and we rehashed the 1965 election campaign. There was no doubt where these people stood – they wanted Diefenbaker gone.

When I was fired from headquarters several months later, I was approached almost immediately by John Meisel, who had become the head of the political studies department at Queen's. He was swamped by administrative details. He and Alex Corry proposed that I be a combination of secretary and administrative assistant in the department, plus serve as a teaching assistant for John in a course he taught on political parties. I was thrilled! I had dreamed of university and finally it was happening. I liked the idea of working in a university setting. It would be very different from anything I had done before. It would, I hoped, take me away from the whole partisan political scene.

Hah! I was soon up to my elbows in politics again. Even before I got to Kingston, I went off to Charlottetown where Conservative Walter Shaw, a vigorous seventy-eight-year-old, had decided to seek a third term as premier in what would turn out to be one of the most famous, closest – and wackiest – elections in the history of Atlantic Canada.

Lowell Murray and I were invited to see if we could help Shaw. We knew it would not be easy. The contrast between the elderly Shaw and the thirty-two-year-old Liberal leader, Alex Campbell, was stark. Campbell was everything Shaw was not – fresh, attractive, and contemporary, with a distinguished political lineage; his father, Thane Campbell, had been premier and chief justice of the province. Lowell and I quickly discovered that Shaw's government had no idea what it wanted to do if re-elected. They did not even have a record of what they had done during their seven years in power. The premier invited us to attend a cabinet meeting. It was bizarre. He went around the table asking each minister what he had accomplished. I was to take notes so we could record the achievements and put them into a campaign pamphlet. Most of his ministers had nothing to say, no accomplishments to volunteer. I had to struggle to keep a straight face.

The election was every bit as difficult as we feared. There were thirty-two seats in the legislature – sixteen constituencies, each electing two members. But one of the candidates in Souris died before election day, meaning the election in that constituency had to be deferred. On election night, 30 May, the Conservatives and the Liberals were tied with fifteen seats apiece and, as I recall, the difference between them in the province-wide popular vote was just fourteen votes. The two seats in Souris would determine the outcome.

Political pandemonium reigned in PEI for the next six weeks, until the deferred election on 11 July.

I went to Winnipeg to help Dalton Camp in the re-election campaign of Duff Roblin's Tory government, returning to PEI for the Souris deferred election. It was one of those times when outside organizers did more harm than good. While Camp, working out of an anonymous motel near Charlottetown airport, wrote speeches for our two Conservative candidates, the two parties turned the deferred election into an auction, each trying to outbid the other for the votes of the 2,500-odd electors of Souris. Never in my experience was so much promised to win the votes of so few. We sent out the road crews with instructions to pave every flat surface they could find. It was hilarious. I drove to Souris with Dalton one day and all along the road there were little signs saying, "I'm a potato patch, please don't pave me."

I came up with an inspired promise that I was sure would win the election. In the 1965 federal election, John Diefenbaker had promised to raise the old age pension from $75 a month to $100. The promise had been especially popular in PEI where we won all four federal seats. We lost that election, of course, and Lester Pearson's Liberal government had not acted on the pension increase. Alex Campbell announced that, if elected, his Liberals would use provincial funds to boost the pension to $100. I was furious. Old age pensions were *our* issue and there was no way I was going to let the Liberals steal it. Campbell could promise anything, but Shaw was still premier. So Lowell and I went to Shaw and pitched my idea. Everyone knew that Ottawa would eventually raise pensions to $100. So the PEI government would pay the extra $25 immediately, and back out of the field later when the feds increased their payment. I did the math. There were about ten thousand old-age pensioners on the Island, so the raise would only cost the provincial treasury $250,000 – a modest investment to keep the Conservatives in office, I thought.

Shaw bought the idea. So did the cabinet. The happy announcement was made. The cheque-writing machines went into overdrive, and we made sure that the first wave of $25 cheques was sent to Souris. I woke up the next morning in a cold sweat. It had been a long time since math class in North Sydney, and I had blown the calculation. The cost of our largesse would be $250,000 per *month*, not per year. The annual expenditure of about $3,000,000 was more than the tiny PEI budget could comfortably accommodate. But it was too late to pull back – the cheques were on their way. The people of Souris, wise to the ephemerality of election promises, cashed their cheques so quickly that the bank in town ran out of money.

In the end, Walter Shaw did not have to find the $3,000,000. The Liberals won both seats in Souris – by a total margin, as I recall, of eighteen votes. Alex Campbell became premier, and he would be unbeatable for the next twelve years. In Ottawa, Diefenbaker told people it had been a big mistake to let "that woman" go to PEI.

Almost before I knew it, I was drawn into the leadership-review campaign that Camp had launched with his speech at the Albany Club in May. Lowell and I were still in Prince Edward Island when he made that a speech. It was remarkable for its clear analysis. "It seems to me there are limits to the power of political leadership and these should, from time to time, be examined and appraised," he said. "Leaders are fond of reminding followers of their responsibilities and duties to leadership. And followers sometimes need reminding. What is seldom heard, however, is a statement on the responsibilities of the leader to those he leads. [...] The party is not the embodiment of the leader, but rather the other way round; the leader is transient, the party permanent. The argument is made that to question at any time, or in any matter, the acts of leaders will invoke a grave question of non-confidence. This is an argument for sheep, not for men."

Diefenbaker was aware of the speech because one of his loyalists, Senator David Walker, had been in the audience at the Albany Club and was seen slipping out of the dinner to phone the leader with the news of Dalton's heresy. But because it had been delivered at a closed event, the press, the general public, and, indeed, most Conservatives, were unaware that Camp had thrown down the gauntlet.[3]

In September, he went public in a speech to the Junior Board of Trade in Toronto. It was a reworking of the Albany Club address, but this time the speech was to a public forum and copies were distributed to the news media. The effect was electric. "CAMP CHALLENGES DIEF," declared the *Toronto Telegram* in a huge front-page headline. The *Globe and Mail* ran the story across the top of page one under the headline, "Camp Challenges Diefenbaker's PC Leadership." Inside, the *Globe* published a partial text of his remarks. Diefenbaker loyalists fired back, and Gordon Churchill made the front pages with a demand that Dalton resign as national president.

For the next two months, my life revolved around the leadership-review campaign. We held a strategy meeting in Kingston.

Including myself, there were six of us. The other five were: Dalton; Norman Atkins, his brother-in-law; Paul Weed, a Camp friend and ally from Toronto; Lowell Murray, who was still working in Senator Wallace McCutcheon's office in Ottawa; and David MacDonald, a young PEI clergyman who had been elected to Parliament for the first time in 1965 and had quickly become appalled by Diefenbaker.

We were the core group of the campaign. Norm Atkins was our campaign manager. He organized Dalton's "pilgrimage" – his cross-country speaking tour that took him into every province in the course of six weeks – and Atkins would also command our forces at the annual meeting in mid-November. David MacDonald (who was no relation to me or to Finlay) had just turned thirty. He was assigned to organize youth groups, and he spent weeks travelling and speaking to young Tories wherever they were.

My job was to contact delegates across the country – all those party members I had dealt with during my years at headquarters. I told them what we were doing, explained our reasons, and asked for their support. The membership lists I had taken with me when I left headquarters proved invaluable; I was able to reach everyone we needed to contact. I spent every night on the phone from my apartment in Kingston, starting in Newfoundland and working my way west.

Then one day there was a knock at my door. Two RCMP officers were investigating why I, a newcomer to Kingston, was making so many long-distance calls. The Mounties apparently suspected I was up to something nefarious – running a bookmaking operation, selling phony stocks, or operating a prostitution ring – I do not know. I could not very well tell them not to worry, that I was merely trying to get rid of a former prime minister. So I said I was working with people in other cities to organize a political meeting. I do not know whether they believed me, but they were very polite and they went away.

Lowell, who had access to free long-distance service on government lines in McCutcheon's office, also did a lot of phoning to British Columbia and Alberta while I was responsible for Newfoundland and Prince Edward Island. We did not worry about New Brunswick. Richard Hatfield, Gordon Fairweather, and Cy Sherwood, our provincial leader, had that province under control. Nova Scotia was Bob Stanfield's political patch – outsiders ventured in at their peril – and Dalton worked with him and Stanfield's deputy Ike Smith. Manitoba was tough. We had strong supporters in Roblin's cabinet, but

Diefenbaker loyalists were fierce. Saskatchewan, Diefenbaker's lair, was impossible. Nevertheless, Dalton took his pilgrimage into Saskatchewan. "Going to Regina was a great success because I survived it," he commented later.

Quebec was an enigma. The Conservative party had no organization to speak of. The new president of the provincial association, Paul Trépanier, who had been our candidate in Shefford in 1965, was unpredictable. He was a great character, but we could not count on his support for more than twenty-four hours at any stretch. Ontario was well organized. Dalton had gathered a group of dedicated supporters. His friend Don Guthrie, a lawyer in Toronto, was our principal conduit to John Robarts, the premier and the most influential Conservative in the province.

So we had an organization. We had a campaign. We were building support, but we still had no focus. Would we be fighting to ensure a secret ballot on the traditional resolution of confidence in the leader, rather than the customary standing vote? Would we be fighting on the issue of the presidency – the re-election of Dalton Camp as national president? Or would we be fighting on the question of holding a leadership convention? We had not thought it through. We still did not have a battle plan, a strategy, when we arrived in Ottawa for the annual meeting.

Diefenbaker and his people made two mistakes that handed us the battle plan we desperately needed. The first mistake was their decision to challenge Camp for re-election as national president. As Dalton told historian Jack Granatstein, he had lain awake nights worrying what would happen if Diefenbaker had simply said, "All right," and allowed Camp to be unopposed for re-election. That would have been the smart thing for Diefenbaker to do. Camp had gone across the country telling Tories that a vote for him would be an endorsement of his approach to the rights and responsibilities of leadership. But if there was no vote, if he was allowed to win by acclamation, his re-election would be hollow, whereas victory in a contested election would strengthen his hand immeasurably. But Camp suspected Diefenbaker would not go the no-fight route – "It wasn't like him to out-think you. He would only try and out-fight you."[4]

And fight he did. Diefenbaker's supporters chose as their standard-bearer Arthur Maloney, a brilliant courtroom lawyer and former Conservative MP from Toronto. Maloney was an inspired choice. He was popular among both pro- and anti-Diefenbaker

Conservatives. He had not taken sides in the leadership dispute. And he could present himself as a conciliator, a person who would be able persuade John Diefenbaker to retire gracefully of his own accord. But by nominating a candidate to oppose Camp, especially one as formidable as Arthur Maloney, the loyalists also established the battle line we needed. The election of the national president would be the test of Diefenbaker's leadership.

The second mistake was to attempt to impose an agenda for the annual meeting that would have given Diefenbaker a huge advantage. As proposed by Jim Johnston, it called for the leader to address delegates on the opening night, Monday. The report of the resolutions committee – including the motion expressing confidence in the leader – would be presented on Tuesday, with the election of the national president and other officers following on the last day, Wednesday. If a powerful speech by Diefenbaker on Monday night led to a positive vote of confidence on Tuesday, who would care about the election of officers on Wednesday?

The Johnston agenda made us focus on our strategy. The party's principal officers met in Ottawa on the Saturday night before the meeting began. Because people were still trickling into Ottawa, Camp asked the group to assemble in his suite at the Chateau Laurier at 10 p.m.; the meeting went on until two o'clock in the morning. Because I no longer worked at headquarters and was not a delegate to the meeting, I had no status. But I attended as a note-taker or as an institutional memory, I do not know. The principal officers accepted our changes to the agenda: Diefenbaker would still speak on Monday night, but the report of the nominations committee – this is where the election of officers would occur – would be presented at 2 p.m. on Tuesday. The report of the resolutions committee – including the issue of confidence or non-confidence in the leader – would come last, on Wednesday.

Once the national executive approved the revised agenda – by a surprisingly large margin of eighty to forty-one – on Sunday, the stage was set. The battle between the loyalists and the reformers, between those who believed that the party was the embodiment of the leader and those who held, as Camp did, that the party took precedence over the leader, would be fought out on Tuesday when the delegates chose their next national president.

I was nervous. I thought Arthur Maloney, a man with a great reputation and no enemies in the party, was the strongest candidate the Diefenbaker people could possibly have put forward. As I wandered around the Chateau Laurier, I grew more anxious. Many people wearing delegate badges were also sporting Maloney buttons. There were too many of them for my comfort. If nothing else, we had the edge in technology. We had booked ten rooms at the Chateau for our key workers, and I was astonished when I got to the room I was to share with Dalton's secretary to find it crammed with communications equipment. Our room was obviously operations central. We had what amounted to our own switchboard. We had walkie-talkies. We had speakers connected to microphones – or bugs – in various locations in the hotel ballroom, on the speaker's dais, and even behind the stage where the dignitaries would be assembling before they made their entrance. We had four spotters on the floor whom we could contact instantly by walkie-talkie if we heard anything that required attention – a wavering delegate, for example.

The PC Women's Association held its annual meeting in the ballroom on Monday afternoon. I was there for that session and I hung around for a while after it ended at five o'clock. I got a bit panicky when I realized that many of the people were not leaving the hall. A lot of the older ones were moving to chairs at the front of the room, even though the evening meeting with Diefenbaker's speech was not due to start for another two hours. I beetled back upstairs and alerted our people to get our supporters to the ballroom where Doug Harkness, the former defence minister, and Jean Wadds, the MP for Grenville-Dundas, were managing the floor for us. According to the media coverage of that evening, the Camp forces packed the front of the hall and sat on their hands when Diefenbaker spoke. That is not what happened. Photos of the crowd show that the front rows on one side of the centre aisle were mostly older people – Diefenbaker supporters – while those on the other side were mainly younger Camp supporters. They were quite evenly balanced.

We put our technology to good use. Our people in operations central listened to the proceedings. When they heard Camp welcome delegates and deliver a report on his stewardship (there were some boos), they signalled Don Guthrie to escort Premier Robarts to the ballroom. Don took him down in a freight elevator, and Robarts made a dramatic entrance. He walked to the stage while Camp was still speaking, paused at the podium, and shook Camp's hand before taking his seat on the platform. Not a word was said to the audience, but the gesture was clear – the powerful Ontario party was with us. It was one of the most dramatic moments in party history.

I will never forget that evening. When Diefenbaker entered the ballroom, Camp motioned to our supporters to rise. But many of the younger ones did not. They heckled Diefenbaker, drowning him out at times.

"Is this a Conservative meeting?" he demanded.

"Yes, yes," they roared back.

His speech was pathetic. He could have risen above the taunts and jeers and called for reconciliation. That is what the delegates wanted to hear. But he could not say anything positive. Instead, he ripped into his enemies, at one point wheeling and jabbing his finger at Dalton as he challenged him to explain why he had betrayed him. It was sad. Diefenbaker's old magic deserted him that evening. The man who had been the most compelling politician in the land had become an angry old man.

That Monday evening, 14 November 1966, become known in Conservative lore as *The Night of the Knives,* a description taken from the title of a book written by one of the fiercest of the Diefenbaker loyalists, long-time Nova Scotia MP Robert Coates.[5] He insisted that Dalton, I, and rest of our group had stabbed the Chief in the back. That was not at all the way I saw it. I saw it as a legitimate exercise in party democracy – when a leader loses the trust and confidence of his or her party, the members who elected them have a perfect right to replace them with someone who does command their trust and confidence.

Camp won re-election the next day. The vote, on a secret ballot, was 564 for Camp to 502 for Maloney. It was closer than most people had anticipated and there were several reasons. Many delegates were embarrassed by the way Diefenbaker had been treated the previous evening. They felt he deserved better than to be humiliated by his own party. A second reason was Camp's speech, which was one of the worst I had ever heard him make. And a third was a magnificent speech by Arthur Maloney. Anyone who heard it will always remember this emotional line: "When John Diefenbaker, former PM of Canada, leader of Her Majesty's Loyal Opposition, when he walks into a room, Arthur Maloney stands up."

I had been looking for ways to get officially involved in the party and when Dalton suggested I run for national secretary, I agreed. It was a real challenge to address the party officials and delegates

for whom I had worked for nine years at headquarters. I was overwhelmed by their applause and praise. I won in a walkover with
Ken Binks, a good man who had the misfortune to be labelled
the Diefenbaker candidate. Members of our group won the other
principal-officer positions, giving us control of the party machinery.

We used that control the next day, Wednesday, when the meeting
turned to the issue of the leadership. Some people said we did not
play fair, that we played fast and loose with the rules. They had a
point. Eddie Goodman lived up to his "Fast Eddie" label that day.
He was chairing the session, and according to the order of business,
the morning would be spent debating amendments to the party constitution and the afternoon dealing with resolutions – including the
leadership. As the morning meeting was about to begin, however,
Eddie got word from Parliament Hill that Diefenbaker was preparing to descend on the Chateau Laurier in an eleventh-hour bid
to rally his supporters. After checking with Camp and Elmer Bell,
the Ontario party president, Goodman announced a change in the
timetable. Resolutions would be considered first and constitutional
amendments later.

He recognized Bell who moved that the motion of confidence
in the leader be taken by secret ballot, rather than by the customary standing vote. That change was approved. Next, with many
Diefenbaker delegates leaving the room to prepare a welcome for
the leader, Eddie recognized Ben Cunningham, a Kingston lawyer, to
introduce an amendment to the usual confidence motion. This was
a tense moment. The night before, a group of us had sat around,
celebrating and trying to come up with wording for the amendment.
We came up with something, or we thought we did, but in the morning none of us could remember what we had agreed on. Fortuitously,
Cunningham had scribbled notes on the back of an envelope. When
Goodman called on him, Ben pulled out the envelope.

The original resolution stated: "That this party expresses its
confidence in its leader, the Rt Hon. John G. Diefenbaker." The
Cunningham amendment made it read: "That this party expresses
its support of the Rt Hon. John G. Diefenbaker, its national leader,
and acknowledges its wholehearted appreciation of his universally
recognized services to the party; and in view of the current situation
in the party directs the national executive, after consultation with
the national leader, to call a leadership convention at a suitable time
before 1 January 1968."

The heated debate had been going on for about forty minutes when shouts, cheers, and the wail of bagpipes signalled Diefenbaker's arrival in the hotel lobby. Goodman cut off the debate. He instructed delegates to vote on both the original confidence motion and on the amendment. The votes on the original motion would be announced only if the amendment was defeated. But the amendment passed easily: 563–186. The Tory party had agreed to thank Diefenbaker, and to replace him.

When the national executive – of which I was now a principal officer in my new capacity as national secretary – met in January 1967, we asked Eddie Goodman and Roger Régimbal to be the co-chairmen of the leadership convention. Eddie approached me to be the secretary of the convention, a role that would have prevented me from being actively involved in any of the candidates' campaigns. But Dalton came to me and said, "Please don't get into anything. We're going to need you when this whole effort comes forward."

I took that as an indication that Camp was considering running himself. But he did not say anything further as the executive spent the winter months organizing the details for the convention; we settled on early September 1967 at Maple Leaf Gardens in Toronto. Dalton was particularly worried that George Hees, the former trade and commerce minister who had resigned at the time of the Bomarc missile crisis, would win the leadership.[6] Although George was Goodman's bosom buddy, Dalton considered Hees, a one-time Toronto Argonaut football player, to be an intellectual lightweight. He was not content to let the leadership go to other former ministers, including Davie Fulton, Alvin Hamilton, Donald Fleming, Mike Starr, and Wallace McCutcheon. And there was the very real possibility that Diefenbaker would decide to run, too.

We waited for a few months to see if other candidates would emerge. John Robarts had no desire to trade being premier of Ontario for leader of the Opposition in Ottawa, but we thought Roblin in Manitoba or Stanfield in Nova Scotia might be tempted. Finlay MacDonald was keeping in touch with Stanfield, who was preoccupied with the provincial election that he would call in the spring of 1967. At that time, his comment back in February 1965 seemed to remain his definitive word on the national leadership:

"I have considered [federal politics] in much the same way I have considered ski-jumping." Duff Roblin at the time seemed equally uninterested.

In April 1967, a group of us met with Dalton in Toronto to explore the feasibility of a Camp candidacy. We put a shadow organization in place. It was essentially the same group that had worked on the leadership-review campaign, although three key people – Lowell Murray, Joe Clark, and Brian Mulroney – were honouring commitments they had made to work for Davie Fulton. There was no doubt in any of our minds that, barring the entry of one of the premiers, Dalton would be superior to any other candidate. Having worked so hard to establish the party's right to change its leader, we did not want the job to go by default to some tired holdover of the Diefenbaker era. The Conservative party needed new blood, new energy, and new ideas. We especially needed a leader who could attract young Canadians.

Dalton was not ready to commit himself at our April meeting. He went to Europe to think about whether he wanted to dedicate the next period of his life to politics – his wife was anxious to have him at home more to help raise their five children – and whether he would have a realistic chance of winning the leadership. He knew he would be anathema to the Diefenbaker wing of the party at a time when most Conservatives yearned for healing and unity. And he would have to answer the inevitable allegation that he had brought down Diefenbaker because he coveted the leadership himself. Camp would be a hard sell, and he knew it.

When he returned from Europe, he seemed disposed to put aside his own leadership ambition for the sake of the party. In June, he and Norman Atkins went to Winnipeg to see if they could persuade Duff Roblin to run. Camp, however, was offended by the coolness of Roblin's response. Roblin dithered. He was not prepared to commit himself, but if he did run, he would welcome Camp's advice and his organization's muscle – so long as Dalton stayed well out of public view. Disgusted, Camp went to Halifax to see Stanfield. He had won his fourth term as premier on 30 May and felt committed to stay in Nova Scotia. The only way he would consider leaving would be if Ike Smith, his number two in the party and cabinet, would agree to take over. But Smith, who had a heart condition, was more interested in getting out of politics.

Discouraged and increasingly worried that Diefenbaker might actually be able to win the convention, Camp began to think seriously about running himself. "As we went closer and closer to the convention itself," he said later, "I became more and more annoyed and more and more concerned."

On his return from Halifax, he called us to a weekend meeting at his New Brunswick cottage at Robertson's Point on Grand Lake. I received Dalton's summons at Queen's on a Friday and scrambled to fly to Fredericton in time to drive to Grand Lake for Saturday morning. Norm Atkins, who had a cottage next to Camp's, was there, as were Richard Hatfield and Gordon Fairweather from New Brunswick, David MacDonald, and Heath Macquarrie, a veteran MP, from PEI, and Torontonian Paul Weed, who also had a cottage in New Brunswick.

Norman, who was really good at this sort of detail, had already prepared an organization chart and a calendar that plotted Dalton's leadership campaign, day by day, from that early July weekend until the end of the convention in September. The strategy was to exploit the fragmented field – no candidate would have enough votes to win on the first or even second ballot – with a short, dramatic campaign that would peak at the convention. We spent two days going over those plans. We knew where Dalton would be every day. We knew what each of us would be doing. We were rolling!

We finished our meeting on Sunday night and decided to take Dalton to Halifax to make his announcement on Tuesday from Finlay MacDonald's television station. In those days, Dalton did not have a phone in his cottage and the party line at the farmhouse up the road was usually busy. So I drove to the nearest village, Jemseg, to use the phone in the general store. I called Finlay to give him the happy news. But Finlay quickly deflated our balloon. He had been trying to reach us to tell us that Stanfield had changed his mind and would be a candidate after all. Ike Smith had agreed to take over in Nova Scotia.

I had to break the news to Dalton and the others at Robertson's Point. Dalton took it badly. He disappeared into a bedroom and we saw very little of him for the next forty-eight hours. He knew, as we all did, that this might be his only chance to be the leader of his party and perhaps prime minister of the country. He came out of his depression before long and immersed himself in Stanfield's campaign. Norm Atkins simply took the organization chart he had prepared for Dalton's campaign, changed the name at the top from Camp to Stanfield and we carried on.

I became the bridge between the Stanfield team in Nova Scotia, which thought it was running his campaign, and our group in Toronto, which was actually running it. John Meisel was wonderful. He gave me all the time off I needed from my job at Queen's. I recruited two Queen's colleagues, George Perlin, an assistant professor of political science, and Michel de Salaberry, a graduate student, to travel with Stanfield across the country. George worked on policy issues, while Michel, who would become an ambassador in Canada's diplomatic service, worked on Stanfield's French.

As the convention came closer, I moved my base to Toronto, to the Westbury Hotel around the corner from Maple Leaf Gardens. My job was to keep in close contact with delegates and party officials across the country. I also kept in touch with Lowell Murray, who was running Fulton's campaign. We had an understanding. If one of our candidates was eliminated in the voting, we would deliver as much of our support as we could to the other.

If Duff Roblin had decided to run when Dalton and Norman saw him in June, he would have won. Stanfield would not have come in against Roblin. But Roblin left it too late. By the time he made up his mind, Stanfield was already in the field and Roblin could not catch up. He came very close during the voting, but he could not get ahead of Stanfield. After the fourth ballot, Davie Fulton, who was in third place, dropped out. I threw my arms around Lowell on the convention floor. Stanfield walked to Fulton's box and shook his hand. On the next ballot Bob Stanfield became the new leader of the Progressive Conservative party, defeating Roblin by 1,150 votes to 969. Diefenbaker, who had made a last-minute decision to be a candidate, embarrassed himself. He placed fifth on the first ballot and withdrew after attracting only 114 votes on the third.

The Diefenbaker era was finally over.

The next era should have been the Stanfield era. He was everything the country could have asked for – intelligent, thoughtful, progressive, considerate. As people who got to know him discovered, he had a delightful dry, often self-deprecating humour. My brother Ron had a favourite Stanfield story that he would occasionally tell when he wanted to embarrass his big sister. It went like this: "On St Andrew's Day in 1974, Bob Stanfield was to speak to the British Columbia Tory annual meeting in Nanaimo and was to be introduced by my sister Flora. She was a great admirer of his and her lavish introduction at the noon luncheon relayed Stanfield's accomplishments in florid language. Stanfield, who admired Flora, as well, was given to poking fun at her. 'I want to thank Flora MacDonald for her most kind introduction. She's a Highland Scot from Cape Breton. Usually by noon on St Andrew's Day, she's blind drunk.' Flora told me later she almost collapsed on the floor she was laughing so hard."

I recall the luncheon and the joke. As to nearly collapsing on the floor, no comment.

Stanfield had all the qualities anyone could have wished for – the same qualities I had noticed in Adlai Stevenson when I was hitch-hiking in California during the 1956 American election. Everything, that is, except being exciting – just like Stevenson. Maybe it was the spirit of Centennial Year or Expo 67, but Canadians seemed to crave excitement. Prime Minister Pearson sensed that when, at the age of seventy, he announced his retirement in December 1967. Delegates to the Liberal leadership convention in April 1968 clearly sensed the same thing as they passed over an assortment of conventional, safe candidates to choose Pierre Elliott Trudeau – new, trendy, and charismatic.

I watched the Liberal convention on television in a Montreal hotel with Richard Hatfield and Lowell Murray. I did not know much about Trudeau beyond the fact that Camp had taken an instant dislike to him prior to our Fredericton conference four years earlier. We assumed, however, that he would waste little time in calling an election, and he quickly proved us right as he called it for 25 June 1968. We knew we were in trouble, and we were right about that, too.

I spent the last part of that campaign travelling with Stanfield on his campaign aircraft, and by then we all knew we were going to be beaten. And we were. The result was definitive: The Liberals took 155 seats to our 72.

I was feeling terrible for Stanfield as the campaign wound down. I had been one of those who had encouraged him to run; I had helped to organize his leadership campaign – and here he was, in his first national election, facing what might be an absolute rout. I decided I should go to him and say, "Look, you've done a good job, and if you're beaten, don't consider it the end of everything. There are lots of people who still support you." I wanted to do anything I could to bolster his spirits. I was all set to do that on the Sunday morning, two days before the election (it was on a Tuesday that year). Then the phone rang, and it was Stanfield asking me to come to see him. He spent the next half-hour consoling me, telling me not to worry, trying to make me feel better about the defeat we were about to experience. It almost reduced me to tears. This man who had not been keen to seek the leadership in the first place, this man whom we had put through so much, was worrying about others, not about himself. If I ever had any doubt about my loyalty to Stanfield, I had none after that day.

9

Launching My New Life at Queen's

For a woman whose formal education ended at secretarial school, Queen's University in Kingston was a glorious experience. It was a new job in a new environment with new issues and problems, new colleagues, and new friends in a new city. As I disentangled myself – temporarily, as it turned out – from the Conservative wars, I became absorbed in causes that would be important for the rest of my life: protection of our heritage, preservation of the environment, equality of women, treatment of prison inmates, Canadian sovereignty, and the issues of poverty and opportunity in the Third World.

Coming to Queen's with the blessings of both the principal of the university and the head of the political studies department smoothed my transition. So did the fact that my arrival coincided with an influx of new faculty members – George Perlin and David Cox in political studies and Jayant Lele in sociology, a new department that my boss John Meisel was helping to launch. I quickly became fast friends with them. Later on, I joined Jayant and Uma Lele in India, where they were from originally. Jean Perlin, George's ex-wife, became one of my closest friends, a confidante and sounding board to whom I turned for advice and support. She worked with me in Ottawa when I was a member of Parliament and ran my constituency office in Kingston. Jean and I have travelled to refugee camps in Africa, trekked the Silk Road together, and skated on the Rideau Canal in Ottawa.

I was caught up quickly in a circle of bright young Queen's graduate students with political stars in their eyes, starting with Tom Axworthy, who was destined to become principal secretary to Prime Minister Pierre Trudeau and later a professor at Harvard, and John Rae, who became executive assistant to Jean Chrétien when he was in the Trudeau cabinet and continued to be Chrétien's key political adviser during his years as prime minister.[1] Before long, I was also involved in a variety of off-campus activities. One was the campaign to preserve the Grand Theatre in Kingston from the wreckers. It was quite a historic building – an old movie house that had been transformed into a "legitimate" theatre for stage productions. They were setting up an advisory board for the theatre and John Meisel proposed that his new assistant join it. Before I could blink, I was secretary of the board and was catapulted into the midst of Kingston's artistic community.

One thing led to another. I got involved in a campaign to save the Kingston waterfront from developers. Bill Teron, an Ottawa developer (and prominent Liberal), wanted to build a string of apartment towers along the waterfront in Kingston. The towers would have blocked residents and visitors from enjoying the lakefront, much as has happened on Toronto's waterfront. Along with John Berry, a Queen's professor, I became co-chair of a citizens' coalition to stop the development. Our goal was to preserve a three-mile stretch of the waterfront for nature lovers and hikers. We eventually got the development stopped and plans approved for a walking trail along the waterfront. Teron was not pleased. He called me from Ottawa to say that he understood I was interested in politics but, given the kind of activities I was involved in, he could assure me that I would never be elected. That sounded like a threat to my ears. A few years later, when I was a member of Parliament, I served on a committee that called Teron as a witness. I took some pleasure in reminding him of his warning. "Well, here I am," I told him.

The apartment I had moved into in August 1966 was only a couple of blocks away from Kingston's notorious Prison for Women. The following year, I was approached to become a member of the Elizabeth Fry Society (named after the nineteenth-century English Quaker and prison reformer), and to join the group's Wednesday evening visits to the prison to socialize with inmates. We had a different program each Wednesday. It might be music, reading, cards, volleyball, or other games. I got to know the president of the society, Renée Hogarth, and when she stepped down a year or so later, she and other members of the executive asked me to become president. I held that position for three years.

As I became committed to the cause of penal reform, my involvement extended to all eight federal prisons in the Kingston area. But the treatment of women offenders was my biggest concern and the Prison for Women – P4W, as it was known – was my main focus. Women offenders had been incarcerated in Kingston since 1835. For the first century, they were housed in basement cells in Kingston Penitentiary, the men's prison. That prison was like something out of Dickens. The cells were cold, damp, and bug infested. Women who broke the rules were treated as brutally as the men. They could be placed in chains or flogged, submerged in ice water, put on a regimen of bread and water, or be forced to stand hunched over for hours in a coffin-like contraption known as the "box."

In 1934, a separate Prison for Women opened nearby. As it was the only such institution in the country, female convicts from all parts of Canada were sent to Kingston where they had to serve their sentences far from their families, friends, and other sources of support. Although it was an improvement over the basement of the men's penitentiary, P4W was controversial from its outset. Four years after it opened, a federal study, known as the Archambault report, cited its deficiencies – not enough space for outdoor exercise, no facilities for the women to pursue their schooling, no training programs, and no meaningful work for them to do. The report recommended that the prison be closed and the women be moved closer to their families and communities.[2]

The Elizabeth Fry Society was one of the outside groups – the Salvation Army was another – that played an important role at the prison. We counselled individual inmates, organized classes, and helped to find employment when the women were released. It was fulfilling work – and we also had fun. One of the inanities at the Prison for Women was a requirement that all inmates learn to operate sewing machines. But they were not allowed to make complete garments – the stated reason being that making entire items of clothing would give them a trade when they got out. I never did figure out what was wrong with that. Anyway, they were supposed to sew prison uniforms for the men in other institutions. They were allowed to make arms, legs, backs, and so on, but they were not permitted to assemble the pieces into whole uniforms.

I had an idea. We went to the warden and got permission for the inmates to use their spare time to make costumes for themselves for a Halloween party, which we would then organize. The prisoners were creative and made some imaginative costumes. We worked for days on the decorations. We built a mystery tunnel and a haunted

castle in which we had skeletons hanging. It was quite elaborate.
Then we thought we should have entertainment. So we went back
to the warden. "What would you suggest?" he asked. Well, we had
records for music, so we proposed that we invite the Queen's Male
Choir to perform. He thought about it, and after a while he agreed
this would be a good idea.

The only catch was that Queen's did not have a male choir. We
posted a notice on the bulletin boards in the department of political
studies and the law school, asking for forty men to form a male
choir to perform at the Prison for Women on Halloween. We got
forty names. One of them was Tom Axworthy. Another was Peter
Raymont, who became an Emmy award–winning filmmaker. We did
not bother with rehearsals because we had no intention of singing.
The choir was just a cover for a dance. As we went into the prison,
I told each of the men, "If anyone asks, you sing bass, you sing tenor,"
and so on. Axworthy said to me afterward, "I was okay until I heard
that door clang shut and realized I couldn't get out." We went to the
gym, turned the music on and had a fine dance.

Tom danced with a young blonde woman who was in on a drug
charge. She had been a student at a private girls' school in Toronto
and had been caught bringing a small quantity of marijuana back
from Pakistan where her father was working on a United Nations
contract. She should never have been in P4W, and later on we managed to get her out. Tom danced with her several times, not knowing
she was involved in a three-way relationship with two butches in
the prison. But one of them, a big heavyset woman, part Indigenous,
part French Canadian, from Northern Quebec, got very angry at
Tom. Her hand came down on Tom's shoulder, as though to say.
"Leave my woman alone!" Tom backed off very quickly.

There were no incidents. We started at eight o'clock, ended at ten,
and everyone left quietly. The next day, however, I got a call from the
warden, who had not been at the prison the night before. He asked
me to come to see him. He was furious – "I'm shocked at you, how
did you think you could fool me, and get away with this?" I was sure
my access to the prison would be cancelled. Within a week, however,
he called me again to say, "We've had the quietest week we've ever
had. Do you think you can arrange to repeat this kind of event once
every few months?"

One of the things that long-time members of the Elizabeth Fry
Society were allowed to do was to take an inmate out for an evening,

or for a Saturday, as part of a pre-release program. Jean Perlin and I would take them on outings. If Jean was with me, we could escort two women. But if I was by myself, I could escort only one. I made a point of taking some of the hard cases. There was a woman from Saint John, New Brunswick, who was serving a sentence for murder. The one thing she wanted to do was to ride a horse. I had never been on a horse in my life, but I found there was a place not far from Kingston where you could hire horses, so off we went and rented two of them. I had terrible trouble getting on my animal, but she was an excellent rider. She yelled at me, "No, you stupid fool! You don't know how to ride a horse!" We set out – gingerly in my case. We were heading into the countryside when she suddenly spurred her horse and took off. She could have ridden to Toronto or Montreal for all I could have done about it. I could see myself being accused of aiding a murderer to escape. But eventually she turned around and came back. She laughed at me.

On another occasion, I took a prisoner – she had murdered her live-in lover – home to my apartment for dinner. She was in the kitchen helping me prepare the meal. When I turned around, she had a knife, which she drew across my throat.

"You know, I could slit your throat if I wanted to," she said.

"But you're not going to, are you?" I replied. I was scared, but she did not hurt me.

One of the problems with the Prison for Women was that it housed many offenders who should never have been sent to a dreadful place like that. There were harmless Doukhobor women from British Columbia who were stuck in P4W because there was no other place to send them. And I remember clearly a seventeen-year-old Cape Breton girl. Her father, who had been a coal miner, suffered from emphysema although he was still a young man. He got no financial support from the mining company, so his wife, a nurse, had to support the family. This young girl was his favourite, and while the mother was at work, she took time off from school to care for him. It was a very traumatic period for her. When her father died, she just exploded. As we would say in Cape Breton, she "ran wild." Although she came from a strict Catholic background and had been well behaved all her life, she got in with a bunch of rough kids. One night they went to Sydney and began to grab items from the counter in a shop. When they ran out, she was caught.

She was just a child and had never been in trouble before. When she went to court, someone advised her to tell the judge that she was very sorry, that she did not realize what she was doing, and that she would never do it again. But the judges in Cape Breton were very strict in those days. "We'll make sure you don't do it again," the judge said. He sentenced her to a year's detention in a Catholic home for women in Halifax. But when she got there, the home was no longer in operation. They sent her back in front of the judge. "What was I to do?" the judge asked me later. "The Catholic home for girls was closed. There was only a Protestant home left, and I couldn't send her there. So I had to up her sentence to two years, and send her to the Prison for Women." (Sentences of two years or more were, and are, served in federal institutions and shorter sentences in provincial ones.)

This poor child was absolutely terrified to be locked away with murderers and other violent offenders. She sat in her cell and cried all day. There was no one she would talk to. The people at the prison asked me to talk to her. I happened to know who her father was; he had been active on the local baseball team. I thought it intolerable that the system had treated this young person so callously. We eventually managed to have her sentence rescinded and we got her back to Cape Breton to be with her mother. But by that time she had been in that horrible prison for three or four months.

What we really needed was a place – a halfway house – where women who were not really criminals or who had already been in the prison long enough could spend the last six months or so of their sentences, where they would be supervised but would still have quite a lot of freedom. The federal Solicitor General's department, which was responsible for corrections, had already tried to set up a halfway house for women within the grounds of Collins Bay Penitentiary in the west end of Kingston. It never got going. There was opposition from local people, and it did not make much sense to take people from a prison setting and set them up in a building adjacent to another penitentiary. That was not going to help them to re-integrate in the community.

At the Elizabeth Fry Society, we made a proposal to the Solicitor General's office for funding to establish a proper halfway house for women in a residential part of Kingston. They had all furnishings – beds, sofas, chairs, dishes, cutlery – in storage from the failed effort at Collins Bay. We said we would find a house at a reasonable rent, if the department would pay for it. These negotiations went on for a couple of years. We finally got the funding approved. But the Elizabeth

Fry Society had to take responsibility for managing the home, and we hired a woman from Cape Breton to be the house mother. On the house mother's night off, I or one of the other Elizabeth Fry members would fill in for her. We found a modest house on a quiet street that was large enough to accommodate six women, and we selected the first group. I persuaded some graduate students at the university to help by getting a small moving van and carting the furniture over. The house had been vacant and the neighbours assumed a group of students was moving in. They did not seem to be concerned. But when all the furnishings were unpacked and the boxes were put out for the garbage collection, the neighbours saw that they had "Correctional Services" stamped all over them. Someone concluded that a gang of ruffians was moving in, and we began to get a lot of flak. Renée Hogarth and I sat down with them one by one to explain what was happening. Most of them proved to be understanding. We got the house set up and some of the inmates from P4W helped us paint the rooms. When we were ready, we held a reception for the neighbours. A lot of them came and some even brought cookies. In time, our halfway house became a prototype for the department.

One of the women we brought to the halfway house was an unusual inmate named Ann Spiller. Ann had been accused of theft in a white-collar crime that had made a big splash in newspapers across the country. She was a very capable woman who had become the assistant manager of a bank in British Columbia. But Ann had expensive tastes. She developed a sophisticated scheme to defraud the bank, buying beautiful clothes and flying to New York for weekends. She managed to juggle her two lives for quite a while, although she told me later that she was relieved when she was finally caught. She was convicted and sent to the Prison for Women, there being no facility in British Columbia for women convicted of serious offences.

At P4W, Ann tried to keep herself aloof from other prisoners, who took to calling her the "White Queen' or "Frozen Queen." After we got her to the halfway house, John Meisel hired her to type the manuscript of a book he was writing. In the acknowledgments in the book, he included her name, which had to be a first for someone from the Prison for Women. She later married and moved away from Kingston.

I got to know one of the professors at the law school, Hugh Lawford, who had previously been a ministerial assistant in Ottawa. Hugh was working on a project with the federal Justice department to put court decisions on computer. It was a huge project. All of the documents had to be typed into the computer system. I arranged to bring a half-dozen women from P4W and the halfway house to take on the typing. It gave them a chance to earn some money while renewing their skills.

My interest in the plight of women inmates did not end when I left Queen's for the House of Commons. Years later, when I was in the cabinet, June Callwood, the celebrated writer, and I became involved in the cause of a woman in her sixties who had been sent to prison for murdering her unfaithful lover. It was a tragic case. The woman had been a war bride who had come to Canada with her husband after the Second World War. Her husband was a department head at an Ontario university. They had no children and were totally dependent on each other. One morning, she woke up to find him dead in bed beside her. He had died of a heart attack.

In her grief, she fell to pieces. She took up with another, quite unsuitable man, but before long she discovered that he was seeing another woman. That drove her over the brink. She took a knife and killed him so she was sent to the Prison for Women. She had committed murder, there was no doubt about that. But if ever there was someone who was not a criminal, she was that person. There was no purpose to be served in keeping her in jail. She would not talk to anyone in the penitentiary. But she would feed the birds through the bars on her cell, and as long as she could see the birds, she felt connected to the outside world. June and I kept trying to get her released or pardoned. We took turns visiting her until she was released under the Crown's prerogative of mercy. She was sent to a women's shelter in Toronto and then was returned to the general community. Sometimes the system can be made to work.

My experiences with inmates made me an advocate of extending the right to vote to prisoners. Originally, "women, idiots, and criminals" were denied the right to vote. It took many years to win the franchise for women, and it was an even harder struggle to persuade the government to let inmates vote. Yet some of these people, locked away for years, did a tremendous amount of reading. They became extremely knowledgeable about the law and about issues outside the prison walls. Some of them were a lot better informed than people in the general population. I asked myself, "Why wouldn't they have the right to vote? Why should anybody be denied the right to vote?" So I made speeches and lobbied until, much later, they got the vote.

I was never very far away from politics in my six years at Queen's. Following the 1968 federal election, Dalton Camp came to Queen's. Dalton had run for the Conservatives and lost in the Toronto riding of Don Valley. After the election, he was badly depressed. He did not know what he wanted to do with the rest of his life. He was trying to write a book, but it was not going well. When I went home to Cape Breton that summer, I stopped off for a few days at Dalton's cottage in New Brunswick. He showed me some of the early chapters and I went through them almost as though I were his book editor. He had the kernel of a good book, but it was a long way from what it would become, the brilliant *Gentlemen, Players and Politicians*, Dalton's account of his early years in politics leading to the election of the first Diefenbaker government in 1957.

As it happened, the political studies department at Queen's was considering reviving its Skelton Clark Fellowship, which in previous years had been used to bring such prominent Canadians as the Liberal politician Charles "Chubby" Power and General E.L.M. Burns to the university for a year of reflection, reading, writing, and mingling with students. I suggested Dalton would be an inspired choice for the fellowship and John Meisel, who knew Dalton, agreed. He convinced the University Senate to appoint Camp for the 1968–69 academic year. It was not a restful year for Dalton, however. His family stayed in Toronto and he commuted back and forth, trying to keep his hand in at his advertising agency and co-hosting, with Warner Troyer, the weekly public affairs program, *W5*, on CTV. When on campus, he immersed himself in his writing, finished the book, and it was published in 1970. I did not see a great deal of him when he was in Kingston but spent more time with him a year or so later, when we were both in New Brunswick for the 1970 provincial election, the one that brought our friend Richard Hatfield to power.

Not long after the New Brunswick election, I had a visitor. Walter Gordon, who had been the Liberal finance minister under Lester Pearson, came to see me with a proposition – would I join him and a group of Canadian nationalists in the building of a new citizens' group, the Committee for an Independent Canada? The CIC, as it was known, was conceived by Gordon, magazine editor and author Peter C. Newman and University of Toronto professor Abraham Rotstein to promote Canadian economic and cultural independence. They recruited book publisher Jack McClelland and Claude Ryan, publisher of Montreal's *Le Devoir,* to be national co-chairmen of the CIC. Gordon asked me to join them as their executive director.

My job was to help them set up the organization. I kept my Queen's connection, working there on Friday, Saturday, and Sunday. On Sunday night, I would drive to Toronto, stay with my sister Jean, and work with the CIC through Thursday, when I would return to Kingston. As well, I did a lot of travelling, working my way across the country to find people to organize local chapters of the committee. We soon had forty-one chapters with ten thousand members. We set out to collect one hundred thousand signatures on a petition calling on Ottawa to impose tougher regulations and restrictions on the foreign ownership of Canadian resources, manufacturing, and cultural industries. By the time we presented the petition to Pierre Trudeau in June 1971, we had exceeded our wildest expectations: we handed him 170,000 signatures.

The CIC had some notable successes as policies it promoted were enacted into law. These included: the establishment of the Foreign Investment Review Agency,[3] creation of Petro-Canada, new controls on land acquisition by non-residents, tougher Canadian content regulations for radio and television, and the elimination of Canadian tax status for *Time* and *Reader's Digest* magazines. The CIC disbanded in 1981 having accomplished most of its major goals.

My life has always been an uncharted map. As I noted earlier, serendipity has played a larger role than conscious strategy in many of my decisions. It happened again while I was in Kingston where I lived in an apartment on Pembroke Street. At the end of the street was a large mansion, which was the residence of the commandant of the National Defence College, Fred Carpenter. I got to know his wife, who was originally from Nova Scotia. Whenever a cabinet minister from Ottawa or some other VIP came to the college, the commandant and his wife would have a dinner party at their home. There tended to be more men than women on their guest list, so from time to time I would be invited to help balance the table.

After I had resumed my normal life at Queen's, following my Committee for an Independent Canada interlude, I received a call from the new commandant, saying it had been proposed by the outgoing class of the college that they include a woman in future classes.

The next one was going to be their twenty-fifth anniversary class – and they had never had a woman student in all those years.

The National Defence College was created after the Second World War with a view to exposing mid-level Canadian military officers – the sort who would be assuming leadership roles in coming years – to the international issues and problems that confront Canada and the world – from the Cold War to human suffering and poverty. Officers from Britain and the United States were added, along with some federal and provincial bureaucrats and a few people from the corporate sector. By the early 1970s, there were thirty-five students each year, about half military and half civilian. Then in 1971, the NDC made its daring leap into the unknown, by inviting a woman to take part.

"We have talked to a few people, and they think you'd be an ideal candidate to come on the course for a year," the commandant said.

I swallowed hard, and said, "Yes."

In the course of the year, students were expected to travel as a group to countries in various parts of the world. In my year, 1971–72, we went to twenty-seven countries in the Western Hemisphere, Asia, Africa, and Europe – including the Soviet Union, the first time an NDC class had gone there. The year was as stimulating intellectually as it was difficult financially. Our travel expenses were paid for by the college, but living expenses were a different issue. All of my classmates had their salaries continued by their employers – the military, a government or, in one or two cases, a big corporation – but I could not expect Queen's to pay me when I was not available to work. The arrangement I made was to work one-third of the time at Queen's for one-third of my regular salary. So I worked at the university from Friday afternoon to Monday noon. Queen's paid me about $3,000 for those twelve months, and I had to stretch the income to cover my apartment rent, food, clothing, and so on. I had not been so poor since my days as a penniless hitchhiker in Europe and North America.

The course could be treated as year-long boondoggle and a few students inevitably approached it that way. But it paid dividends to those who took the year seriously and made the effort to study, observe, and learn. In addition to all the travel, students were expected to make presentations to the class once every quarter. When my turn came, I was assigned to be one-half of a presentation dealing with the projection of the roles of work and leisure in the year 2000. The first half – on work – was presented by a prim and proper brigadier general from the United Kingdom. For my part – on leisure – I put on a sheer red negligee and draped myself over a black leather sofa while addressing the class: "Gentlemen, you asked me to talk about leisure, so I thought I would just relax and enjoy it." The commandant just about fainted, but my classmates loved it and it helped me to win the acceptance of the thirty-four men in the class, who until that point had been somewhat aloof. They began to treat me as regular fellow student, rather than as an exotic interloper.

The year was invaluable for me. It not only satisfied my appetite for travel, it opened my eyes to cultures I had not previously encountered. And it gave me an immersion course in international affairs. I learned far more than I would have learned if I had taken a post-graduate degree at the best university in the land. There were other factors, of course, but I think my exposure to global issues during my year at the National Defence College was one of the reasons why Joe Clark, after we won the 1979 election, asked me to be his secretary of state for External Affairs, or minister of Foreign Affairs, as we call it today.[4]

One of my classmates at the NDC was Hugh Hanson, who had worked as a policy adviser to Premier John Robarts in Ontario. Hugh became a good friend and an invaluable political ally and supporter. He was the person I relied on most when I ran for the Conservative leadership in 1976, and when I became a cabinet minister, I persuaded him to move to Ottawa as my chief of staff.

The NDC course ran from September 1971 to August 1972, but my life took another turn before the course was over. The class was in Hong Kong in February 1972 when I received a cable from George Perlin advising me that he and some other friends intended to put my name forward for the Progressive Conservative nomination in the riding of Kingston and The Islands for the upcoming federal election. "We hope you agree," the cable said. I was stunned.

I had been approached four years earlier to seek the Tory nomination for the 1968 election. But I had only been in Kingston for two years at that point. I was still finding my feet in the community, and felt I was not ready. It was just as well that I declined. The 1968 election was the first Trudeau election and I do not think I could have beaten the incumbent Liberal, Edgar Benson, a powerful member of the Liberal cabinet. But 1972 was different. The bloom was off the Trudeau rose. The Conservatives had their best shot in years of winning – as it turned out, Bob Stanfield came within two seats (109–107) of becoming prime minister in 1972 – and Benson decided not to run again.

I did not have much time to campaign for the nomination. In fact, I had classes at the National Defence College on the day of the nominating convention, getting out just a few hours before I had to appear at the meeting at the Grand Theatre. But my friends were busy in my absence. Michael Vaughan, a student at Queen's who went on to become a CBC national political correspondent, made sure my supporters turned out. By the time I arrived, there were one thousand people in the theatre, including students, women from the various groups I had been involved with during my six years in Kingston, and, in the balcony, my colleagues from the National Defence College. Unknown to me, a senior officer at the college had persuaded everyone on the course to buy a party membership so that they could vote. Even the officers from the US military were there and voting for me, there being no citizenship requirement for nominating conventions.

My opponent that night was an old Kingstonian, Bogart Trumpour, a lawyer and president of the Board of Trade, who had been the Tory candidate in the previous election. His supporters thought he deserved another chance. Some people actually thought I was just in it to create a bit of a contest for Trumpour. But I won the nomination easily. And when it was over, I went to see Bogart, congratulated him, and said, "I need your involvement in my campaign." He gave me his help then, and he continued to support me unstintingly in every election thereafter.

I took two months off from Queen's – without pay – for the election campaign. Most people did not really expect me to win. Benson had made Kingston and The Islands a Liberal fief. My Liberal opponent, John Hazlett, a local physician, had stunned the community by nearly defeating the Conservative incumbent, Syl Apps, a Kingston (and hockey) legend, in the provincial election the year before. It was assumed by many people, including Hazlett, that he would walk all over me, a novice and a woman to boot.

Hazlett's arrogance hurt him. The election was on 30 October 1972. Every fall, the women's auxiliary of the Kingston symphony orchestra held a formal ball to raise money for Kingston General Hospital. All the medical and professional staff turned out for the event. That year, the ball was about ten days before voting day.

Although it was not a crowd I normally socialized with, I wanted to support the women who had worked so hard to organize the gala. The weather was beautiful and I had been out canvassing all day. I rushed home to get into a long dress and dashed to the dance. There was a break in the dancing at the time I arrived and, when the music resumed, to my surprise the master of ceremonies announced, "We're going to have Dr Hazlett and Flora MacDonald lead off the dance." As I walked on to the dance floor, I heard Hazlett declare, "Not on your life. I don't intend to dance with her."

That insult spread quickly by word of mouth through Kingston. The people at the fundraiser were persons of influence in the community, and they expected more class from one of their peers. Meanwhile, I was left standing by myself on the dance floor, not quite knowing what to do. I was rescued by Eric Harrison, the head of the history department at Queen's. He came out on the floor, bowed to me, and asked, "May I have this dance, Miss MacDonald?" I was never so glad to see anyone. I practically fell into his arms.

Although I felt good about our campaign, I assumed the vote would be close and that the counting would extend late into the evening. So on election night, I went out to dinner with George Perlin and Michael Vaughan. We were just starting our dinner when the waitress came to say, "You know, you've just been elected!"

It was a landslide! We had turned a 4,435-vote Liberal plurality in 1968 into an 8,745-vote Conservative margin in 1972. Someone told me it was the biggest voting shift in the country in that election. My picture was on the front page of the *Globe and Mail* the next day with my sisters Jean and Sheila. I had been elected to Parliament! Not only that, I was the only woman among the 107 Conservatives elected that day. It took a while for both facts to sink in.

The Premier and the Pumpkin – No one could say I did not have celebrity support in my first campaign for Parliament in 1972. Here my great friend and ally, New Brunswick Premier Richard Hatfield, and I check out the farmers' market in Kingston. Richard taught me that these weekly markets are terrific places to meet voters. Why a pumpkin as a photo prop? Because the federal election that year took place on the day before Halloween. (*Kingston Whig Standard* Photographic Collection, V142-6-246)

Flora, MP – Fired after years at Progressive Conservative headquarters, I began a new life at Queen's University. But my passion for politics continued to burn. Nominated by colleagues at Queen's, I was elected to Parliament in 1972, the only woman in the Tory caucus. Here I am being sworn in by Alistair Fraser, the clerk of the House of Commons, as Bob Stanfield looks on. (Flora MacDonald Collection)

Flora Power – *Ottawa Citizen* cartoonist Rusins Kaufmanis captured my pitch to delegates at the 1976 Progressive Conservative leadership convention with these bold strokes. Unfortunately, not enough Tories got the message. I finished fifth.
(Rusins Kaufmanis/*Ottawa Citizen*)

Leadership Denied, A Dream Dashed – New Brunswick Premier Richard Hatfield (right) raises Joe Clark's arm in victory while I hide my disappointment behind a frozen smile. I knew at that moment I would never be prime minister. (David Rees-Potter/Library and Archives Canada, Duncan Cameron fonds, DCX 53-23)

A Surprising Development – I was astonished when out of the blue Joe Clark up and married a Tory party researcher, Maureen McTeer (on the left in this photo). I had assumed Joe was like me – far too absorbed in his political career to take time for dating let alone courting. Even people who were as close to him as I was barely knew Maureen – until Joe did what only an incurable politics wonk would ever do. For their honeymoon, he took his bride along on a Commons committee tour to inspect national parks. (Library and Archives Canada, Joe Clark fonds, Acc. 1997-374)

The Soviets Walked Out – One of my first duties as foreign minister was to address a crucial United Nations conference in Geneva on the humanitarian crisis of refugees fleeing their homelands in Southeast Asia following the Vietnam War. The delegation from the Soviet Union walked out when I cited their country's role in precipitating the crisis, and the UN secretary-general dressed me down for causing a fuss. I interpreted the walkout and the lecture as unintended compliments for criticism well placed! (Flora MacDonald Collection)

My First Summit – The crisis of refugees in post-Vietnam Southeast Asia was becoming a global preoccupation when the leaders of the G7 nations met in Tokyo in June 1979. We had barely been sworn into office when Prime Minister Joe Clark, Finance Minister John Crosbie and I, as foreign minister, flew to the Japanese capital. I left the summit determined that Canada would be a leader in relief and rescue efforts.

(Government of Japan/Library and Archives Canada, Joe Clark fonds, Acc. 1997-488)

Two Women Who Smashed Glass Ceilings – Christmas in Washington with Hillary Clinton. (Flora MacDonald Collection)

Canadian Trailblazers – Canada's first female foreign minister (that would be me on the left) with Kim Campbell, our first woman PM and Ellen Fairclough, who in 1957 became the first female cabinet minister in the nation's history. (Flora MacDonald Collection)

Two Canadian Speed Skating Champs – If Gaetan Boucher, winner
of two gold medals at the 1984 Sarajevo Olympics, was nervous that I,
the women's speed skating champion of Nova Scotia in my day, might
challenge him to a friendly race, he did not let it show when we met.
(Flora MacDonald Collection)

Three New Beginnings – Gathered in Brian Mulroney's office in 1984, we three discuss our new roles: Brian, prime minister; Joe Clark, foreign minister; me, minister of employment and immigration. My relationship with Brian was strained at times, but I had his support when I needed it most. He trusted me to carry through on the issue of greatest importance to me – equality of opportunity for women, a principle we enshrined in the Employment Equity Act, which I introduced and he supported unreservedly. (Peter Bregg, CM/Library and Archives Canada, Brian Mulroney fonds, e002713207)

Falling From Grace, Abruptly – Joe Clark's Progressive Conservative minority government was defeated over its maiden budget, in December 1979. In the ensuing election in February, I held my seat in Kingston, but our party was decisively defeated. I was out as foreign minister, and we faced four miserable years in opposition to a new majority Liberal government, led again by its old leader, Pierre Trudeau. (Flora MacDonald Collection)

Last-Minute Strategizing – As the balloting begins, Toronto lawyer Edwin A. ("Fast Eddie") Goodman, a long-time friend, ally, and chief fundraiser of my leadership campaign, offers an optimistic assessment of my chances, while Richard Hatfield, New Brunswick's premier, listens from my left. Our optimism was quickly dashed. I had many fans, but not enough voters. (Peter Raymont, writer and director, from the documentary *Flora: Scenes from a Leadership Convention,* 1977/National Film Board of Canada)

An Unforgettable Moment – The applause and cheers of delegates swept over me. They loved my speech, they were excited by my bagpipers, and hundreds of them put on Flora badges. If badges could vote, I would have been leader. (Peter Raymont, writer and director, from the documentary *Flora: Scenes from a Leadership Convention,* 1977/ National Film Board of Canada)

Flora, MP

I was no stranger to Parliament Hill when I was elected in 1972. During my nine years at Progressive Conservative headquarters, my office had been just a few blocks south of the Hill and I had made the hike to the Parliament Buildings countless times to see caucus members and to listen to debates in the evening. I knew the place well. Yet it was an eerie experience to walk, for the first time as a newly minted MP, up from the Centennial Flame to the Peace Tower, through the great brass doors and into the Rotunda and the Hall of Honour in the heart of the Centre Block. I was both thrilled and scared.

I could not stop shaking as I took the oath of office and signed the register. At my first caucus meeting, all the new members – and we had many of them after the 1972 election – were asked to stand and say a few words about themselves. I was so nervous that I thought my knees were going to buckle. The fact that I was the only woman among the 107 Conservative MPs seems astonishing today. At the time, however, it did not strike me as odd. I was used to being the only woman in the room at meetings of political insiders.

Let me be clear. Being used to something is not the same as accepting it. The under-representation of women in public life had long been a glaring weakness of the political process in Canada. As my father taught me years ago in Cape Breton, girls are as good as boys, women are equal to men, and they have the same right to climb to the top in all walks of life. No cause is more important to me than that.

Some obstacles confronting women with political ambitions were institutional. Politics in Canada had traditionally been regarded as a man's game. Men ran the parties. Men set the rules for nominating conventions. Men recruited new candidates. Men controlled the distribution of campaign funds. Perhaps it was only natural that when men searched for promising candidates, their eyes went first to other men rather than farther afield where they might discover qualified women. It is not that male recruiters were hostile to female candidates. Most of them in those days were not. They simply did not think of women when they thought of candidates. In their eyes, males were obvious candidates whereas females could be risky.

After Brian Mulroney became our leader in 1983, Kay Stanley, who had been president of the Progressive Conservative Women's Association, and I set up classes for Tory MPs on gender issues. Today, we would call it sensitivity training. We assembled caucus members in the leader's boardroom and, using skits and discussions, tried to get the male MPs to understand female voters. We tried to persuade them that if they want women's votes, they had to pay attention to the issues that concern women. You might think that was obvious, but it was not to most Conservative MPs at that time. They assumed the female voter would be interested in the same matters as men – or, at least, would follow their male's lead when it came time to vote.

We demonstrated how candidates should present themselves at voters' doors – acknowledge the presence of the woman of the house, treat her as the equal of her husband, and ask her for her opinions and her support. The caucus really took this training to heart; they understood what we were saying. After a week of this, George Hees, one of the old guard MPs, got up and spoke with great enthusiasm about how helpful our classes had been. "You girls have just done a great job!" he declared. Girls? Well, George was George and I could not help but laugh at his well-intentioned, if not politically correct, words.

Although I knew some of our MPs questioned the need for more women in Parliament, I did not encounter any personal resentment when I joined them in 1972. Many of them knew me. I had been their best friend at headquarters. This is not to suggest that they welcomed me as "one of the boys" – or that I ever wanted to be treated that way. I ate most of my meals by myself, usually at my desk. After hours, I kept to myself. I avoided the late evening drinking parties and card games in members' offices. That scene was not for me.

As the only female among 107 Conservative members of Parliament, I felt a special obligation to be the very best representative I could possibly be. Of course, all MPs want to do well for their constituents; their re-election depends on it. However, I believed I also had to perform well for the women of Canada. There were only five of us in the House following the 1972 election – three Liberals from Quebec, Jeanne Sauvé, Monique Bégin, and Albanie Morin, plus Grace MacInnis of the NDP, and me.[1]

As the party's sole woman in the Parliament, I was called on to do more than my share of campaigning across the country.[2] I was probably also in demand because I was seen to be a member of the inner circle around the leader, Bob Stanfield. Although I shouldered the burden willingly, it sometimes took its toll. During the 1974 election, I was in my apartment in Kingston one morning watering my hanging plants before driving to Toronto to catch a plane to Vancouver. My stepladder collapsed and I fell, cracking three ribs. How embarrassing – and painful! But I picked myself up, dusted off my dignity, took some painkillers, and headed for the West Coast.

The proximity of my riding to Ottawa was a mixed blessing. It meant I could go back and forth easily and spend more time in my riding than MPs from more distant constituencies. But because I was less than two hours away by road, my constituents thought I ought to show up at every event, regardless of any other plans I might have. These were the days before MPs were given allowances to open constituency offices and hire people to run them. But my motto in the 1972 election had been "Keep in Touch," and I was determined to do that. So I set up a constituency office at my own expense. As I recall, Andrew Brewin, a New Democrat from Toronto, was the only other MP to have a constituency office at that time.

It was hard to manage financially. The annual salary of MPs then was $18,000, plus a non-taxable expense allowance of $8,000. That was more than I had been making at Queen's and it probably seemed like quite a lot of money to many Canadians. Out of that amount, though, I had to maintain an apartment in Ottawa and one in Kingston, operate a car, rent and equip a constituency office, and pay the wages of an assistant to run that office. I hired Ian Green, a master's student at Queen's, to work for me part-time.[3] I spent my Saturdays in the Kingston office where a number of women who had worked in my election campaign helped out as volunteers.

Officials from the office of the Speaker of the Commons came to Kingston to inspect our operation. They must have been impressed because it was not long afterward that a plan to fund constituency offices was introduced. At that point, I was able to hire a full-time assistant in Kingston. I also started an open-line radio show on a

Kingston station. We called it "Keeping in Touch with Flora." I did it by phone from my office in Ottawa, taking calls from constituents for an hour every Wednesday morning just before our weekly caucus meeting. And I wrote a column for a little newspaper that was distributed in shopping centres in the riding.

One of the first things I knew I had to do when I was elected was to improve my inadequate French. When I resigned my position at Queen's, the university returned my pension contributions. I used that money to pay for language training at Laval University. Derek Burney, later chief of staff to Prime Minister Mulroney and Canadian ambassador to Washington, was studying French there at the same time. The Laval program worked for Derek and others, but not for me. I found I was not making any progress in French when I took classes with anglophones who reverted to speaking English as soon as the class ended. I needed something more intensive. The padre at the military base in Kingston was from rural Quebec, so I asked him where I might go to learn French in the summer. He recommended a monastery in St Georges de Beauce, but as it turned out they were not offering summer language courses. The monks referred me to the sisters at a nearby convent in St Georges Ouest, and they agreed to take me in.

Given my Methodist roots, I wondered what it would be like to actually live for an extended period in a convent where nuns still wore the habit. "I'm going to do whatever you do," I told the sisters. "You're going to help me learn French, but to learn, I must live with you and I must do what you do." They held a religious service at seven o'clock every morning – it was not officially a mass because there was no priest to celebrate it – and when they said I would be welcome to come, I said I would be delighted, on one condition. "You come out jogging with me afterward because I believe in keeping fit." After the service each morning, we would go for a half-hour run in the countryside or through the streets of St Georges, I in my track suit and they in their habit. I do not know what the locals thought, but it was great fun!

I went back to the convent a number of times. I was there in 1979 when Joe Clark called to offer me the position of foreign minister (or secretary of state for External Affairs, as it was called then) in his new government. Joe swore me to secrecy, and I guess I violated my oath because I did tell the sisters. They were tremendously excited and started making scrapbooks of my career.

One of the issues that bedevilled Parliament during my early years as an MP was capital punishment. There was no question where I stood. I was an abolitionist then and I remain an abolitionist today. I inherited my conviction from my father who had seen people hanged when he was growing up in Cape Breton. He had been appalled and revolted. I felt the same way.

The death penalty has nothing to do with law enforcement, the administration of justice, or the deterring of violent criminals. Plain and simple, it is retribution – society's way of taking revenge on those who break the ultimate rule: thou shall not kill. I never considered capital punishment to be acceptable in a civilized society. It was immoral. It was not even effective. The prospect of being apprehended is what deters would-be murderers – not the distant possibility of being executed. I understood this very well from my years of volunteer work in the prisons of Kingston.

Back in 1859, when British law still ruled in Canada, death was the sanction for a number of offences, including murder, rape, treason, administering poison or wounding with intent to commit murder, unlawfully abusing a girl under ten, buggery with man or beast, robbery with wounding, burglary with assault, arson, casting away a ship, or exhibiting a false signal endangering a ship. Over the years, the list of capital offences was reduced. By 1869, two years after Confederation, the list was down to murder, rape, and treason. In 1961, Parliament passed legislation that reclassified murder into capital murder (premeditated murder, murder committed in the course of a violent crime, or the murder of a police officer or prison guard) and non-capital (or unpremeditated) murder, such as crimes of passion. The death penalty was retained for capital murder only; the sanction for non-capital murder was life imprisonment. The last two people to be executed in Canada were Arthur Lucas and Robert Turpin – Lucas for the premeditated murder of a police informer and witness, Turpin for the murder of a policeman while trying to avoid arrest. They were hanged back-to-back at the Don Jail in Toronto at two minutes past midnight on 11 December 1962. They were the 709th and 710th people to have been hanged in Canada – the only means of execution ever used in this country. Over the years, another 771 people who had been sentenced to death had their sentences commuted to life imprisonment.[4]

Pressure to eliminate the death penalty had built slowly over the years. The first formal attempt to abolish it was in 1914 when a

Liberal MP from Montreal, Robert Bickerdike, introduced a private member's bill to that effect. Although Bickerdike failed, others kept trying. Similar private member's bills were introduced in every parliamentary session between 1954 and 1963. Even after the death penalty went out of use, it remained on the statute books. In 1967, Parliament – by a vote of 105 to seventy – imposed a five-year moratorium on capital punishment, except for the murder of police or corrections officers. That trial period was drawing to a close when I was elected in 1972. After an emotional debate, we voted in 1973 to extend the moratorium – by a margin of just thirteen votes.

It was not an easy issue for me in Kingston and The Islands with its five penitentiaries. Three thousand prison guards lived and voted in my riding. They were overwhelmingly in favour of retaining the death penalty. When their families were factored in, I figured I was up against a pro-capital punishment force of six or seven thousand voters. It would have been a lot simpler and less stressful to have been a retentionist in Kingston.

When I first ran, I was invited to meet with the prison guards and to listen to their complaints – most of them well justified – about their working conditions, their pay, and the lack of direction they were getting from their supervisors. I found the best approach was to tell them off the top that I was categorically opposed to capital punishment and that I would never change my mind on the issue. Once we got that out of the way, we talked about subjects on which we could agree. The guards never walked out on me. They listened to what I had to say. I think they were astonished that somebody would come along and open up in the way I did. It gave me a certain credibility that I would not have had if I tried to temporize or to avoid confronting the capital punishment issue. I told them I believed in prison reform on both sides of the bars – both the treatment of prisoners and the treatment of those who guarded them. The guards realized I was sincere. Some became good friends.

Conditions were unsettled at Kingston-area prisons at the time of the 1973 debate on extending the moratorium. There had been riots at the forty-year-old Kingston Penitentiary, and inmates had been moved to another maximum-security institution, the newly constructed "high-tech" Millhaven Institution. Because of all the prisons in my riding, I was named to a parliamentary sub-committee to hold hearings at the penitentiaries into the causes of the unrest. There were three of us. Jim Jerome, an Ontario Liberal who later became speaker of the House, was our chair; Stuart Leggatt, a New Democrat from British Columbia, and me. We held hearings in the chapel at Millhaven. Inmates came forward with stories of the abuse they had suffered and the beatings they had endured while in federal custody. Our committee documented their grievances in a report to Parliament.

Becoming more deeply involved, I joined the "Twenty-Five Club" at Collins Bay Penitentiary. Collins Bay was a medium-security institution and the Twenty-Five Club was a group of inmates who were serving sentences of twenty-five years or longer, mainly for murder. Many of them had been young men when they were sentenced and were growing old in prison. They knew they would not have many years left to live by the time they were released. The Twenty-Five Club held study sessions and debates; each year the club helped to organize a competition for disabled athletes on the prison grounds.

Although I survived the election of 1974 handily, my popular vote dropped by five thousand votes and my margin of victory shrank from 8,745 votes in 1972 to 3,896 in 1974 – not enough to cause me to panic but enough to make me worry. My opposition to capital punishment may have been a factor – sentiment in the riding was ten to one against me on the issue – but I knew the major reasons were more national than local. We had come within two seats of winning the country in 1972, but 1974 was a very different election. We were stuck promoting an unpopular policy, wage and price controls, to combat inflation, and the Liberals ran away with the election.[5]

We were still not finished with the capital punishment dilemma. It came up again in 1976 when the Liberals scheduled a free vote on Bill c-84, legislation to remove capital punishment permanently from the Criminal Code. I took it on myself to organize support for the bill among Tory MPs. Warren Allmand, the solicitor general, did the same thing with the Liberal caucus. Leggatt was the point man for the NDP, but he had a much easier job of it than Warren or I because his entire caucus intended to vote for the bill.

Although Robert Stanfield was a firm abolitionist, he did not have much influence with his caucus. A majority of our MPs favoured retention and some of them were strident on the subject. A majority of Liberals supported abolition. Allmand and I had several anxious meetings as we did our head counts, identified the waverers, and went off to woo them.

As the day of the vote neared – 14 July 1976, or Bastille Day, as I thought of it – it became clear that the outcome would be desperately close. We knew we had to make sure that every supporter would be present. I was worried about Lincoln Alexander, a Red Tory MP from Hamilton who would later be a federal cabinet minister and then lieutenant governor of Ontario. Linc was having serious back trouble. He was in such agony that he was hospitalized in Hamilton. I phoned him in hospital and begged, "Linc, please, get up here. We need you. Just get an ambulance and get them to put you on a plane. We'll have an ambulance meet you at the airport in Ottawa and bring you into the House." But his wife Yvonne and the doctors put the kibosh on that. We had to get along without Linc.

We were frantic as the roll was called. In the end, we won, by just six votes. With the passage of Bill C-84, capital punishment was eliminated from the Criminal Code.[6] It was eliminated, I might add, without the help of John Diefenbaker, the self-styled champion of human rights. Diefenbaker had been a passionate advocate of abolition throughout his years as a defence attorney and politician. But when the issue was put to a vote in 1976, he abandoned the principle he had embraced for so long. Although he said it was because he feared the new law would not protect prison guards, I have always suspected it was because he did not want to alienate his supporters in the caucus, almost all of whom were fervent retentionists.

A sensible person would have thought that the 1976 vote had put the matter to rest, but, of course, it did not. Capital punishment is one of those causes that is so fraught with emotion, political ideology, and religious conviction that it simply refuses to die. We could knock it down, stomp on it, and beat it senseless, but we could not kill it. To no one's great surprise, the issue came before the Commons again in 1987 with a debate on a motion to reinstate the death penalty. There was a free vote again, but this time the abolitionists won by a wider margin, 148–127. Finally, in 2001, the Supreme Court of Canada ruled, in a deportation case, that the death penalty is unconstitutional in Canada. That seemed at long last to close the book on a historic struggle.

The 1974 general election was a terrible disappointment for the Progressive Conservatives. Having come within two seats of victory in 1972, we found ourselves two years later facing a majority Liberal government again. The election was not a rout. We managed to elect ninety-four members, only thirteen fewer than in 1972, but looking across the aisle we saw 141 Liberals. We knew we were in for four or five hard years in opposition.

As much as many of us would have wished otherwise, it was clear that Stanfield would not be around to lead us into another election. Having lost three elections in six years to Trudeau, he knew it was time to move on. The party knew it was time to look for a new leader. Mine may not have been the first name to spring to Conservatives' minds when they thought about the leadership. But why not?

The rumour mill began to spread names – Claude Wagner, Jim Gillies, Paul Hellyer, Jack Horner, Heward Grafftey, Sinclair Stevens, and several others. What, I asked myself, made any of these men – eleven of them eventually entered the race – so special? What could they conceivably bring to the job that I could not? For starters, I knew as much about the party and the country as any of the men – and a lot more than most of them!

No one individual talked me into running, but some of my caucus colleagues, especially Gordon Fairweather from New Brunswick and David MacDonald from Prince Edward Island, were extremely supportive. So were former Ontario MPs Ron Atkey and Terry O'Connor, who had lost their seats in the 1974 election, as was my great friend Richard Hatfield, the premier of New Brunswick, and Hugh Hanson, who had been on the National Defence College course with me and would later serve as my chief of staff in Ottawa.

Gender was definitely a factor in my decision. There had never been a female leader of a national party in Canada. There had never been a serious female candidate for the leadership of either the Liberal or Progressive Conservative party.[7] Surely, it was time to give a woman a chance at national leadership. Ideology was another factor. Stanfield was a progressive, as I am. Most of the men who wanted to succeed him were to the right of centre, with the exceptions of Joe Clark, John Fraser and, arguably, Brian Mulroney.

No one pushed me into seeking the leadership. No one coaxed me. I made my own decision. I decided to run because I honestly believed I would be a better leader than the rest, and because I felt I owed it to myself and to the women of Canada to demonstrate that a woman could lead a national party. And I decided to run because I intended to win!

I I

The Flora Syndrome

I had never lusted for political leadership. It was only after Robert Stanfield decided to leave that I seriously considered the possibility of succeeding him. In my view, the party needed a leader who could carry on where Stanfield left off, who would emphasize progressive values and continue his efforts to appeal to Canadians of moderate views. As I looked around at the caucus and the party, I could not see anyone who would be as comfortable as I wearing the Stanfield mantle. Most of the other prospective candidates – all of them male – were too right-wing for my taste.

Before I made my decision, however, I sought advice and guidance. At the suggestion of Ron Atkey, the Toronto MP who had lost his seat in the 1974 election, I agreed to test the waters to see what support I could expect. In early February 1975, a group of potential supporters met at my apartment in Ottawa. In addition to Atkey, they included Terry O'Connor, an MP from Oakville, Ontario, who had also lost his seat in 1974; three former Queen's students with whom I had become friendly in my years there, Michael Vaughan, Murray Coolican, and Michel de Salaberry; Patrick Martin, at twenty-three the youngest of the group and an aspiring freelance writer; and my caucus colleague from Alberta, Joe Clark. The group expanded later, but these early supporters formed the nucleus of my campaign organization – all except Clark who soon withdrew from my team to seek the leadership himself. The others were young and relatively inexperienced, but they were eager, committed, and more than willing to work twelve or sixteen-hour days. And one other thing: they all believed as fervently as I did that I could win.[1]

A few weeks later, the Progressive Conservative party organized
a forum at St Lawrence Hall in Toronto to showcase four MPs who
seemed likely to be candidates at the leadership convention, to be
held in Ottawa's Civic Centre in February 1976. The four were Clark
from Alberta, Heward Grafftey from Quebec, and Sinclair Stevens
and myself from Ontario. We were invited to speak our minds, and
we did. Sinc Stevens called for reducing federal spending, shrink-
ing the size of the government, and turning Crown corporations
over to private enterprise. Grafftey, as always, was entertaining if
not entirely comprehensible. He wanted a "citizen-property owner
democracy" to replace the "socialist statism" of the Liberals. Clark
argued that the Liberal government had ignored the real problems
of the country by concentrating on centralizing power in Ottawa.
Using speech notes prepared by Patrick Martin, I expressed my
concern about uncontrolled growth in society, the erosion of public
confidence in our political institutions, and the alienation of the individual from big business and big government.

Writing in the *Globe and Mail*, columnist Geoffrey Stevens placed
me on the extreme left of the four MPs. The audience, he wrote,
seemed impressed by the depth of my commitment, although he
commented: "On most questions, she is very short on specifics."[2]

A long period followed in which little seemed, on the surface,
to be happening. In the fall, candidates began popping out of the
woodwork. The irrepressible Grafftey was the first to declare and
I was second, on 8 October 1975. I deliberately declared early
because I wanted to show that I was a person with an avid interest in winning, not a token female who had to be coaxed to run at
the last moment. I was heartened by the people who volunteered
to help. O'Connor and Atkey became campaign chair and deputy
chair, respectively. Eddie Goodman, my old friend and ally from the
Diefenbaker wars, joined us as fund-raiser. Michael Vaughan, who
had helped me win the Tory nomination in Kingston and The Islands
in 1972, became my personal assistant while Murray Coolican
organized my tour. Another former Queen's student, Les Foreman,
was my voting-day coordinator. He worked with Michael Hatfield,
a brilliant young man, who developed a sophisticated system for
tracking delegate preferences and intentions. Michael, who had
earned his master's degree at Queen's, was the nephew of my great
supporter Richard Hatfield. My Kingston friend Jean Perlin, who

ran my parliamentary office in Ottawa, took charge of volunteers across the country. Patrick Martin looked after media relations and helped with speech writing.

David Crombie, the mayor of Toronto (and soon to be MP), was a big supporter, as were John Crosbie, the smartest man in the Newfoundland cabinet (he would win a federal seat in a by-election a few months later) and my caucus colleagues Gordon Fairweather from New Brunswick and David MacDonald from PEI, along with Egan Chambers, a former MP and party president, from Montreal, Ellen Fairclough, Canada's first woman cabinet minister, Senator John M. Macdonald from Nova Scotia, and my old ally, Lowell Murray, later to be a cabinet minister and senator himself. John Diefenbaker did not support me, of course. That would have been too much for both of us. But one day, about a month before the convention, he took me by the arm and told me how proud he was of my populist campaign. Coming from the old populist himself, that was no mean compliment. It was the first time we had spoken in ten years.

The key person in my campaign was Hugh Hanson, who had become a good friend when we were at the National Defence College together in 1971–72. He was on leave that year from the Ontario government where he had been deputy secretary to the cabinet under Premier John Robarts. He knew how to run an organization. Hugh was one of the first people I contacted when I decided to seek the leadership. Officially, he was my policy adviser. In reality, he was also my campaign manager, chief strategist, speechwriter, and closest confidant.

I knew I faced three obstacles to overcome in the four and one-half months between the time I announced my candidacy and the leadership convention in Ottawa. The first and most obvious obstacle was my gender. I was the only female candidate in the race for the leadership of a party that had never had, or even thought of having, a woman leader.[3] Many Conservatives assumed women were content to stay in the political wings, pouring tea, or stuffing envelopes, not on stage competing with male politicians, let alone campaigning against them for national leadership. It would be a few more years before the perception of women in politics would begin to change in Canada, and I think the election of Margaret Thatcher as the British prime minister had a lot to do with that change – however thoroughly I disagreed with her right-wing ideology and many of her policies.

The second obstacle was that I did not have a conventional political resumé, the sort of background that parties traditionally looked for in their leaders. I was not a lawyer or business owner. I had worked at a university – I had even done some lecturing to political science students – but I was not a professor. I did not have a university degree. I was an office administrator, a graduate of a business college in Cape Breton. True, I had been a member of Parliament for four years, but I had never been a cabinet minister nor even a parliamentary secretary. I knew how to run an office, but was I qualified to run a national political party, a government, a country?

The third obstacle was my political philosophy. I was very much in the progressive wing of the PC party – a Red Tory, and proud of it. It never bothered me in the slightest to be identified as being to the left of other Conservatives, but I know it bothered many of them. I was opposed to capital punishment when most Conservatives were strongly in favour of it. I believed abortion should be left to the decision of the woman and her doctor – which was very much a minority view in our party in those days. In the eyes of many Tories, I was a little too radical, a little too unconventional, for them to feel comfortable with the prospect of me as their leader.

These perceived "deficiencies" in my gender, resumé, and political orientation might, I knew, weigh heavily on the minds of some of the male delegates at the convention. What I did not anticipate was that they would weigh just as heavily on many of the older women delegates who, though they counted themselves among my supporters, could not in the end bring themselves to vote for me. Did the women simply follow their men when it came to cast their ballots? I don't think so. I think they made their own choices. And I think the women of the Tory party in the mid-1970s were even more cautious and conservative than the men. They were sympathetic and encouraging to me. They liked the idea that I was running, and I think they would have been happy if I had won, but they could not quite bring themselves, personally, to take a chance on me.

If the obstacles were mountains to be climbed, I set out to climb them by emphasizing my unique strengths and attributes for leadership. First, having spent so many years in its service, I knew the party inside out. I knew the members. I understood their problems. I had worked with them in victory and defeat. I had fought alongside them in thirty-eight federal and provincial elections and by-elections. To thousands of Tories, I was simply "Flora" – their friend and ally.

Second, I had a track record from my work in Kingston and in Ottawa of being able to reach out to others – to youth, to the poor and the elderly, to frightened immigrants, to Indigenous and other disadvantaged Canadians. As leader, I would be able to give the Conservative party – often stiff, distant, and seemingly uncaring – the human face it had appeared to lack for much of its history.

Third, as a woman, I could give the party a new look, a different style. I offered the potential of being able to open new doors and of attracting new supporters to a party that had too long been dominated by dour men in serious three-piece suits.

I set out to address these issues when I declared my candidacy. "Let me make the point before anyone else does," I said in my announcement:

I'm a candidate with a difference. I am a woman. I represent no single region. I'm neither a lawyer, nor a business executive, nor am I an academic. But I understand politics and how it works. How it really works. I understand people, how they make their decisions and shape their lives. And I care, care passionately, about what is happening and what is being allowed to happen to my country. ... [T]he label put on me is that of Red Tory. So be it. So be it, that is, if what is meant by "Red" is that I see red when I see injustice. I am outraged by the exploitation of the disadvantaged; by discrimination against women, against Canadians living in regions outside the big cities, against the old who are made to feel unwanted and unneeded.

It was not the sort of rhetoric that Progressive Conservatives were accustomed to hearing from leadership candidates, but I made a bow to traditional Tory values as I continued: "I am incensed when I see public waste, intrusions in private rights, the deadening weight of bureaucracy, the larcenous effects of inflation." I unveiled the principal themes of my campaign – the recapture by the people of their own institutions and government, and the rediscovery of our sense of national purpose, adding: "My campaign will have a third theme. By the party. With the party. For the country. It is not a new commitment. It was given to us a century ago by the first member of Parliament for Kingston and The Islands, the first Red Tory, Sir John A. Macdonald."

I was pleased with my campaign launch and with the way I had positioned myself for the race to come. I would not play second fiddle to any other candidate when it came to my experience in the party, my understanding of the needs and concerns of ordinary Conservatives or my ability to establish a personal connection with them. Here is how I put it in a speech to one group of convention delegates:

> Because I understand what the philosophy of Conservatism means, I'm able to understand the concerns, needs and hopes of the people who are the Conservative Party. It is not simply because I am one of you and have been for many years. It is because I have shared your thoughts and worked with you throughout that time, in the most basic, elemental sense, and in every province of this country. I have typed letters, stuffed envelopes, knocked on doors, walked miles, and driven and flown thousands more. I have answered telephones, answered mail, answered questions. I have made coffee, made speeches, made policy. I have celebrated our triumphs with you and wept with the most broken-hearted worker among you when we've suffered defeat.

The *Globe and Mail's* Stevens ranked me as one of the two strongest contenders, along with our foreign affairs critic, Claude Wagner, the former provincial Liberal cabinet minister and judge from Quebec,[4] but he still had reservations. "Everyone knows Flora MacDonald," he wrote," but how much does the country really know about what she would do with her party as its leader, what sort of Canada she would try to create if she became prime minister? Miss MacDonald has had an extremely high political profile, but on a relatively narrow range of issues – prison reform, native rights, status of women. What does she think about the economy, about labour unrest, about the development of natural resources, about transportation policy, about Canada's place in the world?"[5]

That is a problem with journalists: they always want politicians to spell out every last detail in our policies so that they can either pick them apart or accuse us of boring audiences to distraction.

Money was a constant worry for me and my campaign workers. Among my opponents, Brian Mulroney ran the most lavish campaign. He had the Power Corporation's Paul Desmarais backing him and Desmarais gave Brian the use of one of the corporation's executive jets to transport him quickly and comfortably across the country wherever and whenever he wanted to travel. Brian also hosted the most extravagant party of convention week when he hired the renowned

Quebec singer Ginette Reno to entertain delegates. Reno's performance cost the Mulroney campaign $10,000, which was a fortune
in 1976. She was a great hit at the convention, but her appearance
actually hurt Brian's chances. As was his tendency in other aspects of
his public life, he overdid it. He spent too much money, and he spent
it too conspicuously. Many delegates saw him as the candidate of big
business. That backlash would doom his campaign.

Claude Wagner, a former judge who had been a provincial Liberal
cabinet minister in Quebec, was a formidable candidate and everyone
expected that he would be in the lead on the first ballot, which he was.
He, too, was well-financed, with affluent backers in the business communities of Montreal and Toronto. Paul Hellyer had personal wealth
and Sinc Stevens could tap contacts on Bay Street. But the two of us
who came into the race as outsiders, because we were clearly not part
of the political establishment – Joe Clark and I – had to raise campaign money the hard way, a few dollars here, a few dollars there.

At one point, I became so concerned that Clark would be forced
out of the race for lack of funds that I went to Lowell Murray, who
was supporting me but was also a friend of Joe's, to see if he could
help. He wrote Clark a cheque, and he also helped by preparing
some French speech material for Joe.

As for me, we had so little money that we had to make a virtue out
of frugality. When I traveled, Hugh Hanson and Michael Vaughan
usually accompanied me; when my schedule included important
media events, Patrick Martin would come along to deal with the
press. We went everywhere by the cheapest means possible – by
car, bus, train, and economy flights, although on one occasion we
managed to borrow a helicopter for a quick visit to the Haliburton
region of Ontario.

The four-and-a-half months before the convention became a
blur of cities, airports, bus stations, meeting halls, and delegates'
faces. I was worried. I had always maintained a good attendance
record in the House of Commons and it bothered me to be away for
lengthy periods. My weekend attendance in my constituency office
in Kingston was also something I had attended to assiduously. What
would my constituents think when I failed to show up? And what
about my wardrobe? How could I keep my clothes in proper condition as I traveled? In public life, what a woman wears, and how she
wears it, is more closely analyzed than the attire of a man.

These concerns receded as the pace intensified. The variety of the audiences and their question-and-answer sessions stimulated me. Although I spoke before some large groups, including the Empire Club in Toronto, most of my campaigning was with smaller groups of delegates and party supporters. I think I was at my best in these more intimate settings.

I was astonished by the number of people who came up to me and pressed a dollar bill or two into my hand after meetings. They knew I did not have a large war chest; they were pleased that I was running, and they wanted to show their goodwill by giving me a few dollars. One day, mid-way through the campaign, I was in Kingston talking to Hugh Hanson, Michael Vaughan, and Patrick Martin when I reached absently into my pocket and pulled out a fistful of small bills. "Everywhere I go," I said, "people push money into my hands. 'It's just a dollar, a few dollars,' they say. 'Take it for your campaign.'" A light bulb came on. I do not know who came up with the words first, but the "Dollar for Flora" campaign was born.

The next day we called a press conference in Toronto and announced that we were inviting Canadians to send a dollar, just one dollar, to assist my campaign. The response was astonishing. Nearly twenty thousand Canadians mailed me a dollar, and some enclosed more than that. Many included notes of encouragement. Writing in *The Canadian* magazine, journalist Harry Bruce observed, "[F]or weeks now, the small crumpled bills had been flopping into Flora's office on Parliament Hill. Funny, loving notes, jingles, and slogans accompanied the money. The authors were not all Tories, and they were not all women. Some were kids, husbands, housewives, students, old men. Some were NDP supporters, and a few were even Grits. Some hadn't contributed a nickel to any political party for years, and were therefore the political equivalent of lapsed Christians who'd become part of 'the lost.'"

The Dollar for Flora was a gimmick, of course, but it raised about $40,000, and my campaign needed the money badly. More important, nearly twenty thousand people, most of whom would not otherwise have become engaged in the leadership competition, got involved, albeit in a small way. It was a means of reaching out to people and touching them. It reinforced the perception that I was not an establishment candidate, that I was not in the pocket of any special interests, that I was a populist.

Unfortunately, populist credentials do not pay the bills. Even with
a bare bones budget of $120,000 – decidedly modest by today's
standards – we needed to raise more money in denominations larger
than one-dollar banknotes. Eddie Goodman introduced a variation
on the Dollar for Flora theme and pitched it to prospective donors
with deeper pockets. He called it "Five to Fifty for Flora," and that
campaign was quite successful. In the end we spent about $140,000
and had a deficit of $15,000–$20,000, which Eddie's good pal, John
Bassett, the media magnate, helped us to pay off by hosting a fund-
raising skating party and dinner at his TV station in Toronto.

One of our few extravagances was to send every delegate a
long-playing record for Christmas 1975. We had recorded many
of my speeches and interviews. Hugh Hanson and Patrick Martin
gathered those tapes and arranged to get others from radio stations
around country. They chose the best bits. Patrick, who had learned
tape editing at the CBC, assembled the pieces. When they felt I had
delivered a particularly effective line or made an especially telling
point in an interview or speech, but had not been interrupted by
applause, they shamelessly borrowed an ovation from some other
speech and edited it in. CBC announcer Russ Germain, a friend of
Patrick's and a supporter of mine, recorded the introduction and the
transitional passages.

They had the finished product pressed into a 33-1/3 rpm record
(there were no CDs in those days). They designed a record jacket
in terra-cotta, my signature colour. They bought three thousand
padded envelopes and a machine to heat-seal them, along with an
Addressograph to run off labels and a Pitney Bowes stamp machine.
Soon they had huge piles of records stacked, ready to send, in a
donated office we were using as a headquarters in downtown
Toronto. As Hugh and Patrick recall, there were only two problems.
Once the envelopes were stamped, they had to be delivered to the
post office by midnight the same day or the postal authorities would
not accept them. And a monster December blizzard hit Toronto that
day. Buses and streetcars were not running, and there were no cars
or taxis on the roads. Most of the downtown streets were impass-
able. How could they get the recordings to the main post office on
Front Street, nearly a mile away?

The solution? They found a sporting goods store nearby where
they bought a toboggan. They carted stacks of the recordings down
in the elevator to the street, loaded them onto the toboggan, and

pulled it to the post office. It took several trips, but they had all three thousand in the mail by midnight. I have no idea how many delegates actually took the time to listen to my recording, but the scheme was innovative. Like the Dollar for Flora, it helped to mark my candidacy as something different and distinctive.

Austerity ruled our campaign through the convention in Ottawa in late February. While other candidates threw fancy receptions for delegates and poured free drinks in their hospitality suites, my supporters, led by Mayor Crombie, did it differently. They set up soup kitchens in church basements and outside on the cold street corners. Delegates and anyone else, including homeless people in the nation's capital, could get a bowl of hot soup and a pitch for Flora MacDonald.

I, too, had hospitality rooms in the delegates' hotels, but we did not serve anything stronger than coffee. Some of my Kingston friends baked cookies, cakes, and breads that they sent to Ottawa every morning. Not having $10,000 or so to hire a Ginette Reno, we came up with something better. I invited my Cape Breton friend John Allan Cameron, who was known as the "Godfather of Celtic Music," to bring a group of fiddlers to Ottawa for a great bash on the Friday evening, the day before the candidates were to address the convention. My mother, white-haired and seventy-five, was there as was my brother Ronald and my three surviving sisters. We sang Scottish and French-Canadian songs. We sang in English and in Gaelic. I wore the costume of the original Flora Macdonald – long tartan skirt, green velvet jacket with white lace – as I led the Scottish country dancing with John Allan. It was the best-attended, most enthusiastic party of convention week – and John Allan did it for free! It illustrated the down-home, down-to-earth tone of my entire campaign. The press noticed and a number of reporters and columnists made a point of observing that I was a unique candidate with a unique campaign.

Two events remained. The candidates' speeches on Saturday and the voting on Sunday. The speeches are always crucial. A great speech cannot turn a weak candidate into a frontrunner, as Joe Greene learned at the Liberal convention in 1968. But a superior speech can put a strong candidate over the top – as happened with Bob Stanfield in 1967 and Pierre Trudeau in 1968 – while a disappointing speech can doom the chances of a strong candidate – witness Paul Hellyer at both the Liberal convention in 1968 and the Tory convention in 1976.

We were sure that Wagner would be the early-ballot leader and were reasonably sure that Mulroney would be second. We also knew that large numbers of delegates would never vote for either of them. It was going to be crucial to place no lower than third on the first ballot. If I were in third place, I was confident that the supporters of Joe Clark and John Fraser would come to me, giving me the momentum to come up the middle. But if I finished behind Clark, he would get the momentum. I might get to play kingmaker, but I would not be leader.

I needed to deliver the speech of my life.

With Hugh Hanson and Denise Ashley, my French language coach, I went to a borrowed chalet north of Quebec City to work on my speech, which Hugh wrote. When we returned to Ottawa, I practised my delivery in my hotel suite where we set up a podium that was a replica of the one in the Civic Centre. On Saturday morning, Hugh was there and Richard Hatfield came in. I guess the stress of the long campaign and the pressure of convention week caught up to me. I was so tired I could barely stand up. I experienced a meltdown, an incredible anxiety attack. This was just hours before the final great effort, but I knew I could not go on. I could not face thousands of Tories that day. When I said I wanted to withdraw from the race, a voice like a whiplash cut through my moaning. "Stop that!" It was Richard. "I've worked so hard for you. I've neglected my own responsibilities – and you're not going to pull this sort of stunt now."

A jug of cold water over my head could not have had a more sobering effect. Richard brought me to my senses. "Pull yourself together," he ordered me. "You haven't come this far to back away from it. Buck up." The way he said it was enough. I straightened up. After I went through the speech a couple of times, he said, "Okay, that's fine." Richard was great that way. There was never any sentimentality to him. He just said, "Do this," and I did it. Ours was a relationship where we could support one another in a brutally frank way.

I was pleased with the speech. I thought I touched all the important bases, including the need for political renewal:

The old ways don't work for us any more. Unless we as a party rejuvenate ourselves, the people won't respond. And yet they will respond to something new. They will answer an appeal to get involved. I know, because when I asked for support, I got a response from as many people as contributed to the entire party last year. Now maybe the amounts weren't as big, but the numbers are. What a base to build on! And we need such a base. The first priority of thousands of Canadians I have spoken to recently is to get a new prime minister. They are now looking to the Conservative party to see what alternative we have to offer. And a real alternative is what we must offer. Not just someone new, but someone who is truly different.

Without singling out opponents about whom I had grave misgivings, I made it clear that I felt they fell well short of the party's needs:

We need a leader who can attract thousands of ordinary Canadians with their extraordinary strengths. We need someone who will win support on the farms, in the factories, from young and old, and gain respect on the buses as well as in the boardrooms. As a party, we need a leader who has a proven ability to work with others, who can bring all our energies together in an overwhelming onslaught on the malaise of this country and on the divisive deceit of its present government. I am confident that as leader I can do these things.

I am not a candidate because I am a woman. But I say to you quite frankly that because I am a woman, my candidacy helps our party. It shows that in the Conservative party there are no barriers to anyone who has demonstrated serious intentions and earned the right to be heard. It proves that the leadership of this great party is not for sale to any alliance of the powerful and the few.

I talked about the need to ensure economic stability with balanced prosperity, to help the provinces to use their vast resources to build new industrial corridors in the western provinces and the Maritimes. I promised to implement a sensible policy of bilingualism – this in a party that was not always sensible on the issue – to return Canada to a position of prestige in the world, to re-equip the military, and so on. If I did not touch every single base, I think I hit most of them.

When Hellyer addressed the convention, he made the fatal error of emphasizing what he saw as divisions in the party. It was an evening when delegates wanted to hear about unity, about the bright future that awaited us in the months ahead. They did not want to rake up old differences and old grievances. Paul misread the mood entirely. Looking directly at me, he called on the delegates not to allow the Red Tories to take over the party. That was a huge blunder and Hellyer knew it instantly when a large number of delegates – not all of them my supporters by any means – booed vigorously. And they cheered when I looked straight at Hellyer, reminded the crowd of his defection from the Liberal Party after he lost his bid for its leadership, and declared: "I am a Conservative by conviction, not convenience."

Although I thought I got the better of the exchange that evening, it probably did neither of us any good in the voting the next day. But at least my vote increased between the first and second ballots, while Hellyer's collapsed. Senator Grattan O'Leary, the grand old man of the party, told me afterward that my speech was the best of the evening. Coming from Grattan, a great orator, it was a compliment to treasure.

I suspect, however, that most delegates did not remember what I said so much as they remembered the way I entered the arena. We decided we wanted to do something dramatic. In the normal course, a candidate is introduced, his delegates cheer and his youthful supporters jump up and down, shouting and waving lollipop signs. These floor demonstrations are all pretty much the same, and when they go on too long, they steal precious minutes from the candidate's speech. We told our supporters not to demonstrate, cheer, or even applaud. We wanted silence.

When my name was announced, the spotlight picked out a solitary piper standing in the entrance, playing "The Skye Boat Song" – the saga of the first Flora Macdonald. As he moved onto the floor, other pipers and drummers moved in behind him until there were forty-nine of them, volunteers recruited from across Eastern Ontario. The haunting music swelled, filling the arena, as only the pipes can. The pipers and drummers formed a corridor through which I walked to the stage – I felt as though I was floating. As I passed, they fell in behind me and, when I reached the podium, they switched from "The Skye Boat Song" to "Mairi's Wedding" and quick-stepped out of the hall. It was just spectacular!

How I wish I could say the same about the voting the next day! We were confident we would be where we wanted to be, in third place on the first ballot, behind Wagner and Mulroney. Michael Hatfield and Les Foreman had been tracking all committed and uncommitted delegates at the convention. They were convinced I had 350 delegates absolutely committed on the first ballot – 350 sure votes. A CTV survey put my delegate count at 325. And when Claude Wagner's workers counted the number of delegates wearing Flora buttons in the lineups to vote, they came up with 328.

Anything in that range – 325, 328, 350 – would put me comfortably in third place, ahead of Joe Clark.

Joe and I both knew we would be standing together on the final ballot against Wagner or conceivably Mulroney. There was no formal agreement of any kind. We understood each other. We understood that when one of us had to drop out, their support would go to the other. We represented the same values, and we both drew our support from the progressive wing of the party. We shared the same friends. Lowell Murray, for example, was working for me, but he was a great friend of Joe's, too. Eddie Goodman made no secret of the fact that the only person other than me he would support was Clark. I knew if I could not win, Joe was the only one I would be comfortable with as leader. And I knew Joe felt the same way. There would be no secret deals, no last-minute negotiations under the stands. We understood how the drama would play out.

While I waited in my box in the stands for the count, I was as confident as I could reasonably be that Joe would be coming to me, and not the other way around. I was dumbstruck when the totals were announced. I was speechless. I could not believe my eyes or my ears. I felt as though my windpipe had been cut. I could not breathe. Or as Hugh Hanson put it, "Flora was gob-smacked. She was eviscerated."

I had only 214 votes. I could not understand it. Where had my other votes gone? If 328 Flora buttons went into the polling booths, why did only 214 Flora votes come out? It could not be. I turned to someone – to Kathy Davis, I think, the wife of Ontario's premier – and said, "There's a mistake." When Hugh looked at me, I shook my head and told him, "No, no. This is wrong." We all thought that the announcement had been wrong, that the announcer meant to say 314 not 214.

At 214, I was finished – I knew that. I was 63 votes behind Clark. Worse, I was actually in sixth place, behind Wagner, Mulroney, Clark, and even Jack Horner and Paul Hellyer. The first ballot looked like this:

Claude Wagner: 531
Brian Mulroney: 357
Joe Clark: 277
Jack Horner: 235
Paul Hellyer: 231
Flora MacDonald: 214

Sinclair Stevens: 182
John Fraser: 127
James Gillies: 87
Patrick Nowlan: 86
Heward Grafftey: 33
(A nuisance candidate, Richard Quittenton, got no votes.)

We stared at one another in horror and disbelief. The disappointment, the feeling of betrayal, was almost too much. Some of my
people, including Eddie Goodman, were urging me to withdraw at
once and go to Clark as our best chance of stopping Wagner or
Mulroney. "Now's time, got to go, got to go," Eddie shouted, "Got
to make your move right now."

I guess it all went in one ear and out the other. Although it was
obviously over for me, I could not make the move. Part of me clung
to the hope that the first-ballot count had been wrong. I felt I owed
it to the people who had made such a huge emotional investment in
my campaign to stay on for another ballot. I even thought we might
be able to close the gap a bit on the second ballot. So I stayed on,
and I think it was the right decision. My vote did grow. Although
I picked up only twenty-five votes, it was enough to let me march to
Joe's box with my head high.[6]

On the second ballot, Clark moved ahead of Mulroney into second
place. On the third, he closed to within thirty-four votes of Wagner,
and he won it on the fourth, 1,187 votes to 1,112.

They have a term to describe what happened to me at that 1976
convention. It's known as the "Flora Syndrome." People say they
love you. They promise to vote for you. They even wear your campaign button into the polling booth. Then they vote for someone
else. They do not tell you what they intend to do because they do
not want to hurt you.

We will never know for sure, but the best analysis I can offer
is that I was let down, not by men delegates deciding at the last
moment that they did not want a woman leader, but by older women
delegates who could not quite bring themselves to accept that one of
their own gender really could lead a national political party or government. As I observed earlier, this was before Margaret Thatcher
became Britain's prime minister (in 1979). Perhaps if Thatcher had
come on the scene a few years earlier, the outcome would have been
different on that February Sunday in Ottawa in 1976.

Whatever the complicated explanation might have been, Hugh Hanson had a simple, blunt one of his own when he told Harry Bruce of *The Canadian* magazine: "The Progressive Conservative party proved today that it hasn't got the balls to elect a woman leader."

POSTSCRIPT

Defeat is never easy to accept. I know it was hard for me after the convention. It was particularly hard for Brian Mulroney. Two years later, in 1978, I was in Quebec City to attend a conference on Canada's future that Mulroney was chairing. I was seated next to my old friend and supporter Tom Sloan throughout the proceedings, and as they ended, Tom suggested we have dinner together. We found ourselves in a very nice restaurant where Mulroney and some of his friends were dining. During the evening he came over to speak to us. He was in a black mood. He launched into a tirade against me for having supported Joe Clark two years earlier: "We've been friends for a long, long time. We've worked together, and you deserted me." I was completely taken aback. Tom felt he had to intervene, so he stood up. Sloan may have been a gentle giant, but he was a good deal bigger than Mulroney. Brian calmed down pretty quickly, and Tom and I left the restaurant. Some weeks afterward, I received an apologetic note from Brian. The next time I was speaking in Montreal I went to his house to see him.

12

Joe Clark

The next three years were my most miserable in public life. I was depressed following the leadership convention. My spirits did not recover until we got into the campaign for the general election of 1979. Some friends worried I had lost my zest for politics. I had put every ounce of my energy and ambition into the pursuit of the leadership. It was not until I heard those first-ballot results that I realized how deeply I wanted to be leader. Now I had to buck up and face reality. I was an ordinary member of Parliament, with an ordinary member's duties as an opposition critic and committee member, and with an ordinary member's responsibilities to her constituents.

No one had to tell me that I had almost certainly missed my only chance at the leadership. I was about to celebrate (if "celebrate" is the word) my fiftieth birthday. Joe Clark was only thirty-six. There was every reason to expect he would be our leader for many years to come.

It would have been unbearable if the new leader had been anyone other than Clark, but Joe was someone I could live and work with. We were not close friends – not in the way that I was close to Lowell Murray, Richard Hatfield, or Dalton Camp. We were political comrades, philosophical allies, and on a personal level we were comfortable with each other. We knew we could trust each other.

We were both elected to Parliament for the first time in 1972, and I can remember going out to Alberta to campaign for him in Rocky Mountain riding, which he won from an incumbent Liberal. In my early years in Parliament, I was the Conservative critic for the department then titled Indian Affairs and Northern Development and Joe was my deputy critic. We both served on the parliamentary committee to which the department reported – I because I was the spokesperson for the official opposition and Joe because the committee's mandate included national parks and Banff was in Joe's riding. It was during this period that Joe married Maureen McTeer, who worked in our caucus research office.

I was stunned by their marriage. I had assumed that Joe was like me – so consumed by political life that he would not let his attention be diverted by dating or courtship, let alone marriage. When Joe got married, the parliamentary committee was about to take off on a tour of parks in the Northwest Territories. Joe brought Maureen along so that committee trip could double as their honeymoon. How many other politicians would bring their new wife on a tour of northern parks with a group of middle-aged, mainly male parliamentarians? How many brides would agree to go? Joe and Maureen would, and they did.

Having worked together so closely over the years, Joe and I had become soul mates on many issues. He was more conservative than I on economic issues, but that was to be expected: His Alberta and my Maritimes had different needs and priorities. But we agreed on most social issues, including the rights of women. It was not just a matter of Maureen keeping her own name, although that did hurt Joe among some Conservatives, but he was truly committed to the equality of women in the party and in the country. He displayed genuine leadership on that issue.

After the leadership convention, I had asked Joe to make me the opposition critic for foreign affairs. He explained he could not do that. Claude Wagner had been our foreign affairs critic before the leadership race, and Joe knew that Wagner, a proud and sensitive man, would regard any other position as a demotion, a slight. Quebec was a very difficult province for us in those days. No matter how much time, effort, and money the party plowed into campaigns there, we harvested almost no seats. With Wagner as our Quebec leader, we had a star, a celebrity on whose coattails we hoped to ride to victory. So Claude remained our shadow foreign minister.[1]

What was my role to be? Joe asked me if I would agree to be our critic for federal-provincial relations. I was not enthusiastic. It struck me as a made-up job, a make-work project for poor Flora. We had not had a federal-provincial critic in the past. In fact, the Liberals in those days did not even have a minister of federal-provincial or intergovernmental affairs for a shadow minister to hold to account. For all practical purposes, that job fell to the prime minister. So without a flesh and blood minister to shadow, I became by default opposition critic to Pierre Trudeau, at least as far as constitutional matters and dealings with the provinces were concerned.

It was not as straightforward as that, unfortunately. Shadow cabinet ministers can be every bit as turf conscious as real cabinet ministers are. It did not happen every day, but disconcertingly often I would be preparing to brace Trudeau on some issue that I felt fell within the purview of federal-provincial affairs, only to have a Conservative colleague object. No, no, that involves farm policy. You should not ask about agriculture. Leave that to our agriculture critic. Or energy critic. Or health or communications critic. The problem with my assignment was that it had no definition, no handle that I could grab and say, "Aha! This is mine," and go after the prime minister on it. I had to carve out a niche for myself.

There was another problem. I had no background in constitutional issues or other aspects of federal-provincial relations. It is not a field in which I had any philosophical or political positions, although I was comfortable with Clark's general approach. I agreed with him that the Liberals were obsessed with building and maintaining the prerogatives of a strong federal government, that they had concentrated too much power in Ottawa, and that they had no respect for the constitutional rights of the provinces or for the political needs of provincial governments. It was not simply a matter of being opposed to whatever the Liberals stood for. Under Clark, the Progressive Conservatives embraced the concept of a more decentralized federation. Joe called his vision of Canada "a community of communities." The Liberals did not see Canada that way. They mocked Clark, saying his ambition would turn the prime minister into a headwaiter or doorman for the premiers.

Despite my misgivings, the federal-provincial assignment turned out reasonably well. It gave me an opportunity to help position the party for the next election. The constitution began to show up on the political radar in the second half of the 1970s. Over the course of the next five years, it would become the most divisive issue in the country. There would be a pitched battle between Ottawa and the provinces, a reference to the Supreme Court of Canada, the patriation of the Constitution from Britain, and finally a negotiated agreement – accepted by all governments except Quebec's – that included the adoption of the Canadian Charter of Rights and Freedoms as part of the Constitution of Canada.

My aim, as the Tory critic, was to make our party's voice heard in a debate in which the prime minister and the premiers were the principal protagonists. I took the first step in September 1977, when I organized a one-day meeting in Kingston between Joe Clark and the four Progressive Conservative premiers: Frank Moores of Newfoundland, Richard Hatfield of New Brunswick, William Davis of Ontario, and Peter Lougheed of Alberta. We held it in the hall where Sir John A. Macdonald had first been nominated as a candidate for Parliament.

Although the conference was more for show than for substance, we were able to achieve a couple of objectives. One was to present Joe, the opposition leader, on the same platform as the premiers – meeting them as equals – and to show that he was every bit as capable of dealing with provincial leaders as Prime Minister Trudeau was. Of course, the fact that all four of the premiers were Tories simplified the effort, as some journalists were unkind enough to note. The second objective was to set out some policy approaches that would distinguish our party from Trudeau's Liberals.

At the end of the day, we produced a joint statement, endorsed by the five participants, entitled, "Making Canada Work." The statement was not actually written during the day of the meeting. Joe's staff had prepared it weeks in advance, and three drafts had been circulated to the premiers before they arrived in Kingston. Once there, they deleted some bits and reworded others. If the document fell some distance short of inspirational prose, it did contain two proposals designed to set us apart from the Liberals. One was a proposal to entrench in the Constitution of Canada the principle of equalization – the financial obligation of richer provinces to support poorer ones. The second was a constitutional restraint that we proposed to impose on the federal government's spending power to discourage Ottawa from invading areas of provincial jurisdiction. Both of these proposals spoke to Clark's belief that, under Trudeau, too much authority had been concentrated in federal hands and that the federation would work better if more powers were distributed among the provinces.[2]

Although the Kingston conference did not strike fear into the hearts of many Liberals, it did annoy Trudeau. He chose the day of our meeting to announce a cabinet shuffle. As shuffles go, it was a puny one, but it served to divert some media attention from us in Kingston.

The conference disappointed me in one respect. I had hoped that we would take the leadership on Senate reform, a perennial issue that successive governments had attempted to address, with a uniform lack of success. The model I preferred would have converted the Senate of Canada into a House of the Provinces. Ottawa would surrender its patronage power to appoint members of the upper house. Instead, provincial governments would choose senators to send to Ottawa as delegates. The idea was to balance the power of the rep-by-pop House of Commons with an upper house that would clearly speak for the regions, especially the smaller, less populous provinces. The change, if accepted, would have gone some distance to weakening the federal hold on the levers of political power, a hold that we maintained was becoming a stranglehold under the Trudeau Liberals.

Alas, the House of the Provinces was dead on arrival in Kingston. Alberta's Lougheed, the most determined of the four provincial leaders, was having none of it. He jumped on my proposal with both feet and stomped it to death. He believed in executive federalism. If Alberta had something to say to the federal government, he, the premier, would say it to the prime minister. Or his cabinet ministers would say it to their opposite numbers in the federal cabinet. There was no way an obscure bunch of anonymous senators was going to speak for his province. I had always liked Peter Lougheed, but I felt bruised by his rough rejection of my plan.

As I have said, the years from 1976 to 1979 were tough ones for me. I felt as though I was drifting without a compass. It took the prospect of the next election, which we expected to be called in 1978, to keep me focussed. We knew Trudeau was in trouble again, as he had been in 1972. He seemed to have exhausted the patience of the electorate. He was in danger of letting power slip away from him again.

We could feel the momentum moving our way when we won two key by-elections in 1976. John Crosbie, who was destined to be a senior minister in both the Clark and Mulroney governments, won in St John's West in Newfoundland. In Ontario, Jean Pigott stunned the Liberals by taking Ottawa-Carleton, a Liberal fief that had just been vacated by John Turner, Trudeau's finance minister.[3] As 1977 unfolded, it was clear the Liberals did not know what to do. In the normal course, Trudeau would have called a general election in 1978, four years after the last one. But he procrastinated. By the fall of 1978, with fifteen vacancies in the House, he was forced to call what was in effect a mini-general election. On 16 October, voters in the fifteen constituencies went to the polls, with devastating results for the Liberals. They lost all twelve of the by-elections outside Quebec. We took ten of them, including two long-time Liberal seats that were won by future Tory ministers David Crombie in Toronto Rosedale and Robert de Cotret in Ottawa Centre.

We were buoyant as 1978 turned into 1979 with still no election in sight. We knew we were running ahead of the Liberals in most parts of English Canada, although not in Quebec. We were confident we could win the country if we did not make any mistakes. The question we could not answer was whether we would be able to elect enough members to form a majority government. Or would it be a minority?

Trudeau finally called the election for 22 May 1979. Clark ran an exceptionally cautious campaign. He attacked the Liberals for their budget deficits, for inflation, and for the country's high unemployment. "It's time for a change," he declared, without being precise about the changes he was advocating. He avoided making specific promises that would invite Liberal fire. It was very much a defensive, front runner's campaign, designed to protect our party's lead, and avoid errors. If Joe had campaigned more aggressively, he might have managed to eke out a majority. But he was determined to protect what he had and not risk it by stretching for a majority.

We won 136 seats, falling six short of a majority.[4] Thirteen days later, Joe Clark was sworn in as Canada's sixteenth prime minister. He was one day shy of his fortieth birthday, making him the youngest prime minister in history. For the first time in sixteen years, Canada had a Tory government – and I was going to be part of it!

13

Foreign Minister

Following the 1979 election, what I needed most was to get out of Ottawa and away from the crazy, swirling rumour mill during the government transition. While Joe Clark worked on his cabinet, I returned to "my" convent in St Georges Ouest, telling people I wanted to work on my French. I was not worried. I knew Joe would call and I was confident he would have an important portfolio for me. I was elated when he phoned to ask me to be his secretary of state for External Affairs (or minister of Foreign Affairs, as we call it nowadays). It was the job I had longed for, and I accepted instantly. While the nuns celebrated, I went to Montreal to shop for a new dress with my friend Greta Chambers. The appointment certainly called for a new dress. Not only would I be Canada's first female foreign minister, I would be one of a very few women in the world to hold that position in their government.

When I returned to Ottawa, I was stunned to discover how frantic the next few weeks were going to be. Ten days after we took office, I was off to Paris with John Crosbie, our finance minister, for a meeting of the Organization for Economic Co-operation and Development (OECD). Next came Tokyo with Clark and Crosbie for the annual summit of the leaders of the G7 industrial nations, followed by Geneva for a United Nations conference on refugees, then a tour of African nations with Clark, including the Commonwealth Heads of Government Meeting in Lusaka, Zambia. It was a good thing I loved to travel.

As a new government, we faced urgent international issues we had to address without delay. One was the plight of the Asian "boat people" – including an estimated eight hundred and forty thousand Vietnamese who fled their country following the end of the Vietnam War in 1975, risking their lives in a desperate search for safe havens.[1] How many boat people would Canada accept? A second urgent priority was to find a way to extricate the government from an ill-advised promise that Clark had made during the election campaign in a bid to win votes in the Jewish community, primarily in Toronto. Under pressure from Ron Atkey, our immigration critic (and soon to be immigration minister), Clark had pledged a Tory government would move Canada's embassy in Israel from Tel Aviv to Jerusalem – a symbolic move fraught with significance in the troubled Middle East. Although the promise did not produce the dividend in Jewish votes that Atkey and Clark hoped for, it touched off a firestorm in the Arab world. One of my first chores as foreign minister was to put the fire out.

Just as we were getting these issues under control, Iran erupted, and it became our third urgent priority. In early November 1979, students and Islamic militants, followers of the Ayatollah Khomeini, rebelled against the Shah, overthrew his regime, and physically overran the United States embassy in Tehran. Many of the embassy personnel were taken hostage. Six managed to escape and sought sanctuary with Canadian diplomats. For the next twelve weeks – until we could smuggle them out of Iran – the presence of the six Americans was a tightly guarded secret in Ottawa and Washington. It came to be known as the "Canadian Caper," and I was caught up in the centre of it.

As a new and inexperienced government, we were so busy putting out fires that we did not do what we should have been doing. We should have acted boldly. We should have taken the political initiative. We should have exploited our election momentum by calling Parliament without delay, presenting a speech from the throne and establishing our priorities while our opponents were still in post-election disarray. Instead, we chose to be cautious – and painfully slow. We waited four months, until 9 October, before meeting Parliament. Meanwhile, as we stumbled and made the mistakes new governments tend to commit, the opposition parties were able to regroup. By 9 October, they were ready for us.

All this was in the future on the day Joe Clark called me at the convent. First came the swearing-in of the new government on 4 June. I could not believe how nervous I was as I waited with my colleagues at Rideau Hall to take the oath of office from Governor General

Ed Schreyer. My hand was shaking as I signed the registry. My old nemesis, John Diefenbaker, was in the front row. I foolishly thought that Diefenbaker, now that our party had returned to power, might have mellowed toward me. After all, he had made a point of complimenting me on the populist leadership campaign I had run three years earlier. But old animosities do not die that easily.

As Diefenbaker and I walked out of Rideau Hall side by side, I recalled that he had been sworn in as prime minister for the first time in another June – 1957. I turned to him with a big smile. "Mr Diefenbaker, this is a glorious day. I remember what it was like for you twenty-two years ago." And he turned and looked at me and said, "You! You! They should never have made you foreign minister. They could have made you postmaster general. Or minister of Immigration. But not External Affairs!" He turned on his heel and walked away. It was the last time I saw him or heard from him. Two months later, he was dead.

As a senior minister, I was expected to attend Diefenbaker's funeral. That required a personal concession: I had to wear a hat to church. I am not and never have been a hat person. Only twice in my adult life have I ever worn one. Diefenbaker's funeral was the first. The second was when I was in Brian Mulroney's cabinet and the Queen came to Kingston; I had to be "properly" attired to show her around. Grudgingly, I bought a new hat for each occasion. I still have both of them and have never worn either since.

Diefenbaker's funeral was extraordinary. He had personally and meticulously planned and plotted every detail of the service and every minute and every inch of the route as his body was carried by a special train from Ottawa, across Ontario and his beloved Prairies to Saskatoon, where he was buried beside his late wife Olive outside the Diefenbaker Library at the University of Saskatchewan.

It was a beautiful afternoon for the funeral in Ottawa. Cabinet ministers and other privy councillors walked with the hearse to Christ Church Cathedral, an Anglican church, where the service was held. Everyone – the cabinet, MPs, senators, Supreme Court judges, and provincial premiers – was seated according to Diefenbaker's precise instructions. Joe Clark and Maureen McTeer were in the first row on the right, with Governor General Schreyer and his wife Lily on the left side of the aisle. I was in the row behind Joe and Maureen. The coffin was brought in, and the service was about to begin, when suddenly I saw the government's chief of protocol come over to speak to Clark. They whispered for two or three minutes, as we all waited for the service to begin. Then Joe stood up and looked around. He scanned the congregation, turned and then spoke again to the chief of protocol, who nodded and disappeared. Joe sat down, and the service began. I was puzzled and later I asked Clark what had been going on.

"Well," he said, "the chief of protocol came in, and he said, 'Prime Minister, we've just been advised that there's a bomb in the basement of the church.'" And Joe, being kind of startled by this, asked, "Well, what are my options?" That's something Joe would say! The chief of protocol told him, "Well, we can take it seriously and people will have to leave the cathedral while we search the whole church and see if the bomb is real and remove it. So that's one option. The other is, you could ignore it as a hoax, and go ahead with the service."

Joe said to me, "I stood up and I looked at all these people, the members of the cabinet, the caucus, the provincial premiers, the Supreme Court, all of these dignitaries. I turned to the chief of protocol, and I said, 'There's only one person who would like to see the end of all these people, and he's lying right there in the coffin.' So I told him to go ahead with the service."[2]

THE BOAT PEOPLE OF SOUTHEAST ASIA

My first test as the new external affairs minister came at the three-day G7 economic summit in Tokyo at the end of June. The first ministers, foreign ministers, and finance ministers all met together on the first and third days. On day two, the foreign ministers and finance ministers split off for separate meetings. We met without aides or advisers in the room. Joe Clark, United States President Jimmy Carter, Britain's new Prime Minister Margaret Thatcher and the other four leaders had one advantage we did not have. Under each leader's desk was a button they could press to summon an adviser to help if they were unsure about an issue. The foreign and finance ministers had no magic buttons. We were expected to fly solo.

We had been briefed, of course. Before leaving for Ottawa, I was given several huge briefing books. One dealt with crisis of the boat people of Southeast Asia. It was not an issue I knew much about. I used to tell people that I regarded my ancestors and the other Scottish highlanders who braved the North Atlantic to reach places like Cape Breton to be the first boat people. Their hardships, however, paled in comparison to the ordeals experienced by refugees from Vietnam, Laos, and Cambodia in the wake of the Vietnam War.

A CBC report captured the panic and pandemonium when Saigon fell to the Communist North Vietnamese in 1975:

> The scenes were wrenching – people trying and failing to force their way into the US Embassy, men being punched down as they tried to board American helicopters, Vietnamese babies being passed over fences to open hands and an unknown future. Those South Vietnamese allies left behind faced years of hard labour, imprisonment and death. The same was true for American allies in Laos, where an estimated 10 per cent of the Hmong tribespeople were killed by Communist forces.

Those who could, fled – by air, land, or sea. In the spring of 1975, one hundred and thirty thousand refugees escaped Vietnam. Tiny boats full of South Vietnamese soldiers and their families set off down the Mekong River in the hopes of surviving the six hundred-mile journey to the Malaysian coast. They were the first wave of Vietnamese boat people. But they were not the last.

An estimated 25 per cent perished in the effort.

At Tokyo, the foreign ministers were asked what their countries were prepared to do in the face of this humanitarian crisis. Between 1975 and the end of 1978, nine thousand Indochinese refugees had come to Canada. The Trudeau Liberals then announced the government would resettle an additional five thousand refugees by the end of 1979 – a welcome commitment but a small one given the magnitude of the need. Of course, it was not as simple or straightforward as throwing open the country's doors and saying, "Come on in!" The concerns of bureaucracy and the niceties of the federal system had to be served. We had to notify the provinces that refugees would be arriving and how many each province could expect to receive. Then federal-provincial agreements had to be negotiated for such things as health care, housing, schooling, welfare, and so on.

I began to realize the complexity of the issue. There were major foreign policy implications for the whole of Southeast Asia; the boat people came to symbolize the struggle for control of the region. The people who were fleeing from Vietnam were descendants of Chinese who had settled there much earlier. While the Soviet Union had control of the North Vietnamese, China had ties to many other countries in the region. When the Chinese-Vietnamese began to be expelled from Vietnam, China came out against the Soviet Union, with whom they had had a more or less compatible relationship until then. As these complications became evident, I realized I needed to educate myself about the underlying causes; from then on, I made sure to be well briefed.

Thousands of people were dying. They shoved off from the coast of Vietnam in small, leaky craft; if overcrowding did not cause them to founder, they were sunk by pirates. Or they landed on some remote island with no food or no water. The impact of television was startling. We had never before experienced a major international humanitarian crisis that played out day after day on the screens in our living rooms. The TV coverage had an immediate and continuing impact on people across Canada. We felt we were right on the edge of an incredible disaster.

The public response was intensifying. We could feel it. The Canadian people expected their government to do something, and they wanted to be involved themselves, in some direct and personal way. Humanitarian assistance has been an enduring feature of Canadian policy, and I left the Tokyo summit determined that Canada must do our fair share, and more, to relieve the plight of the boat people. On the flight home, I talked to my deputy minister, Allan Gotlieb, about ways the government could involve the Canadian people in an unprecedented humanitarian effort. At the time, Canada was experiencing an economic downturn and the government was facing some severe financial problems. There was no spare cash lying around. Yet we had to do something, and we needed to do it right away. I told Gotlieb about the offerings envelopes we had in church in Cape Breton when I was young. One envelope had black printing; it was for the maintenance of the church, the minister's salary, buying coal to heat the building, and those sorts of operating expenses. The other envelope, with red printing, was for the missionary and maintenance fund, to send missionaries overseas and to help the people in Third World countries. My father always told me, even when times were tough – as they often were in Cape Breton – "We've got to do both!" And, I thought, this is what it is really all about: as a government, we must pay our own bills, and we must help others who have nothing at all.

The officials in External Affairs were supportive. They proposed we raise the Trudeau government's target of five thousand refugees for 1979 to twelve thousand, and we announced a decision to do so in June. But that was not enough, as Clark and I acknowledged when we were in Tokyo. Back in Ottawa, I took a proposal to cabinet that we increase the number to forty thousand. My Red Tory colleague and friend, David MacDonald, the new secretary of state, who in private life had been a United Church clergyman in Prince Edward Island, urged the cabinet to make it sixty thousand. In the end we sawed it off at fifty thousand – a figure that was readily acceptable to Atkey whose Immigration Department would be in charge of settling the refugees in Canada.

Two days after that announcement, I was in Geneva to address the United Nations Conference on Refugees. It was a short speech, just ten minutes, but I think it was the best speech I ever made. It was crisp and sharp – and it provoked the Soviet Union representatives to walk out in the middle of it. Speaking from the podium in the main meeting hall of the old League of Nations building – a venue that had known its share of frustration and failure – I tried to tell it like it was. I told the delegates that we could not resolve the humanitarian crisis in Indochina without addressing the underlying political issues that caused the crisis. "[A]lleviating the suffering is not solving the problem," I said. "To lower the fever is not to eradicate the infection. It is the cause of the problem we must address. We must identify the reason for this crisis and deal with it."

The reason for the outflow of refugees, I reminded the conference, was the "flagrant [and] outrageous violation of human rights" by the so-called "countries of exodus" – Vietnam, Cambodia, and Laos – which persecute their citizens, especially their ethnic Chinese, and force them to flee. I did not have to state the obvious: that the violation of human rights was taking place with the knowledge and support of those countries' patron, the Soviet Union.

Canada, I said, demands that the countries of exodus "deal with their citizens without discrimination and in a humane manner." I continued: "The international community holds them responsible for the fate of all their citizens. Certainly, their citizens must be able to exercise the fundamental human right to leave their homeland if they so wish. Canada has repeatedly stressed the obligation of all countries to honour this basic right. [...] The international community rejects as an unconscionable violation of human rights the attempt to expel or otherwise eliminate any ethnic community or any socio-economic group."

That was tough talk coming from the foreign minister of Canada – and a brand-new minister in a brand-new government, at that! While the Soviet representatives walked out, the Chinese delegation came over en masse and embraced me. Kurt Waldheim, the secretary general of the UN, was seated above and behind me while I spoke. I could not see him, but I knew he was not amused. I thought he might use his gavel to hit me on the head to make me shut up. He did not, but later in the day he called to remonstrate with me for injecting a dose of political reality into a humanitarian conference. I got through that dressing-down relatively unscathed.

When we got back to Ottawa, we set about honouring our refugee commitment. We did something unique. We invented a sponsorship program. We invited the Canadian people to sponsor Vietnamese families – to welcome them into their homes and communities and to cover their expenses until they were settled. If individual Canadians would sponsor one family, the government would match their commitment by sponsoring a second family. The response was overwhelming. Whole communities banded together to raise money to sponsor refuge families. We used military aircraft to fly them to Mirabel Airport, north of Montreal, and to Edmonton for processing and medical examinations. Our target of fifty thousand was quickly exceeded. When the total reached sixty thousand, I was forced to cap the program. We were out of money.

Money or no money, the boat people kept coming with private sponsorship – one hundred thousand of them in the end. The largest numbers settled in Toronto and Montreal, with significant groups in Vancouver, Calgary, and Edmonton. Cities and towns that had not previously had a Vietnamese community suddenly had one. They went everywhere, even to the Northwest Territories. The majority of the refugees spoke no English or French, yet they adapted. They learned the language, adjusted to the climate, absorbed Canadian ways, found jobs or started businesses, and fitted into the communities that welcomed them with open arms. I could not have been more thrilled.

Canada's intake of Indochinese refugees was the greatest of any country in the world on a per capita basis. It was a unique demonstration of the way Canadians on their own initiative could reinforce and strengthen a government program. And we were recognized by the world community. Each year, the United Nations High Commissioner for Refugees awards the Nansen Medal to the individual who has done the most to alleviate the plight and suffering of refugees. In 1985, it was awarded for the first time not to an individual but to the people of a nation state – to the Canadian people for their voluntary outpouring of generosity toward the boat people in 1979–80.

MOVING THE CANADIAN EMBASSY TO JERUSALEM

Let me backtrack for a moment. After the cabinet was sworn in on 4 June, three of us – John Crosbie, Ray Hnatyshyn, the minister of Energy, Mines and Resources, and I – were called back for a press conference. The very first question, directed to me, was about our campaign promise to move the Canadian Embassy in Israel to Jerusalem. Joe Clark had made the commitment in the heat of the election campaign, in April, four weeks before polling day. He made it on the very day he was to meet in Toronto with leaders of the Canada-Israel Committee whose support he was courting. It came at a crucial moment for the Middle East. Egyptian-Israeli peace negotiations, brokered by United States President Jimmy Carter, had produced an agreement signed by Egypt's President Anwar Sadat and Menachem Begin, Israel's prime minister – an achievement for which Sadat and Begin would share the Nobel Peace Prize. Canada had studiously avoided taking sides, but once the agreement was reached, Clark, Ron Atkey, and other supporters of Israel in our party argued it would not hurt to let our partiality show – and it might help us to make inroads into the Jewish vote.[3] "Jerusalem," Joe declared, "is and always has been the capital of the Jewish people and the Jewish spirit. 'Next year in Jerusalem' is a Jewish prayer, which we intend to make a Canadian reality."

We anticipated protests from the Arab world. We were aware that Carter had made the same promise, to move the US embassy from Tel Aviv to Jerusalem, during his election campaign three years earlier, that he had encountered a firestorm of protest, and that he had quietly shelved the promise once he was in the White House. Even so, we were caught unprepared by the uproar we had created. It began almost immediately following Joe's statement, subsided a little bit in the last week of the election campaign, then intensified the moment we won the election and the move of the embassy was no longer an opposition party policy but took on the force – and, in Arab eyes, the menace – of Canadian government policy.

The Palestine Liberation Organization declared the decision to be "an act of aggression," and the Canada-Arab Federation, a lobby group, labelled it "a declaration of war on 900 million Muslims." Arab ambassadors in Ottawa protested en masse; our diplomats based in the Middle East were called in by their host governments to be lectured about the folly of our policy; Bell Canada was warned that a one billion dollar contract in Saudi Arabia could be cancelled "at the stroke of a pen"; DeHavilland Aircraft, with $600 million worth of business at stake, found doors closed in their salesmen's faces across the region; at home, our friends in the foreign policy and trade communities thought we had taken leave of our senses; in Washington, the State Department official responsible for Canadian affairs registered his government's concern that our policy would be used by other Arab nations to destabilize President Sadat's peace efforts.

I was desperately worried. Here is what I said in a secret memorandum to Prime Minister Clark as we took office:

> This is a time, in the wake the Egypt-Israel peace treaty, when Arab nerves are raw and their reactions emotional and inherently unpredictable. As the collective measures that are being taken against Egypt indicate, moreover, it is probable that any retaliation against Canada would be undertaken by the majority of Arab states in concert, if a leading country initiated action. Their purpose would be to discourage any other government from following our example. Accordingly our action could have serious effects on Canadian interests in the Middle East as well as in our diplomatic effectiveness in connection with the Arab-Israeli conflict.

The words and the warning they conveyed, while written for me by department officials, reflected my true feelings on the Jerusalem issue. Although I had expressed my view to the prime minister in my memo, that advice was secret. I could not state it publicly because it was diametrically opposed to the policy on which our party had campaigned. I certainly could not disown the Jerusalem policy on our very first day in office when I met the press following the swearing-in. So I fudged. I told the reporters that moving the embassy was not a government priority; we had many more urgent issues facing us, so the embassy would have to wait on the back burner for a while. There would be opportunity for stakeholders to be heard. We would not do anything precipitously. There would be lots of analysis and consultation. We would keep Parliament and the public apprised of our plans, and so on.

These obvious evasions did not silence the critics. Nor did they satisfy Joe Clark. His belief in the embassy move seemed to grow stronger as the chorus of critics grew louder. The criticism made him dig in.[4] Within days of taking office, he held a private meeting with all the deputy ministers in the government. He was concerned, with some cause, that the deputies, after servicing Liberal ministers for so many years, might find it hard to transfer their loyalty to their new Conservative masters. He wanted to be reassured that everyone was onside. He told the deputy ministers that if they could not support his government's policies, they were free to look for employment elsewhere. Unfortunately, he chose to cite the Jerusalem embassy issue as a litmus test of the loyalty he demanded. He told them he expected them all to support that policy.

It was at this point that I went off to Paris with Crosbie for the OECD meeting. On the day I got back Ron Atkey went on Cross-Country Checkup on CBC Radio to take calls about why we were moving the embassy in Israel. He stirred up a hornet's nest. It was worse than that. It became a real barrage. I felt as though we were in front of a firing squad. We had to do something and do it quickly.

Actually, we had to do two things. We had to buy some time – enough time for the furore to die down and the public's attention to shift to other matters – and we had to find a way to abandon our foolhardy campaign promise with as little loss of political face as possible.

"What should we do? What can we do?" Allan Gotlieb and I asked each other. As I recall, it was Gotlieb who suggested we appoint an emissary to consult the regimes in the Middle East and produce a set of recommendations for the government. I came up with the name of Robert Stanfield. I went to see Clark, who quickly agreed with the choice. Then he had to talk Stanfield into it.

Bob was reluctant. He was well aware that his true assignment was not to consult with leaders in the region or to prepare recommendations. It was to find an escape hatch to get us out of the mess we had created for ourselves. And that was what Stanfield did. After touring the Middle East and meeting many of the leaders, he delivered an interim report with the recommendation that the embassy move be abandoned.[5]

THE "CANADIAN CAPER"

∽

On Sunday, 4 November 1979, supporters of Iran's new ruler Ayatollah Ruhollah Khomeini overran the American embassy in Tehran, taking fifty-two diplomats and staff members hostage. Six others managed to escape and for the next several days they moved from place to place in the capital, looking for a safe refuge. One of them, Robert Anders, a consular officer, was a friend and tennis partner of John Sheardown, the senior immigration official at the Canadian embassy in Tehran. Sheardown went to Ambassador Ken Taylor who agreed they should take the Americans in. They alerted Ottawa.

∽

It was a Friday morning when I first heard about our American "houseguests," as we called them. At the time I had been more concerned with a different American – President Jimmy Carter, who was scheduled to come to Ottawa that weekend. With my officials, I had been involved in some awkward negotiations with Carter's national security adviser, Zbigniew Brzezinski. The issue was whether Carter's security people would be allowed to bring their guns into Canada and even to the House of Commons. I said, "No, they can't do that. We have our own police, the RCMP, here and they will provide whatever protection the president needs." We had a long argument about that. I said they could not come with their weapons – period. And that is the way it was in my mind until Thursday, as I recall, when Carter went on television to announce he could not leave Washington because of the hostage situation in Iran.

I went to the House to announce cancellation of the Carter visit. The next day, on Friday morning, I got a call from David Elder on my staff to come quickly to my Parliament Hill office where a group headed by Michael Shenstone, the department's director-general of African and Middle Eastern Affairs, were gathered. They told me we had five Americans hiding in the Sheardowns' house – they would later be joined by a sixth – and what should they do with them?

"What are your wishes, Minister?" they asked.

I said, "I'll consult with the PM when the House meets this morning." I asked Joe to stay on after Question Period – "There is something very urgent I have to talk to you about." Our seats were adjacent, and I said, "This is the situation, and my recommendation is we provide refuge for them."

He replied immediately, "Yes, certainly, I agree."

From then on, the houseguests were my responsibility. Joe kind of said, "This is your baby, now run with it." He did not second guess the decisions I made as the "Canadian caper" unfolded.

For the next couple of days in the House, I was pummeled by Pierre Trudeau, the opposition leader, about why we were not doing more than we were to help in the hostage crisis. "We're doing all we can, we're consulting with our Commonwealth partners," I responded, being as vague as possible. With Trudeau not about to let go of the issue, my major concern was to keep Canada's profile as low as I possibly could. We did not want people looking at our operation in Tehran too closely for fear that the presence of the Americans would become public. So I suggested to Clark that he speak to Trudeau, as one privy councillor to another, about what we were doing and why the safety both of the Americans and our own staff in Tehran depended on not attracting the attention of the Khomeini regime.

At the end of Question Period one day, Joe went over to speak to Trudeau, but the cross-examination of me did not stop. What really annoyed me was that this was not by Trudeau, rather it was his foreign affairs critic, Allan MacEachen. I have always thought that Trudeau either did not pass Clark's message along, or he may have said to Allan, "I may have been told this, but *you* haven't been." Anyway, when MacEachen kept raising the issue, it made me furious. I had explained to Joe, and I am sure he explained to Trudeau, how much this would endanger our own embassy people if the facts came out. In my anger, I came close to revealing the secret. "It involves the lives of American human beings who are hostages in Iran," I told MacEachen. "It involves as well the lives of Canadians who are in Iran – and that is something we must never forget." Fortunately, no one in the Press Gallery was paying attention to the exchange, and my indiscretion passed unnoticed.

Two of the six Americans moved in with Ken and Pat Taylor at the ambassador's residence while the other four stayed with John and Zena Sheardown. They were hidden there for the next eighty days, until 25 January 1980, unable to leave the house or communicate with anyone on the outside for fear the Iranian authorities would find them and arrest them. It was especially hard on the Sheardowns, having to accommodate four strangers without the large household staff that the Taylors had at the residence. I worried most about Zena Sheardown. If the worst happened, the Taylors and John Sheardown would have their diplomatic immunity to protect them from Iranian "justice," but Zena did not have the same protection because she was not a Canadian citizen yet. She was from Guyana, a lovely woman. John had married her there, and in those days you had to be in Canada for a period of years before you could become a citizen. She and John had never been back in Canada long enough.

While John and the Taylors were free to move about city as usual, Zena was trapped in that house with four strangers. She lived in fear of discovery, dreading every ring of the phone and every rap on the door, and allowing no one to come into the place. She hardly ever left the house. By the end, she was almost a basket case. Later, when it was all over and we were back in opposition, there was a big dispute over awarding the Order of Canada to the two couples. Ken Taylor and John Sheardown were admitted to the order in 1980, but not their wives, whose roles were as indispensable as their husbands'. Furious that the women were being slighted, I organized a lobbying campaign that had women across the country writing letters to Chief Justice Bora Laskin, who was the chair of the selection committee, demanding that the wives also be recognized. I took the fight to the floor of the House of Commons where I introduced a resolution citing the "courageous and indispensable role" the two women had played in the hostage crisis and urging that they, too, be recognized with the Order of Canada. On 27 January 1981, the House of Commons agreed, giving unanimous approval to my resolution. Later that year, the awards were presented to them. Because Zena Sheardown was not yet a citizen, hers was an honorary Order of Canada, with the word "honorary" being removed in 1986 when she became a Canadian at last.

I must add this. In my view, the real hero of the Canadian Caper was John Sheardown not Ken Taylor. John took the initiative. He ran the real risks when he took in the Americans and sheltered them. In the end, Taylor collected the headlines and the recognition – the Hollywood movie *Argo* made him an A-list celebrity – and he profited financially when he left the diplomatic service for the private sector.

This was far in the future in November 1979 as we tried to figure out how to keep the hostages' presence secret while working out a way to get them safely out of Iran. We let the White House know immediately that we were harbouring these six people. And then we began discussions and negotiations with the Washington intelligence community. We did a lot of spying for them in Tehran. Our staff would fan out around the city to see what was going on. When they came back, we would brief officials in Washington. The Central Intelligence Agency still had some agents operating under cover in Tehran and we began shipping in huge amounts of money in our diplomatic pouch to finance their activities. We had some security people there, too, and they fed us information to pass on to the Americans. I did not have much to do with the spying side of it. I would be told that we've got to do these things and I'd say, "You know what you're doing, go ahead and do it."

One of the first things we had to do was to get communications equipment into Tehran that would enable us to set up a dedicated link with a satellite so that we could pass messages in and out without the Iranians being aware. We sent a specialist to Tehran to operate the equipment.

While that was going in in Tehran, we had a small group in Ottawa working on a plan to extricate the six Americans. We needed Washington's cooperation, but it was slow in coming. I raised the issue on several occasions with Cyrus Vance, the secretary of state. At one point, I warned him, "Either you send somebody up to Ottawa to help us with this exit plan, or I'm going to put these hostages on bicycles and send them across the mountains to Turkey."

Was I serious? Maybe I was. I must have gotten through to Cy, because a few days later they sent a person from the CIA to Ottawa. We had started out with a plan to pass the six Americans off as people from the oil industry in western Canada who were investigating the potential for their companies in Iran. I thought it was a very good idea. As it turned out, the CIA had begun their own construct of a very elaborate exit plan. They set up a whole movie production centre in Los Angeles to make their scenario look real. The people we were holding were supposed to be involved in film production and to have gone into Iran under that guise. Now they would come out of the country using the same cover. Eventually the scheme gelled along the CIA's lines without anybody getting into a snit about whose plan it was.

While this was going on behind the scenes in late November 1979, I was busy preparing for another trip to Europe in December, starting in Paris with Ray Hnatyshyn for an international energy meeting, then on to Brussels with Defence Minister Allan McKinnon for a meeting of NATO defence and foreign ministers.

In Paris, the government of France put us up in ultimate luxury at the Hôtel de Crillon, on the Place de la Concorde at the foot of the Champs-Élysées. My suite seemed to go half the length of the corridor with bedrooms, an office, and a great living room. The morning after the energy meeting, I had a hair appointment. I was to give a speech to the Paris press gallery at noon. I had been working hard on the speech because it had to be entirely in French. I wanted to look my best, assured, and well-dressed. A man the hotel sent to the suite was supposed to be one of the top hair designers in France. He even had his own shampooist. They brought in a stand-up hair dryer that must have been the first one ever made. It had one ring at the top that would get very hot. They washed my hair, put it rollers, and plunked me under the hair dryer. And there I was with my speech, trying to commit as much of it to memory as I could, when suddenly I smelled something burning. My hair was on fire! I screamed for the hair designer, who had disappeared somewhere, as I pulled out the rollers and watched my hair come out in chunks. He had to redo my hair and put it in a different style to try to cover up this ring of burnt hair. It came out not badly in the end. But it was nerve-wracking, to say the least, to try to learn a big speech while your hair is smouldering.

Brussels was a disaster – because of what happened in Ottawa while we were in Belgium for the NATO meeting. On 11 December, Finance Minister Crosbie introduced the first – and, as it turned out, only – budget of the Clark government. The most contentious feature was an increase of eighteen cents per gallon in the excise tax on gasoline. Clark and Crosbie knew at once that we were in trouble. We did not have enough members to defeat a non-confidence motion introduced by the NDP's finance critic Bob Rae, the same Rae who years later became premier of Ontario. With the Liberals and NDP united against the budget, to survive we needed the votes of all Conservative MPs plus the five members of the tiny Quebec party, the Ralliement des Créditistes. But the Créditistes chose to abstain and three Tories were absent – including me, stranded in Brussels. Allan McKinnon had already flown back to Ottawa in time for the vote.

I stayed on for the foreign ministers' part of the meeting on 13 December. That afternoon, Brussels time, I got a call from Joe Clark.

"There's a possibility we could be defeated in the House tonight, can you get back?" he asked.

"Well, I'll certainly try," I replied. "I wish you'd told me that last night, because most of the planes going west will have left by this time."

Hugh Hanson, my chief of staff, and I tried frantically to find a plane going west from somewhere, anywhere, in Europe. Perhaps we could fly from Brussels to London or somewhere else and find a connection to North America that would get me to Ottawa in time. There were absolutely no flights available.

Joe had told me, "If you can't do anything, can you get back to Walter Baker (the government house leader who was in charge of the vote)?" So we called Baker and reported there were no scheduled flights that would get us there in time. "Can we hire a plane?" we asked. And Walter said yes. Hugh asked him, "How high can we go? $50,000?" and Walter agreed. So Hugh got on the phone to Concorde in Paris and offered to rent one of their new supersonic jetliners. We figured that if we could get a Concorde, we could just make it, provided they kept the division bells ringing long enough in the House. Concorde must have thought Hugh was out of his mind. Anyway, we could not get a Concorde. And there was nothing else we could do.

The whole budget affair was badly bungled. Clark could have postponed the vote until I and the other absent Conservatives could get back to Ottawa. The delay would also have given us time to negotiate with the Créditistes and perhaps time for a few wavering Liberals to develop cold feet over forcing another election so soon after the last one. Clark and his political advisers, however, were convinced that we would win the non-confidence vote or, if we did not, that we would easily win the ensuing general election.[6] They were wrong on both scores. We lost the non-confidence vote 139–133. And we were trounced in the election that followed in February.

So I was stranded in Brussels. When we finally accepted that we could not get back, Hugh and I went off to a big dinner and reception that the Americans were holding. Lord Byron would have been right at home with the sound of revelry in Belgium's capital that night. Under the circumstances, what else could we do except party? And we did, for the early part of the night. Back at the hotel, we sat up until four o'clock in the morning, waiting for the results from Ottawa. The next morning, I had to get on a plane and go home.

But something else had happened on my last day in Brussels. While I was still at the NATO meeting, I got a phone call from Washington, to say that Jean Pelletier, who was the Washington correspondent for Montreal's *La Presse* – and the son of Gerard Pelletier, the Canadian ambassador in Paris and a former Liberal cabinet minister – had tumbled to the fact that we were hiding six Americans in Tehran. When Pelletier contacted the Canadian Embassy in Washington for confirmation, they called me and I told Peter Towe, our ambassador, to call Pelletier back, explain the need for secrecy and to say, "If your father were our ambassador in Tehran rather than our ambassador in Paris, would you write that story?" Jean agreed to hold the story back. I promised that if it ever looked like the story might become public, he would be the first journalist to know. And I did tip him off when we finally got the Americans out.[7]

The defeat of the government meant I had to be on the campaign trail, while still running the department and bearing the responsibility for the security and safe return of the houseguests. Jean Pelletier was not the only journalist asking questions. We knew the curtain of secrecy we had thrown around the affair could be penetrated at any moment. The urgency intensified.

I had to get Canadian passports for the Americans. As minister, I could authorize the issuing of special passports in exceptional situations, but I had to get the cabinet's approval to do it. I had already discussed with the prime minister how we were going to get cabinet authorization without having to explain why we needed the passports. Joe made it happen at the next cabinet meeting. He told me he would leave my item to the very end. Just as the ministers were ready to leave the room, he said, "There's just one minor item that Flora has. Flora, could you begin explaining it?" And then he kind of interrupted, and said, "This is pretty routine, we'll just pass it." And we passed it, and everybody left. My knees were still shaking, but we had cabinet authorization to go ahead with the passports.

If only it were that simple! Yes, we could make the passports, but we had not reckoned on the forged Iranian visas that we needed to go with the passports. The visas had to be written in the Farsi language, and among the six people we had working on this, there was nobody who knew Farsi. So we sent the passports down to the CIA, and they came back, not only with the visas in Farsi, but with stamps from all over the world to show where these people had supposedly travelled. It was all neatly doctored up. Since we were unable to read the Farsi, we put the documents in an envelope, and sent them off in the diplomatic pouch to Iran. We held our breath because the day before the New

Zealand diplomatic pouch had been opened by the Iranian authorities. We spent several tense hours waiting for word that the passports had reached the Canadian embassy safely. It was 20 January 1980.

But when our first secretary, Roger Lucy, who could read Farsi, looked at the visas in Tehran, he let out a scream. "The fools! They've made the visas out to the wrong date!" Instead of an issue date in January, the month when the fake filmmakers were supposed to have entered Iran for a twenty-one-day stay, the visas said they had been issued in February. Somehow – with ink remover, I suppose – Roger managed to change the date.[8]

It was two o'clock in the morning of 27 January when the phone rang in my room in Kingston where I had been at an election meeting the evening before. It was somebody from the department calling. "Minister, they're out!" That was all they said, and I think I began to cry. The relief of it was so great. I thought, "Oh, thank God!"

Ambassador Taylor had messaged my department that the six Americans were safely on their way on a Swissair flight to Frankfurt, Germany, the first leg of their trip home. A few hours later, when the cipher machine had been smashed by Claude Gauthier, our embassy security chief, the last four of twenty Canadian diplomats still in Tehran – Taylor, Lucy, Gauthier, and Mary O'Flaherty, the communications officer – left Iran for good, but not until there had been a final exchange of telexes. From Taylor and Lucy in Tehran: "See you later, Alligator!" From John Fraser, responding for the department in Ottawa: "See you later, Terminator."[9]

That evening, I placed a courtesy call to Pierre Trudeau to tell him everyone was safely out of Tehran. "Congratulations, Madam Minister," he replied. I said that in the morning I would be announcing the closure of the embassy, "for reasons of security." I also told him that Prime Minister Clark did not intend to exploit the rescue of the Americans for re-election purposes. Trudeau probably thought we were crazy.

And maybe we were crazy. Twenty-two days later, on 18 February, the most exciting and fulfilling chapter in my life came to a crashing end. Our Progressive Conservative minority government went down to electoral defeat as we won only 103 seats to 147 for the Liberals. Trudeau was back with a majority government. Joe Clark was out as prime minister and I was no longer foreign minister. I held on to my seat in Kingston, but I had to return to Ottawa, once again in opposition. I knew we had at least four bleak years ahead of us.

Brian Mulroney

I cannot recall when I first became aware of Brian Mulroney. It must have been in the summer of 1960 when I was working with Dalton Camp, Finlay MacDonald, Ike Smith, Rod Black, and others in the campaign to re-elect Bob Stanfield's provincial government in Nova Scotia. Brian, who had just graduated from St Francis Xavier University in Antigonish, had decided, rather than return home to Quebec for the summer, that he would stay in Nova Scotia to work as a volunteer in our campaign. He was already establishing a name for himself as an ardent supporter of John Diefenbaker and as a vigorous campus Conservative at St FX. Personable and persuasive when he turned on his Irish charm, he was an effective door-to-door salesman for the party, and his rich baritone made him an obvious choice to read the party's commercials on CJCH, the radio station that Finlay owned.

I still remember that election for an incident when I went canvassing in Halifax with Rod Black, the director of the provincial campaign. We knocked on the door of a frail old fellow who did not look as though he could possibly make it to election day. We tried to talk to him about his vote. All he wanted to discuss was his health. This was the first time that Rod thought we could gain an older voter's confidence if he introduced me as a nurse. The old man beamed. He led me to his bedroom, reached under the bed and pulled out his bedpan. He asked me if I would kindly analyze the contents for him. I almost threw up on the spot.[1]

Mulroney's recollections of that election were somewhat different. With a trace of nostalgia, he wrote in his memoirs of hanging around at the end of the day in Camp's suite at the Lord Nelson

Hotel with Finlay, Rod, and Camp's brother-in-law Norm Atkins, "drinking whisky late into the night and dreaming of days when all of us, we were sure, would be called upon to play important roles in government."[2]

I have mentioned in passing that alcohol was a pervasive presence in politics in those days. Liquor could have been the ruination of Mulroney's career. His fondness for it became a cause for alarm among his friends and supporters during his low period after Joe Clark defeated him for the leadership in 1976. I have already described the ugly incident when Mulroney accosted me in a Quebec restaurant because I had not thrown my support to him at the convention. I am sure it took great willpower for him to give up drinking. But he did. He had to. He would never have become prime minister if he had continued the lifestyle he led in the late 1970s. I never saw him take a drink after he became leader in 1983. I respected him for that.

I do not want to sound like a teetotaler-maiden aunt. I enjoy a drink at the end of the day as much as my male colleagues, but I never let alcohol become important in my life. I never allowed myself to become "one of the boys," like the bunch that gathered in Dalton's hotel suite in the summer of 1960. In truth, I was never invited. My routine was to return to my hotel room at the end of the day's campaigning and wait for Dalton to finish writing the next day's speech for Stanfield. Camp was a night person; his creative juices seldom started flowing before midnight. I would type the final version of the speech in the early hours and have it ready for Stanfield who would be at my door to collect it at 8:30 a.m. sharp. Such was a woman's role in the male world of backroom politics.

People often ask me about my relationship with Brian. For the most part, it was cordial but not close. We were colleagues never friends. He and Joe Clark are as different as night and day. Joe is not a person who goes out brandishing his own achievements. He is not shy about talking about what he might have achieved as prime minister if he had been there longer, or what he did accomplish as foreign minister. But he is not someone who goes about promoting Joe Clark, whereas Brian loves an audience. Unbridled self-promotion was one of Mulroney's flaws. It detracted from his accomplishments. He was a prime minister who got things done. He created change. The Free Trade Agreement with the United States was something that needed to be done. Our trading relationships were hamstrung by the way the tax structure on trade had been skewed. In the same vein, there was no way the country would be able to address the problems of the deficit and the accumulated national debt until the tax system was changed. And Brian did that, over immense opposition, with the Goods and Services Tax.

Brian and I worked together with a certain wariness on my side, and probably on his, too. I am sure he never fully forgave me for supporting Joe Clark when I withdrew from the leadership ballot in 1976. It was an easy choice for me. Mulroney's campaign had been the antithesis of mine – his had a lot of money, the use of a private jet, and all sorts of fancy trappings. While one of my key supporters at the convention, David Crombie, who was the mayor of Toronto at the time, set up a soup kitchen on the street to feed hungry convention delegates (along with homeless Ottawans), Mulroney poured free drinks for delegates in a hospitality suite. During the convention, we had my Nova Scotia friend, John Allan Cameron, unpaid, leading an evening of singing and square dancing. Everyone at Brian's big convention party got free beer and pizza while they listened to singer Ginette Reno earn her $10,000 fee. My campaign paid its invoices with the small banknotes that came in the mail or were stuffed in my pockets during rallies; the bulk of Mulroney's funds came in cheques from corporations. While I reported every dollar I raised and spent, as the party demanded, Brian ignored the rules; he never did disclose how much his campaign cost or where the money came from. When I dropped out, there was no question in my mind. I went to Clark: Joe was my kind of politician. Brian was not.

Having said this, I have no complaints about Mulroney in later years. He wrote me a generous letter after the defeat of the government in 1980, saying that I had been a star of the cabinet.

Everyone knew he was working to undermine Clark in the period between our election defeat in 1980 and the party's national policy convention in Winnipeg in early 1983. His campaign paid to fly delegates to Winnipeg, and one of his big supporters, the Airbus lobbyist Karlheinz Schreiber, handed out shopping money for the delegates' wives. But Brian obviously knew where my sympathies lay. While he approached quite a few of my caucus colleagues to join him in challenging Clark's leadership, he did not come near me.

I was as dumbfounded as everyone else when Joe, after receiving the support of 67 per cent of the delegates in Winnipeg, declared that two-thirds was not enough, and he called for a leadership convention. It was set for Ottawa in June 1983. In the months between

Winnipeg and Ottawa, many of my old supporters urged me to jump into the race. I was never tempted. I had had my shot at the leadership in 1976. I was not going to go through that soul-destroying exercise again. The party had not been ready for a woman leader in 1976. As far as I was concerned, it was still not ready in 1983. As Mulroney was fond of saying about himself, I was "going to dance with the one that brought me." And I did. I worked for Joe and voted for him to the end. Brian knew where my loyalty was. To his credit, he did not try to talk me into supporting him – not that he needed my blessing, as it turned out. When he became prime minister, he did not hold my support for Joe against me. He put me in his cabinet and, although we had some sharp differences along the way, he was fair and for the most part supportive of my work in the two portfolios I held in his government.

Of course, the portfolio I really wanted was External Affairs (or Foreign Affairs, as it has been known since 1993), but I knew from the get-go that my old portfolio would not be mine again. From the day he became leader, Mulroney's focus was on party unity, on putting the leadership differences behind us. It was said that no leader had ever invested as much time and energy in stroking the egos of caucus members as Brian did, and I believe that was true. He particularly needed to get Joe Clark and his disappointed supporters on side. So it came as no surprise to me when Brian offered Joe External, the most prestigious post in the cabinet.

Brian did surprise some of our colleagues when he named six women to his first cabinet. That was quite impressive in the days before gender equality became a political hot button. He knew his political math. If 52 per cent of the electorate was female, having more women on the treasury benches could only help the party at election time.

I had no idea what portfolio to expect. I knew it would not be Finance or Treasury Board because economics was not my thing. It could have been Health, but that department had never attracted me. Not that I had any choice in the matter. If I wanted to be in the cabinet, I would have to take whatever Brian offered. I knew that. I wanted to be able to do real things in the social area, and the portfolio Brian did offer me, Employment and Immigration (as it was known then), was as good as any. It probably had the heaviest workload of any portfolio because its two departments, Employment and Immigration, each came with a huge active caseload.

The next few years were lonely ones. Although I had five female colleagues in the cabinet, I remained something of a loner. The other women all had their own interests; my office was in the West Block while theirs were over in the Centre Block. Some of the other ministers would gather at noon around a table reserved for the cabinet in the Parliamentary Restaurant. I seldom joined them. There was a lot of work to do, and I wanted to get on with it. I spent most of my parliamentary lunch time eating alone at my desk. My only close friends in the caucus were fellow Maritimers, Gordon Fairweather from New Brunswick and David MacDonald from Prince Edward Island.

Unemployment at the time was running at 12 per cent, and in some places like Newfoundland, 25 per cent. At the beginning of every month, on a Friday morning, they released unemployment numbers, and I would wake up at seven o'clock and hear this and I would know what Question Period was going to be all about.

E & I was a thankless job in many ways, and it was frustrating for somebody like me, who likes structure and order, to encounter the horrible hodgepodge of programs in the Employment half of the portfolio. I told my officials, look, you are going to take these fifty-six or ninety-six programs, or however many there are, and you are going to put them all in one of six categories. That is all I am going to be able to understand, six. If I do not understand the system, think about the poor unemployed person out there. How can she or he figure it out? And that is what we did. We simplified the whole system. The sixth category was my idea. I named it Innovations. Nobody had ever tried anything like this before. We allocated $100 million in seed money for people or organizations that came up with innovative ideas for tackling unemployment. We got some great programs out of it. We worked out funding formulas – how much the federal government would put in and how much each province would be expected to contribute.

I had no trouble with the prime minister. Mulroney told me to go ahead. However, I did have problems with the Conservative caucus, which worried about the cost. I told them to regard it as an investment that would help make sure there would be jobs for their children and their grandchildren. The parliamentary committee hearings that followed were grueling. And I had to sell the provincial governments on my plan.

Right after we were elected, Mulroney had called a federal-provincial conference, to be held in Regina. The first order of business was unemployment. All provinces were struggling with it and the premiers were in a mood to welcome any help we could give them. We knew Quebec's Parti Québécois government would be a problem, so we worked out a special arrangement for that province. In the end, I got the support of all ten provinces. Quebec Premier René Lévesque came over to me and said, "We'll do whatever we can."

One of my proudest accomplishments was the introduction of the new Employment Equity Act on International Women's Day, 8 March 1985. Based on the recommendations in 1984 of the Royal Commission on Equality in Employment, headed by Ontario Justice Rosalie Abella,[3] the act targeted systemic workplace discrimination against four groups: women, Indigenous people, people with disabilities, and visible minorities. It became the law for federal departments and Crown corporations and for federally regulated businesses with one hundred or more employees, such as banks, railways, airlines, and broadcasters. In addition, companies bidding on government contracts were required to certify their commitment to employment equity.

Employment equity means equal pay for work of equal value – a cause that I advocated throughout my political life. But employment equity means more than that. As the act states, "Employment equity means more than treating persons the same way but also requires special measures and the accommodation of differences." These "reasonable accommodations," as they are known, are required to remove barriers to employment that disadvantage members of the four groups. The accommodations can include wheelchair access to otherwise inaccessible buildings and washrooms; positive policies to encourage the hiring, training, retention, and promotion of women and visible minorities; recruitment in Indigenous communities; job advertisements in minority-language newspapers or websites; and apprenticeship programs for minorities and people with disabilities.

From the time I was first elected in 1972, in opposition and in government, I had been advocating for legal and constitutional recognition of the principle of gender equality rights. Following the 1980 election, the re-elected Trudeau Liberals picked up a proposal that I and others had been making. They gave it priority, and I was overjoyed when, in April 1981, Section 28 was added to the new Canadian Charter of Rights and Freedoms. It is a very short section, stating: "Notwithstanding anything else in this Charter, the rights and freedoms in it are guaranteed equally to male and female persons." Section 28 did not create any new rights. It simply plugged a potential loophole by making it clear that all rights and freedoms guaranteed in the Charter were to be implemented without discrimination between the sexes. My Employment Equity Act in 1985 gave explicit legal recognition to this principle. The long, uphill struggle for gender equality in Canada is not over. Not by a long shot. But we are going to get there!

Meanwhile, in the other half of my E & I portfolio, there was a mess in Immigration. The number of immigrants had fallen to a catastrophic level at a time when the country needed, and still needs, more immigration to support the economic growth that enables us to pay for our social welfare programs. As with Employment, I revamped the bureaucratic structure. We wanted to attract more people, stream them, and get rid of a huge backlog of applications. To refine the system, I set up the Immigration and Refugee Board. Although I found the work exhausting, it was my good fortune to have as chief of staff the calm and eminently capable Bill Musgrove. My policy chief was a young man named Michael Sabia – the same Michael Sabia who would go on to become head of the telecommunications giant BCE. Years later, when he was running BCE and making a million dollars a year, I sent him a little note saying, "Now Michael, don't ever forget the days when I paid you $40,000 a year."[4]

Michael was well connected to the powers-that-be in Ottawa. His wife Hilary is the daughter of diplomat Geoffrey Pearson, who was Canada's ambassador to the Soviet Union, making Michael the grandson-in-law of Liberal Prime Minister Lester Pearson. Michael is one of those people who never stops working. He is a zealot, almost as bad as I am. The two of us would be working late at night, he in his office and me in mine, when Geoff Pearson would phone me and say, "Flora, would you please send that young man home to his wife?" And I would say, "But, Geoff, he doesn't have to wait for me. He can go any time he likes." I relied on those two, Michael and Bill, tremendously. They got me through a lot.

By then, it was 1986 and Brian decided it was time for a major cabinet shuffle. When he told me I was moving to Communications, I thought it was a real demotion. I suspected he was trying to get rid of me. Actually, it turned out to be an exciting experience. It was terrific! I realized I had always been interested in communications, going back to the war years when my father was a telegrapher entrusted to relay trans-Atlantic messages from Winston Churchill to Franklin Roosevelt. As in Employment and Immigration, I was blessed to have a superb staff. Bill Musgrove came with me as chief of staff, while Michael Sabia went off to Finance, then to the Privy Council Office where Paul Tellier was Clerk of the Privy Council and Secretary to the Cabinet. Michael would eventually move to Montreal and the private sector with Tellier.

I soon discovered the most exciting part of the department was its cultural side. I was responsible for national museums, the National Gallery, CBC, CRTC, film industry, theatre, music, magazine and book publishing, and much more. I got to work with some of the most effective non-governmental organizations (NGOs) in the country and to wrestle with some of the most aggressive lobbyists I had ever encountered. They included Jack Valenti, the hard-pushing chairman of the Motion Picture Association of America.

Valenti was regarded in our cultural community as a bogeyman, a mortal threat to the Canadian film industry. Until I met him, I had a mental image of a big bully. He turned out to be a tiny little man who did not come up to my shoulder. I crossed swords with him over what seemed to me to be a modest measure to protect the Canadian film-production industry by using a combination of import regulations and financial incentives to secure greater screen time for Canadian films in Canadian theatres. At the time, English-language feature films made in this country had only 3 per cent of the total screen time in theatres. Most of the Canadian features were never shown in theatres at all, and those that did make it tended to have extremely short runs. French-language films made in Quebec, protected by their language barrier, did not have the same problem. In relative terms, their industry was thriving while the industry in English Canada was struggling to survive. Producers did not dare to spend even $5 million on a film because they knew they would be unable to recoup their investment.

What I wanted to do was to double the 3 per cent to 6 per cent of screen time. With Canadian producers unable to make money from 3 per cent, I thought the proposed increase was reasonable. In the film industry policy that I unveiled in February 1987, we announced we would use import regulations to make it more difficult for American producers to dump inferior films on the Canadian market. And we offered a carrot – a government subsidy of $200 million dollars over five years – to help Canadian filmmakers produce quality movies. I was not trying to force out US movies. I knew they were here to stay, but I hoped the day would come when at least 15 per cent of the films in Canadian theatres would be made in Canada.

The Americans fought our policy, not so much because they were worried about percentages in Canada, as because they feared it would embolden other countries, especially in Europe, to restrict the entry of US films. Lobbyists representing American interests argued that the reason so few Canadian movies got wide release was that the distributors, the middle men between the producers and the theatres – some of the distributors were owned by American film companies – regarded Canadian movies as inferior to US ones. Canadian films looked cheap, they said, they featured no-name stars, and they simply were not "entertaining" enough.

As I was told repeatedly, the economics of film distribution made the wide theatre release of most Canadian films a losing proposition. Because distributors could secure the rights to Canadian movies for relative pennies, they felt no financial pressure to give them wide release when they could make a modest, risk-free profit by selling the broadcast rights to Canadian TV networks that were always scrambling for Canadian content to meet the quotas dictated by the Canadian Radio-television and Telecommunications Commission (CRTC).

The heavy lobbying by US producers and distributors had some success. We made several concessions between the time I announced our policy in 1987 and the time I rolled out the Film Products Importation Bill in 1988, but I still maintained that 6 per cent was a minimal aspiration, a tiny foot in a large theatre door. But Valenti and the MPAA exploded. You would have thought I was trying to drop a nuclear bomb on Hollywood. Valenti wailed to everyone he could get to in Ottawa, including the Prime Minister's Office. He tried to get Washington to put diplomatic pressure on Ottawa. A force to be reckoned with in United States politics, he even enlisted the White House in his lobbying, and that old movie star, President Ronald Reagan, raised it with Mulroney, asking what our government was doing to his friend Jack.

Reagan sent a three-page private letter to Mulroney shortly before he visited Ottawa in early April 1987. "I am very concerned," the president wrote, "by your recently announced policy to restrict US-owned film distribution companies. This policy seems discriminatory and would impede their long-standing business in Canada." On arrival in Ottawa, Reagan raised it again. He told Mulroney he had been following the dispute personally. "That film decision your government has taken must not happen," he said.[5]

In the end, Brian bent, but he did not break. The free trade negotiations with Washington were at a crucial juncture, and he did not want to jeopardize them by pushing ahead in the face of the president's personal opposition.

Meanwhile, I had managed to win caucus support and cabinet approval for the film policy, despite the opposition of several ministers. I was finally free to introduce the Film Products Importation Bill in the House. It was a big moment for the Canadian cultural community. Leaders of several organizations travelled to Ottawa from Toronto, Montreal, and other places to witness what they regarded as a symbolic event in the evolution of Canadian cultural sovereignty. And then, at the last moment, I was informed by our House leader that the prime minister had instructed that the bill not be introduced. No explanation was offered.

I was utterly taken aback. I was furious. I felt betrayed. I was determined to resign, and I ranted to friends, saying some harsh things about the prime minister. Mulroney had ears everywhere and he must have heard about my outrage. The last thing he wanted was a cabinet crisis. He knew I was coming to see him with my resignation in hand, because he sent his chief of staff, Derek Burney, to head me off. Derek tried to cool me out. "I understand you're upset," he said. "I was just trying to hold this off to a more propitious time." He talked about the delicate state of the free trade negotiations, and the progress Mulroney was making with Reagan on a trans-border pact on acid rain. "We're just not on the same wavelength," I told him. "I think the best thing is I should resign. I believe so strongly that we need to protect our cultural industries. On the very day we are trying to do this, you abandon me."

I think Derek was taken aback by my anger. After we talked for a while, he backed off, saying, "Well, you can introduce the bill next week." Which I was allowed to do, and that headed off my resignation. The problem was, we were running out of time. The session of Parliament was nearing its end, and a new election was on the horizon. The bill was bound to provoke extensive debate in the House; the committee hearings would eat up weeks; and then we would have to repeat the process in the Senate. There was no way we could shorten the procedure to fit the prime minister's pre-election timetable.

The bill never did become law. Although we returned with a second Conservative majority government in the 1988 election, now known as the "free-trade election," I lost my seat in Kingston and The Islands. Free trade was part of it; the public service unions, which were heavily represented in the riding, had declared electoral war on the government; and I guess voters had grown tired of me after sixteen years. Whatever the reason, I was out of the cabinet, and no minister in the post-election administration wanted to embrace the cause of Canada's film industry the way I had. Over time, with a strong US dollar against a weaker Canadian dollar, a number of American production houses discovered it made economic sense to shoot movies, or parts of them, in Canada. They brought in American stars, American scripts, and American-written scores. The economy may have benefitted from this branch-plant production, but the creative side of the film business – the writers, musicians, performers, and directors – was left to struggle to find a place in the American-dominated industry.

What I did not know at the time was that Allan Gotlieb, the Canadian ambassador in Washington, was lobbying against me. As I was pushing ahead with my film industry bill, he was privately warning the PMO that passage of the legislation could scupper the free trade deal. It was essentially the same message that Jack Valenti had been spreading and President Reagan had echoed it in his letter to Mulroney. Of course, it was not my first exposure to Gotlieb. He had been my deputy minister when I was minister of External Affairs in Joe Clark's government in 1979–80. Allan had a reputation for being brilliant, arrogant, and manipulative. I cannot come up with three better adjectives to define him. He had been close to Pierre Trudeau, and I sensed right away that he was not impressed by Joe and especially not by me, a woman with no university degree and no background in his world of international relations. And I was a Red Tory to boot![6] When we were elected in 1979, many senior bureaucrats harboured a sense that our minority Conservative government was not entirely legitimate, that the Canadian public would come to its senses and the natural order – Liberal, of course – would soon be restored. Allan made less effort than others to hide his feelings.

We got off on the wrong foot in 1979. Gotlieb had grown accustomed to reporting directly to Trudeau when he was prime minister rather than through the External Affairs minister. He tried to do the same thing with Clark until Joe warned him off when we were in Tokyo for the economic summit, "There is a minister in charge of these things. Take it up with her," Joe told him. Later, during the Commonwealth Conference in Lusaka, Zambia, Gotlieb went behind my back to set up his own intelligence operation – a daily briefing meeting with members of the Canadian delegation where they sat around discussing what I should be doing that day – without my presence or knowledge. Luckily, my chief of staff Hugh Hanson got wind of it, insisted on being at every meeting, and reported back to me. It is how I kept track of what my deputy minister was up to.

The chemistry between us just did not work. There was too much distrust on both sides. I remember taking Allan to a cabinet committee meeting I was chairing. He got upset about something and walked out and – "slamming shut my briefing books in a rage when she wouldn't listen to me," as he described it in his diary.[7] I have no recollection of the issue we were discussing, but I do remember Defence Minister Allan McKinnon saying to me after the meeting, "If my deputy did that to me, that would have been the last time he'd ever come in my door."

At one point, I did ask Clark if he would replace Gotlieb as my deputy. Joe understood the bad chemistry, but he refused, figuring it made no sense for a minority government to stir up Allan's friends and allies in the upper echelons of a public service whose loyalty we were trying win.

I was hurt and angered in 2006 when Gotlieb published his memoir, *The Washington Diaries 1981–1989*. He seethed with resentment toward me. As the *Ottawa Citizen*'s Paul Gessell observed in his review of the book, "Flora MacDonald is repeatedly vilified. The book's index lists sixteen references to Ms MacDonald – virtually all laced with sarcastic expressions about the 'talons' of the minister or Flora 'in full flower.' Their bad relations dated back at least to 1979, when Ms MacDonald was external affairs minister and Mr Gotlieb was her deputy. Ms MacDonald was 'knifing me in the back' while her staff were inflicting 'petty indignities,' Mr Gotlieb reminisces bitterly."[8]

His accounts of events and issues that I was involved in are unbalanced and dyspeptic. I will not give him the satisfaction of responding in kind to his vitriol. All I will say is that getting away from Allan Gotlieb was one of the few good things about losing my seat in 1988.

Brian Mulroney's comments when he addressed the first meeting of his new cabinet after the election, presented a very different picture of me. "I met Flora thirty years ago," he said. "I know something about fighting the odds, but no one in public life fought longer odds to succeed than Flora. Any book or reference to the PC Party over the last three-and-a-half decades has a place of honour for Flora. She and I sat together in backrooms and in the House of Commons. Her life has been a story of remarkable achievement. There would be few, if any, parallels to rival the impact Flora has made on this party, this country."9

Here I Come, World!

"Devastated" is the only word that adequately describes my emotions when I lost my seat in Parliament in 1988. It was a blow, and it hurt, badly. I did not see it coming. I believed I had been a faithful, conscientious representative for Kingston and The Islands for sixteen years, and I assumed my constituents knew me well and appreciated my efforts on their behalf.

Having a high profile in the party and Parliament was a mixed blessing. It certainly meant everyone knew "Flora," but that recognition could be a liability at re-election time. The party expected me to campaign for candidates across the country, and my absences were noticed by Kingston voters. Many in the media attributed my defeat to public opposition to our government's embrace of free trade. Although that may have been a factor, it was not, in my opinion, the primary one. For several years, the Treasury Board had been dragging its feet in wage negotiations with public servants, and the civil service unions were up in arms. Thousands of residents of Kingston and The Islands worked for the federal government in one capacity or another – as prison guards and administrators and as civilian employees at Canadian Forces Base Kingston – not to mention all the uniformed members of armed forces who were stationed in and around Kingston.

Other public sector workers – teachers, nurses, police, firefighters, paramedics, and so on – sympathized with the federal employees, as did the staffs at Kingston's various institutions of higher education, such as Queen's University, Royal Military College, and St Lawrence Community College. Kingston was not alone in this. Public employees rose up against prominent Conservative incumbents across the country – for example, in Halifax where Stewart McInnis was defeated, in Victoria where Allan McKinnon lost his seat, and in Saskatoon where Ray Hnatyshyn was defeated.

That 1988 campaign was the first time I felt uncomfortable about participating in debates held in union halls. The animosity of the labour movement was palpable. I have returned to Kingston to speak at many functions since that election without experiencing any lingering hostility, so I no longer believe it was a personal vote against me in 1988. Even so, I knew it was time for me to go.

But go where? Many friends asked why the government did not reward me with a comfortable sinecure – something that would pay a secure wage for a modest effort. The federal government has dozens, probably hundreds, of these patronage positions at its disposal, and my old colleague Stan Darling, a long-time MP in Ontario, canvassed everyone he knew, asking why I was not offered one of them. Some people thought I should be governor general; that appointment went to Hnatyshyn. Others urged a Senate appointment. Not many people decline the offer of a Senate seat, but I would have turned it down in an instant. I have nothing against the Senate, but I knew it would constrain my ability to take on other, more interesting activities. Joe Clark, as foreign minister, was active behind the scenes and he let it be known that he was prepared to appoint me High Commissioner to India, if I was interested. I do not know whether that suggestion reached Prime Minister Mulroney, but I was not interested. As much as I love India, I knew the formal and ceremonial obligations of being a high commissioner would make it impossible for me to act independently. I needed to be free to pursue my own beliefs and causes – in my own way.

I heard nothing from the prime minister, and that did not upset me. I did not ask him for anything, did not expect anything, and did not get anything. Although my relations with Brian in those years were, for the most part, cordial, they were never warm. He nurses grievances, and I knew he would never really forgive me for supporting Joe Clark at the 1976 leadership convention. I had served him in two portfolios between 1984 and 1988, and if our relationship was not close, it was professional and supportive. I was never a confidante or someone he would look to for advice. Nor did I want to be. Our natures were too dissimilar. We were simply not empathetic. The truth is, we did not like or trust each other very much. Despite his generous words about me in cabinet after I lost my seat, I have seen very little of him in the years since I left Parliament.

Among my first decisions after the defeat was to move my permanent residence to Ottawa. I could no longer afford apartments in both Ottawa and Kingston. The commuting was stressful and could be dangerous. Not long after the election, while I was driving back to Ottawa from Kingston on a cold, stormy early March night with drifts of blowing snow – having ignored warnings to stay off the roads – my car slid off the highway, over a bank and into a heavy fence. I was taken to a hospital where I remained for ten days while my face was stitched up. If I had not been wearing a seat belt, I might have been killed. I never saw my wrecked car again.

That episode brought me to my senses. I stopped feeling sorry for myself and started asking what I wanted to do with the next phase of my life. As I asked around, I began receiving suggestions. I was asked to join an OXFAM mission to assess the escalating conflict in Namibia (the former German colony of South West Africa). So in June, I took off for Sub-Saharan Africa on what would be the first of many trips abroad on behalf of non-governmental organizations (NGOs).

I spent a month in Windhoek, the capital of Namibia. I went with the naïve idea that, because it is warm in Canada in June and July, it would be warm everywhere. Instead, I found myself in the middle of the Namibian winter. Our group was billeted in a house that had precious little furniture. We slept on cots in unheated rooms, in a bitterly cold city 1,700 metres above sea level.

Not long after that mission, I was invited by the Department of Canadian Studies at the University of Edinburgh to become a Visiting Fellow in the autumn of 1989. I accepted with pleasure and had three great months back in an academic setting. I spent weekdays discussing Canada with students and faculty members and weekends roaming the Scottish countryside becoming reacquainted with the land of my ancestors.

I mention this period because it indicates how quickly the defeat at the polls receded into the background. New interests were awakened. Then, in 1992, I was approached by Mulroney's former chief of staff, Derek Burney, to become chair of the International Development Research Centre (IDRC). A part-time position, it paid an annual salary of five thousand dollars, plus a stipend for attending four two-day meetings of the board of directors each year. I certainly did not accept the post for the money, but for the opportunity to lead one of Canada's little known but widely respected research and project-oriented institutions.

Prior to my IDRC appointment, several NGOs working with destitute and marginalized people in developing countries suggested I become involved in their causes. I did, and I can truthfully say the years after politics have provided some of the richest experiences of my entire life.[1]

It would take three books of this length to chronicle all the activities I became involved in and to describe the adventures I experienced during these years. I will try to compress them by country or continent, starting with Africa.

AFRICA

The month in Windhoek in 1989 for OXFAM was the first of many missions on the African continent. Before long, I returned to Namibia with a group monitoring the new country's first democratic elections following its independence from South Africa. From 1990 to 1995, I hosted a program called *North-South* for VisionTV, a Canadian multi-faith, multicultural specialty channel. The program aired six to eight times a year, and for each hour-long episode VisionTV would send me, a director and a cameraman for a month to the country where the segment was filmed. Many of the programs were set in Africa with others in Brazil, India and Nepal. Although we operated on a shoestring budget, sometimes staying with local residents, we covered cutting-edge topics – such as climate change, an issue that did not command the public attention in those days that it does today.

I went to South Africa with a group of Canadian observers who had been invited to report on the first parliamentary elections of the post-apartheid era: the 1994 election that made Nelson Mandela the nation's first Black president. It was a tremendously exciting time. The district to which I was assigned was in the vicinity of Nelspruit (now known as Mbombela), a city of about two hundred thousand in northeastern South Africa, close to the border of Mozambique. In all the elections I have been a part of, I have never encountered people so absolutely determined to exercise their franchise. Almost 80 per cent of the votes cast in my district were for Mandela – a result that was replicated far and wide in the country.

In the coming years I would have opportunities to monitor elections in Mozambique, Zimbabwe and Rwanda. While I have many vivid memories from those experiences, nothing could top the evening in South Africa when Mandela won. The celebrations swept the county. Villagers' beds went unoccupied as dancing, singing, shouting crowds thronged the roads until dawn and well beyond. Within days, the new South African flag was hoisted on flagpoles across the country.

There are few people for whom I would give up the exciting life I have lived. Nelson Mandela is one of the few. Following his victory, the expectations that fell on Mandela's shoulders were enormous – and some would argue they remained unfulfilled – but they were met by the hope and energy that had taken over the country and its people. While South Africa had its fair share of issues during his presidency and continues to experience serious problems of crime and poverty today, Mandela's message of peace and his unrelenting effort to break down the previously impenetrable colour barrier inspired the nation.

What I admired most about him was how he remained his open and empathetic self, without pomposity and without seeking glory for himself. A few years after his victory, I ran into Mandela in a neighbourhood close to Pretoria. He was strolling down a street, pausing frequently to say hello to friends, neighbours and strangers. After a brief chat, he invited me to the president's mansion in Pretoria. There, he talked to me as if I were an old friend, interrupting our conversation only long enough to greet a delegation led by the head of the Orthodox Church in Egypt. With each encounter with him, I fell more and more under his spell; I often wonder how great it would be if other world leaders could have borrowed some of his abiding faith and respect for humanity.

In August 1994, I flew to Rwanda with a VisionTV crew and a reporter from the *Ottawa Citizen*. We landed first in the port city of Bujumbura, at that time the capital of Burundi. We quickly realized we were in a dangerous part of the world. Just after arriving, we were accosted by a group of bandits who tried to take my purse and camera. The reporter and I, with our hands and feet striking out in all directions and yelling at the top of our lungs, managed to frighten off our accosters.

That experience was nothing compared to the devastation we witnessed while filming in Rwanda. In the course of just one hundred days in the spring and early summer of 1994, an estimated five hundred thousand to one million Rwandans were slaughtered in one of the most brutal genocides of our generation.[2] Years of tension between the country's two biggest ethnic groups, the Hutus and Tutsis, blew up into the mass murder of Tutsis and moderate Hutus. When we arrived in August, human remains were still scattered around.

When I met Canadian Lieutenant-General Romeo Dallaire, the commander of the United Nations Assistance Mission for Rwanda (UNAMIR)[3] we talked about his efforts to organize a reconstruction effort. It was not easy, "We have 110 registered NGOs here," he told me. "You try to understand who these people are, but a lot of them sort of say, 'All right – we're going to set up an NGO and go out and help these people' – without much background or understanding of the issues, why they should be here, or how they can fit in [to the reconstruction effort]." It quickly became apparent to me that rebuilding endeavours would be monumentally complicated.[4]

In another situation in Africa, the NGOs on the ground did know what they were doing, and what needed to be done, but they were not listened to. For many years CARE Canada had worked in the former Zaire – now known as the Democratic Republic of the Congo[5] – and in Burundi, two of the countries that border Rwanda. The people at CARE understood the historical tensions between the Hutus and the Tutsis. Prior to the genocide, they tried to warn the United Nations High Commissioner for Refugees of an impending mass influx of dispossessed Rwandans fleeing to safety in Burundi and Zaire. Before and during the early stages of the genocide, one-and-a-half million refugees crossed those borders. They needed emergency assistance, but no one had paid heed to CARE's warnings. It was not until April 1994, when the mass killings were well underway, that the UN arrived and belatedly began to organize a relief effort.

On my return to Canada, I did my best to tell the story of Rwanda, a shattered country, torn to shreds by fighting between Hutus and Tutsis – a story of how the world had turned its back on the small African nation. I am still haunted by what I witnessed myself and heard from the people I interviewed on that trip.

My involvement in Africa intensified when I became chair of the twenty-one-member board of IDRC from 1992 to 1998. Eleven board members were Canadian and ten represented countries that IDRC was assisting. Most Canadians are sadly unaware of the positive impact that small Canadian agencies like IDRC have in the developing world.

I was able to coordinate my part-time position at IDRC with my ongoing work for VisionTV. On one trip, I filmed a segment in Eritrea for VisionTV, then headed for Kenya, stopping en route for a day in Ethiopia to discuss IDRC concerns with officials at the Canadian embassy there. After eating a salad at lunch at the embassy, I became extremely ill. I have never felt such pain as I did that evening in Addis Ababa.

I had to catch a plane to Nairobi early the next morning, but I was still throwing up when I arrived at the airport. When we landed, I was so weak I could hardly walk off the plane. The Canadian high commissioner to Kenya, Lucie Edwards,[6] met me. She took me to a hotel where I slept for the next 24 hours. Then I felt fine. Coming down the hotel elevator the following morning, I encountered a man wearing a badge that said, "United Nations Development Program Conference." After exchanging pleasantries, I told the man, who was from Thailand, that I was the chair of the IDRC. He looked at me and exclaimed, "Oh! IDRC? We know all about IDRC in Thailand! It does such great programs." I remember thinking to myself that I could come down in a hundred elevators in Canada and if I mentioned IDRC, people would stare at me blankly. Yet here I was in a hotel elevator in Kenya, with a man from Thailand whom I had never met before, and he extolled the virtues of IDRC. It said something about the high regard in which this Canadian agency is held in the developing world.

I have seen first-hand the impact that small groups of motivated individuals can have on a region. I can offer no better illustration than the time I spent as a member of Partnership Africa Canada (PAC). Formed in the mid-1980s, the original purpose of the organization was to handle the distribution of money from Canadian International Development Agency (CIDA) programs to various NGOs. By 1996, when I became a board member of PAC, it was handling upwards of $100 million in aid money every year.

About the time I joined the partnership, however, PAC's role abruptly changed. CIDA essentially told the organization, "There's no need for you people. We can dispense the money ourselves." In short order, PAC had to transform itself from an organization that worked closely with CIDA and dealt with hundreds of millions of dollars into one that had a budget of just over $100,000, and was expected to be a policy-oriented advocacy organization that spoke out on issues of importance. Although many members of PAC left the partnership then, a number did hang on in the belief that they could help shape government policy toward Africa.

During the late 1990s, I worked with groups that kept bringing me stories and pictures of the mutilation, particularly of children, in the civil war in Sierra Leone. I struggled to comprehend the causes of the exceptionally brutal conflict that killed an estimated fifty thousand Sierra Leoneans between 1991 and 2002 and destroyed much of the country's infrastructure. While government corruption was one factor, nobody seemed to have a definitive answer about the causes. Sierra Leone is comprised of at least sixteen different ethnic groups, yet ethnic violence had never been a major issue. At one meeting where I spoke, three men were present: Adrian Labor, a young man from Sierra Leone who was working with IDRC; Ian Smillie, a Canadian who worked at IDRC; and Bernard Taylor, who ran the office of Partnership Africa Canada. Adrian told us, "You will never settle the factionalism and fighting in Sierra Leone, until you settle the question of diamonds."

Diamonds were indeed the key, but we had never paid a great deal of attention to their political significance. Ian Smillie's first overseas experience many years earlier had been as a teacher in Sierra Leone, and he kept in touch with what was going on in that country. With the support of CIDA and other organizations, Ian set up a team to look into the connection between diamonds and the funding of wars throughout Africa. It became clear that the political leadership of Sierra Leone, as well as other diamond-rich countries, was using the profits from diamond sales to purchase military equipment. The more we looked into it, the more we thought something should be done about it.

The report we wrote went all the way to the United Nations Security Council, which then organized its own study, of which Ian Smillie became the key member. The result was what we now know as the Kimberley Process Certification Scheme (KPCS or simply "Kimberley Process"), because the first meeting involving government officials from southern African diamond-producing countries was held in Kimberley, South Africa, the place where diamonds were said to have been first discovered. Created by a UN General Assembly resolution in 2003, the KPCS seeks to block "conflict diamonds" from entering the international diamond market.[7]

The future success of the Kimberley Process, which now includes representation from seventy-five countries, will ultimately depend on the leaders of the nations involved. While I have been fortunate to get to know great leaders such as Nelson Mandela and to observe the positive effects they can have on a nation, I have also seen the damage that corrupt politicians can wreak on their countries and their people.

One of those was Robert Mugabe of Zimbabwe. Back in 1979, shortly after I was appointed foreign minister, I accompanied Prime Minister Joe Clark, to Africa, where we attended the Commonwealth Heads of Government meeting in Lusaka, Zambia. Zimbabwe was already the subject of grave Commonwealth concern. While various leaders within Zimbabwe had stepped forward, only to be knocked down, one ruthless man, Mugabe, managed to seize power.

When I first met him in 1979, Mugabe was still struggling to gain control of the country, which had been locked in civil war since 1965. Ian Smith, the white supremacist leader of Rhodesia, as it was called then, had declared his country's independence from Great Britain. But that independence was not recognized internationally, and Smith never really had control of the population. Mugabe initially impressed me with his conviction that he could lead the people of Zimbabwe. By the time Brian Mulroney was prime minister five years later, however, Mugabe was displaying extreme and autocratic behaviour. Anyone who dared oppose him was thrown into the jail. And worse was to come.

Zimbabwe was once the breadbasket of southern Africa. Today, it depends on foreign aid to feed its citizens. While recurring droughts have devastated the country's agriculture, observers – from farmers and scientists to diplomats and journalists – blame Mugabe's land seizures from white farmers in 2000 for causing the food crisis that persists today. Mugabe's decisions over the decades – notably jailing political opponents, participating in regional conflicts such as the Second Congo War,[8] and perpetually blaming "The West" for the country's problems – have left Zimbabwe in crisis.

The triumphs and failures of the leaders of various African countries since the decolonization of the continent began after the Second World War have been well documented in the media. For every Mandela, there has been a Mugabe.

Yet leadership, while critical to Africa's future, may no longer be its gravest issue. There is another, more deadly menace that has plagued the continent, one that has taken the lives of millions and jeopardizes the future of Africa and its people: the AIDS pandemic. The numbers, while slowly coming down, speak for themselves. Sub-Saharan Africa has 6.2 per cent of the world's population but

54 per cent of its HIV sufferers. To look at it another way, roughly twenty million people in the region are living with HIV and about three hundred thousand die of AIDS each year.

Millions of orphans have been left behind, forced to rely on their own survival skills or perish. Their major caregivers are the generation that is termed "Africa's Newest Mothers" – grandmothers who, after a lifetime of struggle to survive themselves, are now forced to bear the burden of the care and nurturing of their orphaned grandchildren. And they do so without access to social welfare, pensions, or medical insurance – or even society's gratitude for their sacrifices. AIDS does more than kill when it takes people in the prime of their lives. It leaves businesses without employees, schools without teachers, and children without parents. One of the most chilling conversations I had was with an elderly African woman who told me, "You must realize that we are the last 'older generation' for many years to come."

Think about that for a moment. Country after country without elders to support and impart advice to the young, without income earners and taxpayers to bear the costs of schools and hospitals, without future statesmen like Nelson Mandela to lead their nation, and without any real future for the majority of the working population. We cannot visualize such an abject situation in Canada.

INDIA

Of all the countries I have come to love, the one I know best is India. I made my first trip there back in 1969, when I was working at Queen's University in Kingston. This was after I had been fired from my job at Progressive Conservative party headquarters and before I was elected to Parliament. One of my friends at Queen's was John Trent, who was then a doctoral student in political science.[9] He was involved with the International Political Science Association, which was holding a conference in India that year. John asked if I would like to attend as a delegate, along with two others from Queen's: Jayant Lele, a political scientist and specialist in development studies, and his wife, Uma Lele, an economist. Both were from India originally and had been graduate students together at Cornell University in New York State. They promised if I would come, they would show me around India. Of course, I went.

After a couple of days in Bombay (now Mumbai), we went to Trivandrum (now known as Thiruvananthapuram), on the west coast near the southern tip of mainland India, where the conference was being held at the University of Kerala. I am afraid we were not especially conscientious about attending the sessions, preferring to rent a car and explore that fascinating part of India.[10] One of the greatest sights I have ever seen was Kovalam Beach, which is actually a series of three pristine crescent-shaped beaches. It is spectacular. If you stand on the beach and look west across the Indian Ocean in the direction of the Persian Gulf, you can watch the sun drop suddenly into the sea – the colours are astounding! In 1969, there was not a soul around – just this huge bay, gorgeous white sand, blue sky, and the setting sun. Now tourists have discovered Kovalam Beach and each night large crowds congregate at sunset, and they shout a countdown, backward from one hundred, to see if they can get to zero at the precise moment that the sun plunges into the sea.

After the conference, Uma and Jayant returned to Bombay while I flew to Madras (now Chennai) on my own. Across from me on the plane was an American man who had been at the conference. He was a professor in the United States, but he had decided to do research in Madras. He offered to show me around. I had made a reservation at one of those international chain hotels, but he said, "Surely you're not staying in a Western hotel in a city like this. How can you ever absorb anything of India? I'll go with you while you cancel the booking, and I'll show you where you should stay." Once we got into the centre of the city, he said, "You must ride in a rickshaw." We went to a little hotel where he stayed. It was about two o'clock in the afternoon, and he said, "I will take you out to see the market." It was an incredible covered market where you could walk for miles; it had everything you could possibly think of finding in a market. My new friend spoke fluent Hindi. He seemed to know every bookseller in the market, asking if this or that order was in. Later, we went back to his hotel. He invited me to come to his room before dinner. When I got there, he had changed from his North American suit into traditional Indian attire, those long white sheets of cloth known in Hindi as a dhoti. He was squatting on the floor, smoking. He said I should try it. I thought, all right, he has been very pleasant, I should humour him. I did not realize it was hashish he was smoking. Knowing nothing about hashish, I inhaled and regrettably, swallowed the stuff. Before I knew it, I was out of it.

I can remember his voice to this day, as it had a mesmerizing quality to it – "Now, how are you feeling at the moment?" He was writing in a notebook; he was probably doing research on how people reacted to hashish. I just happened to be a case study he had picked up along the way. I could hear this voice coming through like a great fog. "You're in the second stage now. ... You're in the third stage. ... You'll go through seven stages, then you'll begin to come back down." I remember clearly thinking something was happening, that it would all stop if I could just silence that voice. How do I stop that voice? I kept thinking, if I can get my hands around his neck, I could choke off the voice.

But when I got to the seventh stage and started coming back down, I became very, very ill – all over the room, all over everything belonging to the professor, and likely all over him. He thought he had better get me back to my room. I remember him helping me down the stairs. Then he got the door open and sort of shoved me in. I lay there until, bit by bit, I began to gain some consciousness. The thing I will always remember is how I could hear sounds from miles away. I could hear dogs barking and chickens chirping throughout the night. Everything was magnified. And I never did get any dinner or sleep.

The next day I left the hotel, and I left the bill for him. I figured he deserved it. I bought some beautifully woven silk and went to the airport to catch a plane. I felt fine, charged with energy – and vowed to myself never to try hash ever again – a promise I have kept, by the way!

I flew to Bangalore. A small city in those days, it was destined to become the high-tech centre of India. I found a tiny hotel and that night I got into conversation with the receptionist; he might have been the owner for all I knew. "You're from Canada?" he asked. When I said I was, he said, "I met a Canadian once. I think his name was Michener. He was here on holiday with his wife and their two cats, and he commissioned me to get cat collars for them. But he never came back. I've had these cat collars ever since. He paid for them and everything, but I don't know what to do with them."

I told him Roland Michener had been the Canadian High Commissioner to India. While he was vacationing in Bangalore, Michener received a phone call from Prime Minister Lester Pearson asking him to hurry home to step in as governor general to replace Georges Vanier who died in March 1967, just as Canada's Centennial Year was ramping up. "Well, if you know this Governor General, could you take the collars to him?" he asked. And that's how I got to deliver two cat collars from a small hotel in India to Rideau Hall in Ottawa.

Later that night, I went to a hymn service at the Church of Scotland in Bangalore. I was the only non-brown person in the church. By the time the service was over, it was probably 1 a.m. and I was left to find my way back to the hotel. It was a beautiful night. There was no traffic, so I walked along the middle of the road, singing at the top of my lungs in English the hymns I had just heard. Two young fellows on a motorbike passed me, then stopped and came back. "Do you need any help? Where are you going?" they asked. Fair questions to put to a strange red-haired white woman walking in the road and singing in the wee hours. "We're students and we're just going back to our dormitory," they said. "Can we give you a lift?" One jumped off the bike and I got on and the driver proceeded to take me on a tour of the city at night. He showed me the university, told me about the courses he was taking, and a couple of hours later deposited me back at my little hotel. I never saw either of them again.

I have returned to India repeatedly since my "retirement" from politics. My most public involvement was with the Shastri Indo-Canadian Institute, of which I was the chair from 1992 to 2004. The aim of the organization, founded in 1968,[11] is to organize exchanges of academics and artists between Canada and India. One of my primary roles was to negotiate funds for Indian scholars coming to Canada which, as the organization continued to grow, became an increasing challenge. Nonetheless, the rewards were worthwhile; as I write this, more than one thousand academics and artists have taken part in the program.

While administrative work is not exotic and does not generate the same attention as working directly on the ground, it serves a very important purpose. Well-run organizations can achieve amazing results. When I was chair of HelpAge International, an international NGO that assists the elderly to overcome poverty, one of the agencies we funded was HelpAge India. Among other things, it operated massive regional eye clinics where seniors throughout India could go for the removal of cataracts and other eye operations. HelpAge workers in New Delhi, for example, organized the testing of villagers in a forty-mile radius, bringing those in need of treatment to their clinic in the capital, and helping them to return home afterward. Largely free of government interference, this NGO is highly organized and delivers real results that benefit people immensely.

I have also been deeply involved with the Commonwealth Human Rights Initiative (CHRI). The organization was formed in 1987 by Commonwealth associations from various countries to promote human rights. It reports on abuses by police, the courts, or other authorities and encourages legislators and political leaders to respect the fundamental rights and democratic freedoms of their citizens in India and elsewhere.

One day, I stumbled into a demonstration of India's vibrant and unpredictable democracy. I was sitting on a sidewalk, having my hiking boots cleaned, in Guwahati, the largest city in Assam state in India's north-east region. When I looked up, I saw hundreds of women marching along the main thoroughfare. It suddenly dawned on me that it was 8 March, International Women's Day. Never one to miss out on a Women's Day event, I ran to join them. The marchers not only welcomed me, they pushed me up to the very front of the parade where I helped to carry their large banner. Being unfamiliar with their language,[12] I had no idea what the banner said or what the words meant on the huge badge they pinned on me.

The march ended at an open area where robust speeches were delivered about the issues and the opportunities that women in that part of the world face daily. I was among the impromptu speakers, and afterwards I rushed off to rejoin my travelling companions for a flight back to New Delhi. One of them, who came from the north-east region, looked at my badge and gasped in amazement. "Flora," he said, "do you realize you were out demonstrating with the Women's Division of the Communist Party?" To me, it was just a gathering of Red Tories! Those women had the right to speak up, regardless of their political affiliation.

India's Parliament is quite a sight to witness. Having spent sixteen years as an MP in Canada and having travelled to over one hundred countries, I have witnessed my share of debates. I believe strongly in the power of debate, although perhaps not in the charade that parliamentary debate has degenerated into in Ottawa. In India, there is no more unique, yet democratic, vehicle of expression than "Zero Hour." It occurs every day at noon in the lower house of the Indian Parliament, the Lok Sabha (meaning House of the People).

During this hour, any member of the Lok Sabha – which has as many as 552 members[13] – may rise and speak in either of India's official national languages (Hindi or English) or one of its eighteen official regional languages.[14] What's more, he or she can do so at the same time as other members are speaking. The chaos is about what you would expect from a Tower of Babel. The system, however, does have its advantages. Because it is impossible to distinguish who is saying what to whom during Zero Hour, no record can be kept. Members can go back to their constituencies and, if asked, state emphatically that they raised the matter in the Lok Sabha, even if they did not. Zero Hour also seems to me to be a great way for members to let off steam, after which the house can settle down to serious business.

My most memorable visit to India – bar none – was in 2004. On 26 January – India's Republic Day – I got a phone call informing me that I had been awarded the Padma Shri, India's fourth highest civilian honour, in recognition of my humanitarian work. It was the first time the honour had been accorded to a Canadian.[15] It is rare privilege. In a nation of more than one billion people, only fifty Padma Shri awards are bestowed in a given year.

I was particularly pleased when I was notified that I would be allowed to invite two guests to accompany me to the awards ceremony at the president's palace, known as the Rashtrapati Bhavan. I settled on two people, both unique and special individuals in my life. One was Omak Apang, a vice-chair of Future Generations, a non-governmental organization (NGO) dedicated to conservation, research, and development in high mountain areas of the world. He now serves in the legislature of the north-eastern state of Arunachal Pradesh, and he doubled as my translator for the awards ceremony. My other guest, also from Arunachal Pradesh, was an extraordinary woman by the name of Biri Meema. Of all the people I have encountered in India, Biri's story may be the most compelling.

I first met Biri on a visit with Future Generations to Arunachal Pradesh in the early 2000s.[16] Our primary goal at the time was to provide training for villagers in health, hygiene, and environmental programs. Travel within the state is not easy. Most villagers live in the deep and fertile valleys that bisect the high mountains of the eastern Himalayas. To reach their isolated villages, we travelled along the Brahmaputra River in a small Zodiac for hundreds of kilometres, often sleeping on the riverbank at night.

Within these villages, hundreds of women with no formal training and without the support of nurses or doctors – and often functioning without heat or electricity – work together to provide the health care services their communities need. Biri, whom I met in her village of Palin, shared her story with me through a translator.

Born to an impoverished family, Biri was married off when she was six years old. Her husband, far older, made life miserable for his child bride. "Those days were nightmares for me. I don't even want to recall them," she said. "I was prepared to do any amount of hard work by day but the very thought of spending the night with my husband sent chills down my spine."

Having very little contact with other people, even neighbours, Biri spent most of her childhood toiling in the fields and performing household chores. Making matters worse, her husband was an alcoholic. "He was such a drunkard that he sometimes had difficulty reaching home at night and slept on the roadside. Before I was twenty, I had lost two children as babies and a third was a stillborn," Biri told me.

Her life would change dramatically after she came across a group of women who were discussing topics such as childcare and how to keep fit during pregnancy. Biri became an active participant in the group. Within a year, she was selected by the other women to go to Jamkhed, in the state of Maharashtra, for training in coordinating village projects. "That training session was an eye opener for me," Biri said. "The other women trainees were known as 'village health workers.' Most of them were illiterate, as I was, but they were doing excellent jobs."

Upon her return to Palin, Biri became a team coordinator for various projects in her area that were administered with the help of organizations like Future Generations. She learned to read and write. Within a few years, she secured a paying job as a field coordinator – helping various villages with their reports and regional projects. Furthermore, she has seen a turnaround in her personal life. With newfound confidence in herself, Biri was able to stand up to her husband – and convince him to stop drinking. He was elected Gaon Bura[17] – or "head leader" – in the village of Palin.

Women like Biri have shown me that, given courage and determination, there is no challenge women cannot tackle. She and her colleagues are transforming their corner of the world, working for equality and recognition for women, better health care, and greater protection of the environment. And slowly but surely, they are seeing their visions turn into reality. In three sites in Arunachal Pradesh where Future Generations carries out health care projects, infant mortality cases declined from just over two hundred in 1997 to twenty in 2009 – thanks to the efforts of the village health workers.

On that wonderful day, 30 June 2004, when I accepted the Padma Shri, I could not help but look at Biri and think what an improbable journey her life had been. Until that day, she had never been to New Delhi – she had never been very far from the tribal villages of the eastern Himalayas. Neither she, nor anyone else, could have imagined in those years, when she lived in fear by night and laboured in the fields by day, that she would one day be a guest at the Rashtrapati Bhavan, there to meet her country's president and its prime minister. During a media interview later that day, I invited Biri – who was wearing a new tribal costume that the women in her village had sewn for her – to describe some of the health and nutrition programs she was teaching to other women in north-east India. Her interview was carried on national television that evening. Biri could hardly wait to return to Palin to tell her friends and family.

So what have Biri Meema and the women of Arunachal Pradesh meant to me? I think back to the hurdles and obstacles that confronted me when I first contemplated venturing into the political arena. I had proven I could run campaigns for others, but to be the person out front, the one who was the focus of attention, was something I had to steel myself to do. It did not come easily. What if I made a mess of it and let my supporters down? And how was I to disprove the never spoken but ever-present and insidious questions: Can a woman really do this? Will she have the staying power, the fortitude, the guts to make tough political decisions?

These issues of confidence and gender are obstacles that continue to impede women. The barriers I faced in politics decades ago still exist for many women in Canada. But when I consider what Biri Meema and others like her have managed to accomplish given the difficulties they face on a daily basis, I know that my road was easy by comparison. Biri showed me that when qualities of courage and determination are given free rein, there is nothing women cannot tackle. She and her colleagues are transforming their small corner of the world. Such values as greater equality among persons, recognition of the role of women, vastly improved health care, and greater protection of the environment are slowly becoming the norm.

India is also the country where, through a chance encounter, I had the opportunity to unlock my dream of travelling to the top of the world in Tibet and Nepal. I had been speaking at a conference on conservation in Ahmedabad, the largest city in the state of Gujarat, in February of 1994 when a stranger came up to me during a tea break. "I am American," he began. "You're Canadian. Do you know anything about the Shastri Institute?"

"Yes," I replied. "I chair its board of governors." The man went on to tell me that the Shastri Indo-Canadian Institute had helped to arrange his first trip to Tibet, and he had been grateful to them ever since. "Tibet is the country of my dreams," I replied.

"I'm leaving for Tibet in two months' time," he said, adding, "If you want to come, you will be more than welcome to join me."

Let me ask: Would you, as a sensible, mature woman (sixty-seven years old at the time), have dropped everything to go off to Tibet with a man you had never met before?

Of course, I did! And I have never regretted it. His name was Daniel Taylor, and he was president of Future Generations, the non-profit humanitarian organization he had founded in the early 1980s.

Two months later I was hiking with Daniel and his crew in Tibet. Little did I know then that in coming years I would have a number of adventures with him as a member of his organization.

TIBET

I have never shied away from adventure. As a young woman hitch-hiking across Europe, I was captivated by the sights and sounds of Spain, Portugal, and other countries. I also began to read more about other exotic parts of the world, especially the Middle East and Asia. I remember reading James Hilton's *Lost Horizon*; the way he described Tibet made that remote and mystical Himalayan land come alive. It seemed like the most exotic place in the world, and I dreamed of seeing it for myself some day. Following my chance encounter with Daniel Taylor in New Delhi in 1994, the dream became a reality.

Daniel, who had received his PhD in development planning from Harvard in the early 1970s, had spent considerable time in Tibet. In the 1980s, he worked with his father and grandparents in India and Nepal; his father, a medical doctor who was the first head of UNICEF in China, had spent many years establishing public health projects in villages in the Himalayan region. Daniel's work took him to Tibet, where he formed a group called the Mountain Institute, which studied the rivers that flowed out of Tibet into Nepal. Daniel was anxious to do more work in Tibet, but his colleagues wanted to move on to Nepal. So Daniel left the Mountain Institute, and soon afterward he founded his own non-governmental organization, Future Generations.

One of Daniel's great interests was the preservation of the environment. Under his leadership, Future Generations worked with government authorities and local villagers to establish nature preserves in Tibet. The largest was in eastern Tibet where the four great rivers of Tibet – the Yangtze, Mekong, Salween (known in China as the Nu), and the Yarlung Tsangpo (which becomes the Brahmaputra in India) – fall off the Tibetan Plateau and flow down into China, Vietnam, Cambodia, Burma, and India. These four rivers provide the water for one-fifth of humanity. I would spend six years working with Daniel Taylor in the Future Generations campaign, supported by both Tibet and China, to protect the rivers by preventing, or at least sorely limiting, the deforestation of their watersheds.[18]

My initial journey to Tibet and Nepal – the first of six such trips I would make – was in April 1994. It began with Daniel taking me to Lhasa, the administrative capital, 3,490 metres above sea level, of the Tibet Autonomous Region. By this time, Future Generations was well established in Tibet and had operations in villages all along our way. We stopped to see what these people were doing. The meetings we attended, where men and women discussed community issues, were held outdoors. It was late winter, and it was bitterly cold at such a high altitude. Despite shivering through the meetings, I was fascinated to hear the villagers describe their problems.

Among their many pressing issues were family planning, infant mortality, and how to keep newborns warm and healthy in an extremely cold climate.[19] Listening to these conversations, I learned that NGOs face a number of unique challenges in high-altitude regions. One is to persuade families to abandon traditions detrimental to their young children. The experience I would gain on future trips to Tibet would prove invaluable later when I volunteered to work in the mountainous regions of Afghanistan.

Daniel and I drove through southeastern Tibet into Nepal, where I got my first look at Mount Everest. Of the many photos I have taken over the years, my very favourite is a spectacular picture of Everest taken early one morning when Daniel and I were driving up a riverbed towards Everest's south base camp.[20] The clouds that had been obscuring the view suddenly cleared and Mount Everest stood out in all its glory.

The base camp consisted of an array of tents set up by teams of climbers from around the world. I saw a Canadian flag flying over one group of tents, so I said to Daniel, "Let's go over there, there must be Canadians around." As we were talking, a man popped his head from a tent and exclaimed, "I know that voice!" It was a climber from Calgary.

He was a key member of a large Canadian expedition, in charge of communication with climbers at all levels of the mountain. Back home, he was a high-school teacher who had been granted a leave of absence on condition that he continue to teach his class while he was away. He would teach from the base camp, using a satellite phone to tell his students what the Canadian excursion was doing that day. I learned that this was the first Canadian team to try to reach the summit of Everest without the aid of oxygen![21]

I used his sat. phone to talk to the Canadian climbers who were at various levels of Everest. I was fascinated by their courage and their determination to conquer the mountain. In their world, as they saw it, anything was possible.

What about my world? Here I was, now a sixty-eight-year-old woman on her first-ever visit to the Himalayas. I was a retired politician, not a mountaineer. I had no training whatsoever. But why, I wondered, should any of that stop me from climbing Everest?

I may not have been entirely rational when I asked myself this question: Why could I not join their team and try to scale Everest with them? So I did. I managed to climb another 305 metres in the thin air before I had to stop for want of oxygen. If I had not been committed to returning to Canada in a few days, I think I would have stayed on, rested, and tried again. Instead, I went home, but I will never forget my first encounter with Everest.

While Daniel and I were driving down from Everest, we went through a high pass and, as we were going down the far side, I noticed a solitary person on a bike coming up. I saw that the young man had Canadian flags on his saddlebags. "Stop, stop!" I said. "We've got to see what this fellow is all about."

Daniel reached him first and said, "There's somebody here who wants to meet you."

The chap stepped off his bike, looked around and exclaimed, "Flora MacDonald! What are you doing here?" It turned out he was from Oakville, Ontario, had a job in the computer industry, and was so bored that he challenged himself to take his bicycle and pedal across all seven continents as a fund-raising project. He was into his third year by the time Daniel and I encountered him. He was on his way to take a look at Mount Everest before going down through Nepal to India.

He said he was not sure how he was going to get across Antarctica, but he had done pretty well on the other continents. I took his name, and his parents' address and telephone number. When I got home, I phoned them and passed along his messages.

Eighteen months after my initial foray into the Himalayas, I came back. I joined Daniel Taylor and eleven others, including his family members, on a three-week trek from Shegar, a small Tibetan town where backpackers often stop, to the Everest base camp. Our goal was to reach the Gama Valley, an isolated valley in the National Nature Preserve of the Tibet Autonomous Region, which is known for its rich display of wildflowers, ancient forests and spectacular views of some of the world's highest peaks.[22] Future Generations was working on conservation management projects in this region, notably an endeavour to stop the Chinese government from clear-cutting trees in the region.

Before leaving Shegar, I attended the graduation ceremony of twenty-one Tendaba – a Tibetan word for people who take care of the village. They had just completed a six-week program in basic health care. Future Generations had persuaded a young American doctor, Sam Meyers, and his wife to move to Shegar that winter to train these Tibetans in the elements of health care, training that they would share with their villages. The knowledge passed on from these small training sessions can result in a significant improvement in the quality of life of villagers. The completion of the program was an achievement to celebrate.

I also met a group of twenty women who had come to Shegar from many villages for health care training. When I tried to film them for VisionTV, the women were so shy and unaccustomed to foreigners that they would barely lift their heads to look at me.

Jumping ahead for a moment, three years later, in 1998, when I went back on a major trek across Tibet, China, and Pakistan with six women friends – we called ourselves the "Silk Road Seven" – I invited the same twenty women to come to Lhasa, where we held a three-day training session for a larger group of women. There was a special dinner at which I and my Silk Road companions were recognized as very special people who had come from afar to see how the training program worked. It was a great night. The shy women I had met in Shegar took turns entertaining us with their songs. I could not get over the transformation. Women who had been unable to look at me three years earlier could now entertain an audience of strangers and discuss their ambitions without inhibition. Their training program had given them confidence and a new awareness of their potential. It was wonderful to see!

To backtrack, to my second Tibetan trek – the one in October 1995 with Daniel and eleven others – it was more ambitious than the one the year before. Our plan was to leave our vehicles at the eastern approach of Mount Everest, trek along the slope of the mountain, then climb up to the Gama Valley. We had to climb three passes to get to where we were going; the last one was at 5,791 metres.[23] The journey was very difficult for me physically. From the time I was a child, I have had difficulty breathing in dry air and been subject to fierce nosebleeds. To make matters worse, I had just come from a long journey in China, where I had suffered a severe leg injury.

Let me explain. I had originally travelled to China in August 1995 to film a North-South segment for VisionTV about two women's conferences taking place in Beijing. While there, I had met a woman named Chun-Wuei Su Chien, who was the head of a Future Generations women's group. We made plans to travel across China together; I had always wanted to see the west of China, where the silk roads ran in the days of Marco Polo.

We were to meet in Urumqi (pronounced y-rym-chee), the largest city in western China and the capital of the Xinjiang Uighur Autonomous Region, then head west from there. Two days before we were to leave, however, Chun-Wuei fell very ill and could not travel. I was left with two options: cancel the remainder of my China trip, or try to go on alone, even with no knowledge of Mandarin or any other Chinese dialect. After mulling it over for a day, I chose to keep going.

Urumqi has a number of artificial lakes with seemingly endless fleets of very large boats, which are lighted at night. I decided to take some photographs. With many other people doing the same thing, I looked for a vantage point with a clear view of the boats. I climbed up on a wall that ran around the lake. I took my photos, but when I went to get down from the wall, I stepped onto what I thought was a small platform. Unfortunately, it turned out to be a round barrel, and when I put my weight on it, the barrel rolled in one direction while I flew in another. I was more concerned about my cameras than my body. Rather than try to break my fall, I protected the cameras and I immediately felt an excruciating pain. I thought I had broken my leg. As it turned out, the leg was not broken but my shin became badly swollen. It looked like a huge egg.

I hobbled back to the hotel, where I tried to communicate, charade-fashion, to the staff that I needed some ice by making gestures of wringing out towels in cold water. That did not work. Although the leg was excruciatingly painful, I headed off the next day, with directions provided by a couple I encountered who happened to speak English, to Tian Chi Lake, a spectacular crater lake roughly one hundred kilometres east of Urumqi that is popularly known as the Heavenly Lake of Tianshan. Years later, when I was finally able to read author Vikram Seth's book *From Heaven Lake: Travels through Sinkiang and Tibet*, I was reminded of the beauty I was blessed to see that day.[24]

Though my leg never properly healed, I was soon back in Tibet with Daniel and his companions and on our way – with a dozen porters and thirty yaks – to the beautiful Gama Valley at the foot of Mount Everest. It rained steadily, day after day. Our days were long and regimented. They began with tea at 6 a.m. and ended with dinner around 9 p.m. Things could be chaotic. One day I was following what I thought was the correct path, when I suddenly realized I was alone with Karma, one of our porters, on a steep slope of bramble bushes and other prickly shrubs. There was no trail in sight. We clawed our way straight up through the bushes until we found something that resembled a path. After getting back to level ground, we had to search for our original trail, which we found after climbing over huge boulders. My leg was throbbing terribly. Eventually, Sally Warner, a tiny, wiry woman of sixty who was a major financial backer of Future Generations, came to find me and led us back to where the others were getting settled for the night.

The constant rain meant we had to wear waterproof pants over our slacks to protect us from mud that came above our knees. Our theme song became, "Mud, mud, glorious mud, nothing quite like it for cooling the blood." At one point my trusty walking stick became stuck in the mud and began to sink. I had to get two others to help me pull it out.

After a week, my body began to give out. Lack of sleep, sinus problems, and the altitude – we had ascended beyond four thousand metres – all conspired to sap my energy. I could not go any further without assistance. Mike Shranahan, one of the directors of Future Generations, gave me a "Gamow bag" – a large, durable nylon bag reinforced with circular straps. Mike told me that if I crawled into the bag for a while, it would help my body to recover by stabilizing it at a lower altitude. The contraption was invented in 1990 by Dr Igor Gamow, a microbiology professor and avid outdoorsman. By inflating the bag with a foot pump, the effective altitude a person feels can be reduced by as much as 1,500 metres. I can attest that it works; after a few hours of reading and dozing in my sleeping bag inside the Gamow bag, I felt fully recovered.

I was relieved to be able to carry on. If I had not, I would not be able to boast now that not only had I tried to climb Everest at age sixty-eight, I took my maiden ride on a yak at sixty-nine. (Who says the young have all the fun?) It was not as easy as it may sound. Karma, the porter, led the yak, while two others were at my side in case I fell from the hard wooden saddle. In addition to discovering how agile yaks are when climbing steep slopes, my time with the porters was quite educational. I learned a lot more about Guru Rinpoche and how he brought Buddhism to Tibet.[25]

Once you discover Tibet, it is next to impossible – for me, at least – to stay away for long. As I have mentioned, I came back in 1998 with our Silk Road Seven group of Canadian women. Jean Perlin, a great friend from my days at Queen's University, and I had talked for years about trekking the Silk Road. Others heard us and wanted to come. Our visas were arranged, with some difficulty, by Ian Burchett, a friend of mine since his days as an undergraduate at Queen's, who by this time was on the China desk in Foreign Affairs. When the visas were issued by the Chinese, we were all on one document – and it listed our occupations as "housewives!"[26] The "Seven Housewives" had a good laugh about that! As we went along, I showed them some of the work Future Generations was doing. But for the most part, it was an exploration trip for me. After seeing Mount Everest, we headed north and west into areas where I had never been.

The trek took six weeks – from Lhasa in Tibet to Kashgar in far western China, through the Karakoram Pass and down the Karakoram highway to Karachi in Pakistan. It remains one of the highlights of my life. The trip incorporated several of my keen interests – travel, exploring new places, discovering real examples of sustainable development, and seeing how local populations, increasingly often led by women, can bring about meaningful change in their communities' lives.

One of the places we visited was the Rongbuk Monastery at the foot of Mount Everest. At an elevation of 4,980 metres, it is said to be the highest or second highest residence in the world. This Buddhist monastery was destroyed during the Cultural Revolution, and the monks and area villagers worked for years to restore it. We thought we could get accommodation for the night, but the few beds the monastery had available in a hostel for travellers were filled when we arrived. The monks gallantly vacated their tiny cells, gave us mattresses and invited us to sleep there. The cells were spotless. I shared with two other women – Jean Perlin and Jean's Geneva-based British friend Jenny Raper – the three of us stretched on the floor in our sleeping bags. From time to time during the night, a curious monk would pull aside the curtain that served as a door and peer into the cell. We would hear a whispered exclamation – "Women!" – as he withdrew. It was a surely a night to remember – the night we slept in a Buddhist monk's cell on Mount Everest!

From Rongbuk, we headed in groups along the Tibetan plateau toward Mount Kailash, the holy mountain of Buddhists in Tibet and Hindus in India. Jean, Jenny, and I stopped at noon one day at a small rock enclave where a Tibetan family of three was enjoying their midday meal – a yak bone with some meat on it. They offered to share with us. We politely declined with the salutation, "Tashi deLek." In Tibetan custom, we were expected to offer something in return. Rummaging in our backpacks, we came up with a bag of small individually wrapped Swiss chocolates. "Tashi deLek," they declined.[27]

Mount Kailash was something I especially wanted to see. Tibetans regard it as the centre of the world, the home of the gods, and the source of life. Every year, thousands of Buddhists make a pilgrimage to Mount Kailash. So our Silk Road Seven joined a group of pilgrims and set out to climb the holy mountain.

Kailash is a unique, rectangular-shaped geographical formation. Devout Buddhists try once in their lifetime to make a circumambulation of the mountain by following a steep, rocky trail that wraps its way around the mountain as it climbs toward the top. The climb is not for the faint of heart. Although many pilgrims make the ascent in three days, it took us four days with our guides and yaks to work our way through the patches of snow and ice on the trail. The yaks went ahead with our tents and food. We followed, making the entire circumambulation on foot.

We paused along the way to inspect a large burial ground, a place where Tibetans leave their dead for vultures to dispose of. Where we would leave flowers, this burial ground was decorated with prayer flags and the possessions of the deceased – clothes, shoes, rings, jewelry and assorted trinkets – to wish them safe passage to the afterlife. We were a subdued group as we contemplated the place. Even I was at a loss for words!

Mount Kailash rises to 6,638 metres, but pilgrims do not attempt to climb to the summit, because they fear they will disturb the gods who make their home there. They stop at the highest pass, known as Dolma La Pass, about one thousand metres short of the peak. We stopped there, too, and examined a particular rock that has a smooth surface about two feet square that pilgrims believe represents the footprint of Buddha. If they touch their foreheads to the footprint, Buddha will grant them 108 years' forgiveness for their sins, past, present and future. Or so they believe. Who were we to question their beliefs? We knelt, touched our foreheads to the footprint and joined the pilgrims as they celebrated the successful completion of their pilgrimage. There were flags, prayers and food, to which we contributed some yak butter tea. When we completed the descent from Mount Kailash, we had our own Silk Road Seven celebration. No yak butter tea this time. I passed around a flask of single malt Scotch that I had been carting around in my backpack.

The trek had another memorable and, for me, nostalgic moment as we passed through Pakistan near the end of our trip. It took some finagling on my part, but we managed to secure a special permit for our group to travel – with an armed military escort – to the Khyber Pass. The others could not possibly have felt the emotions that overcame me as I stood on what may have been the precise spot where my uncle, Scout Sergeant Alexander MacDonald, of the fabled Black Watch Royal Highlanders, had stood ninety-three years earlier, gazing down at the hostile land below.

He was looking at Afghanistan – the rugged, never conquered, often cruel and always dangerous nation where before long I would open the next chapter of my life.

Glorious! – Early morning sun on Mount Everest following a night in 1998 when our Silk Road Seven slept in monks' cells in Tibet's Rongbuk Monastery, elevation 4,980 metres. (Flora MacDonald Collection)

In the Beginning – My dedication to humanitarian work dates to a 1989 visit to Namibia on the eve of its independence from South Africa. I visited a school, met the children – and was hooked! (Flora MacDonald Collection)

Africa's Greatest Leader – I admired Nelson Mandela immensely. Here we are in Pretoria on one of my trips to South Africa. (Flora MacDonald Collection)

Future Generations – Daniel Taylor (centre), is the American environmentalist and humanitarian who founded Future Generations. His example inspired my volunteer work in high-altitude regions in India, Pakistan, and Tibet. On the left is Mahmood Jaghori, a volunteer working in Afghanistan. (courtesy of Daniel Taylor/Flora MacDonald Collection)

Educating Women in India – In March 2000, we opened this Future Generations Training Centre in the state of Arunachal Pradesh ("the land of dawn-lit mountains") in the northeastern corner of India, up against Bhutan, Myanmar, and China. We brought women from remote villages to the centre where we taught them to read and write and provided instruction in such things as agricultural methods and ways to improve the health and nutrition of their children. When the courses finished, they returned to their villages to share these life skills with other women.
(Flora MacDonald Collection)

Film Maker – In the early years following my involuntary departure from Parliament, I was able to finance my international travel by doing freelance television work, starting with VisionTV. I hosted a documentary series for them called "North/South" that took me to some of the poorest, most troubled countries on earth. (Flora MacDonald Collection)

Honoured in India – One of the thrills of my life was being awarded the Padma Shri in 2004 by the government of India for my humanitarian and educational work in that country. The "Padma" is among the highest civilian awards in India and is rarely given to a foreigner. My guest for the presentation at Rashtrapati Bhavan, the president's palace, was Biri Meema, an extraordinary woman from the northeastern state of Arunachal Pradesh. (Government of India/Flora MacDonald Collection)

Children, Children, Everywhere – Refugee camps are miserable places. They can be soul destroying for adult refugees, so many of whom despair of ever returning to their old life at home or starting a new life in another country. But the children are irrepressible. Their excitement when they see me and the joy in their faces never fail to melt my heart. (Flora MacDonald Collection)

At School in Afghanistan – Future Generations opened schools wherever we could find room in a building or just a sheltered spot outdoors. This one is in a mosque in a village in the Shahidan Valley. (Abdullah Barat/Flora MacDonald Collection)

A Tribute from Canada's "boat people" – On 3 May 2015, Flora MacDonald was honoured by the Canadian Vietnamese community at "The Vietnamese Boat People: a 40-Year Journey Comes to Life," a cultural show and exhibit in Ottawa. With Flora are, from left: Dr Tri Hoang, president (2014–15) of the Vietnamese Canadian Federation (VCF); Luong Le Phan, board member of the Vietnamese Canadian Community of Ottawa; Tuyet Lam, president (2010–14) of the VCF. Sadly, it would be Flora's last public appearance. She died less than three months later at the age of 89. (Trieu Bao/Flora MacDonald Collection)

Creating Afghanistan's First National Park – When I first saw the six beautiful travertine lakes at Band-e Amir in the Hindu Kush mountains, they took my breath away. I set out to persuade the Afghan authorities to declare the site a national park on the model of Banff and Jasper. If peace ever comes to this troubled land, Band-e Amir will be a huge tourist attraction. (Abdullah Barat/Flora MacDonald Collection)

Flora Footbridge – After chewing over the idea for 112 years, the city of Ottawa finally built, and in 2019 opened, a footbridge over the Rideau Canal, where Flora loved to skate in the decades before her death in 2015. A long stone's throw from her apartment, and named in her memory, it is 123 metres long and cost a bit less than the budgeted twenty-one million dollars. (City of Ottawa)

16

Afghanistan

Nothing I have been involved in since I left politics – or politics left me, as I prefer to think of it – consumed me the way Afghanistan did. That country and its people became my obsession, my greatest cause. Over the course of a decade, I made an average of one extended trip to Afghanistan every year at my own expense. When I was back in Canada, I spent much of my time raising money to finance the work that Future Generations Canada, the teaching institute I founded, was doing in the mountain villages of Bamyan province. We helped build hospitals and schools, promoted public health measures, trained teachers and nurses, and taught village women, who had been denied schooling during the dark Taliban years, to read and write and to take control of their households and communities. We did all this on a minuscule budget of $75–80,000 a year. I raised money by making speeches and presenting the Afghan story to audiences across Canada. Some funds came from contacts I had made through politics or my work with other NGOs. When I had to dip into my parliamentary pension to cover a deficit, I did that. On more than one occasion, we asked the Government of Canada for financial help, but they said they were not interested.

The Canadian people were more helpful than their government. David Suzuki, the celebrated scientist and environmentalist, and I co-sponsored a fundraising concert in Calgary in 2007 featuring Rain, a popular Beatles tribute band. We called it "Rain for Afghanistan – A concert to raise funds and awareness for the people of Afghanistan." We charged $250 for the concert with a VIP reception, or $75 for the concert alone. Concertgoers were invited to come early to stroll (and spend) through an "Afghan Marketplace" that we set up.

The concert netted $48,000 for Future Generations Canada, and it drew public attention to our work in Afghanistan. We got more attention the following year when Carole MacNeil brought a CBC crew to Afghanistan to make a television documentary that showed what we were doing on the ground – bringing electrical light, clean water, health care, and a chance for education to impoverished villagers. The program was broadcast several times. We were astonished, and delighted, to receive $60,000 in spontaneous donations from people who saw it and wanted to help.

I first visited Afghanistan in 2001, not long before the terrorist attack on New York's World Trade Center on 11 September. The Taliban was still in power. As a woman, I had to accept the local dress code, which meant being almost completely covered. Even though I carefully complied, I was given a frosty welcome when I met the country's deputy foreign minister. His demeanor was so severe, so forbidding that I did not bother to tell him I had once been Canada's foreign minister, although I suspect he knew. It may have accounted for his veiled hostility.

That first visit was on behalf of CARE Canada, which had been carrying out projects in Afghanistan for a number of years. In the wake of twenty-five years of conflict, the last seven of which had seen the country devastated by drought, CARE was running a food distribution program for ten thousand war widows and their children. This might not seem like a balanced diet to Westerners, but it provided desperately needed sustenance for the long-suffering people – every month, a bag of wheat flour, cooking oil, lentils, and a small amount of sugar.

My involvement in Afghanistan increased exponentially after 9/11. In retaliation for the destruction of the "twin towers," the United States launched Operation Enduring Freedom and, with the support of Canada and other nations, invaded Afghanistan. The invasion had a dual objective: to eradicate the Al-Qaeda terrorist organization and to overthrow the Taliban regime in Kabul. At that time, I was a volunteer with Future Generations International, the US-based NGO that I had worked with in Northern India, Nepal, and Tibet. When Future Generations arrived in Bamyan, poppies were being cultivated everywhere. As late as 2005, Afghanistan produced an estimated 90 per cent of the world's heroin supply. Its annual street value in Europe was said to be one hundred billion American dollars. Poppies have since been eradicated in Bamyan, replaced by grains and other cash crops.

The key to this success was the involvement of the local councils, known as shuras. They made the decisions and generated support among people of the province. Our role was to provide the people and their leaders with the resources to make major decisions on their own. In those days, the area was home to thousands of former members of the Mujahideen – those Islamic warriors who had been in the mountains and deserts of Afghanistan for years, waging guerrilla warfare against the Taliban and Soviet invaders. By the time I got there, they were trying to transition to civilian life. They needed money. We knew that, but we also understood that money was only part of it. They needed tools to take charge of their own futures, free from the control of leaders in the cities. While the cities of Kabul, Kandahar, Herat, and Mazar-e-Sharif dominate the headlines, 75 per cent of Afghanistan's thirty million people live in small towns and villages.

In 2003, we invited thirty-six former Mujahideen members to a picnic and a discussion of the future. One of them told us: "We have been fighting for years to own our future, but now our future is in the control of the NGOs who have arrived [since the American invasion]. We have followed our leaders and now they are in Kabul living like kings. We are hungry and poor, just living like beggars waiting for UN agencies to give us food so that we do not starve and to give us tents so that we do not freeze from the cold. They are not helping us to live like human beings. We should stand on our own feet and tell them what *we* want, not what *they* want."

As a result of this meeting, Future Generations assisted the ex-Mujahideen fighters to form their own political party, the Pagal party. They adopted a slogan: "If you believe the future will be better or if you are crazy enough to work for the betterment of your future, you will join the Pagal party." Not very punchy by North American standards, yet the slogan worked in Afghanistan. Soon thereafter, Pagal party members built a school, where the former combatants began teaching hundreds of students to read.

The "Pagal School" was where the leaders from the seventy-two villages in the Shahidan valley[1] met from 29 January to 2 February 2005, for a conference on their and their children's futures. By this time, every one of the seventy-two villages had its own council and governance system. The structure of each council had been chosen by village people, not imposed on them by outsiders. At the end of the five-day conference, these community leaders agreed to establish a central shura,[2] to coordinate projects throughout the Shahidan valley. I vividly recall how, after the creation of the central shura, more than five hundred women flocked in from the high pastures of the region to meet with it. They complained that NGOs would come to their villages, start programs, get local residents excited, then disappear, leaving the people high and dry with projects they could not afford to continue. They did not want the central shura to allow an NGO to set up in their valley unless they had a clear understanding of what the NGO was going to do, how long it was going to stay, and what ongoing funding it would provide when it left.

The central shura model of governance produced results almost immediately. By the end of 2005, four new schools had been built and more than one hundred thousand willow trees had been planted for fuel. Eventually, we planted 850,000 willows.

Our work was truly fulfilling. The seeds of change germinated. In 2007, Bamyan Town[3] became the first community in the country to elect a female as head of its shura (four of the ten shura members that year were women). In the midst of war and religious violence, women can now look to other women as role models. They can assert their right to be as involved as men in local decision-making. While some men still resist women playing a larger role, others are delighted to have them as active participants in the advancement of Afghan society.[4]

I have never thought of myself as a feminist, but encouraging institutions of male power to correct historic gender imbalances has been a recurring theme in my life. In 1971, I was the first woman admitted to a course at the National Defence College in Kingston – the only female in a class of thirty-five. The class travelled to twenty-seven countries that year, and I became acutely aware of the absence of women in decision-making roles. At the end of the term, our college commandant commented, "You know, I don't think the next class trip will be quite like this one because we won't have Flora with us to say to our hosts, 'That's all very nice, but now please tell us about the situation of women in your country.'"

My advocacy of women's causes continued during the sixteen years I spent as the member of Parliament for Kingston and The Islands. Working in a male-dominated Conservative caucus – which, with the exception of a few sensitive individuals like Joe Clark, was virtually oblivious to the concept of gender equality – I never hesitated to make my voice heard. I was not afraid to offer myself for the leadership of my party. And I have never believed it is necessary to have a cabinet minister responsible for the status of women. The status of women should be the concern and responsibility of every cabinet member, male or female. In my days as a minister, I made a point of ensuring that women received their proper status in every project that my departments undertook.

Whenever I met women in developing countries – notably in Rwanda, Somalia, Bosnia, Kosovo, and Afghanistan – I found that they had a stronger desire for peace and stability than men had. Men do most of the fighting, but when women lose their husbands, their lives change dramatically. The widows become not just the sole parental support for their children, but the breadwinners for their extended families, even in societies where women are not traditionally income earners.

In Afghanistan, the need for women to play a larger role has never been greater. A quarter-century of war has killed two million men. Women are becoming aware of the importance of being prepared to be their own advocates and to take an active role in the governance of their towns and villages. They recognize the importance of education. As recently as 2005, 90 per cent of women in the rural areas of the country were illiterate. Even in Kabul, the capital, the illiteracy rate among adult females was 75 per cent. One widow told me what this meant in terms of political participation: "We are illiterate, we do not have radios or TVs, so we cannot learn about any of the candidates. For most of us, the thousands of election posters that decorate Kabul are simply pictures of strange faces and odd symbols." This was one very good reason why I and my colleagues at Future Generations worked so hard to enroll widows in literacy classes.

International assistance is essential to build the democratic institutions that will empower the Afghan people to govern themselves. But until the curse of the Taliban is lifted from the nation, any effort by NGOs or by domestic organizations, if the effort encourages the advancement of women, will be dangerous. In 2006, Safia Ahmed-jan, provincial director for Afghanistan's Ministry of Women's Affairs, was murdered at the gate to her home in the outskirts of Kandahar. Her killing was widely believed to be retaliation for her support of education for women.

Not long before that murder, I had my own scare on the road to Bamyan, as I related at the beginning of the book. Afghanistan was, and remains, a dreadfully violent place. Many humanitarian organizations have pulled out, concerned for the safety of their employees and volunteers. That is what Future Generations International, on whose board of directors I served, decided to do in 2007. I made the opposite decision. I concluded that our work was too important and too necessary to be abandoned. That is why I started Future Generations Canada, a registered charity, and set my own priorities. I carried on as before, although I began to travel by air rather than by road when moving about the country. When friends and colleagues urged me to stop going to Afghanistan, I refused. I had simply invested too much of my life in my work to give it up. I took precautions, but in my view helping the people of Afghanistan, especially the women and children, was worth taking risks for.

I guess I have always been this way. I took to heart my father's admonition that no matter how hard life seemed to be in North Sydney in the Great Depression, we had an obligation to donate to our church's overseas missions. We must always help the poor, the weak, and others who are struggling with life's obstacles. It is how I felt when I saw how poorly women inmates were treated in prison in Kingston. I knew I had a moral obligation to help them, and I did. It is how I felt during the refugee crisis after the war in Vietnam. I knew our government had no money to spare, but I insisted that we find funds somewhere because we had to help the boat people. And we did, we really did. On a per capita basis, Canada took in more Southeast Asian refugees than any other country. It was a proud chapter.

I felt the same way whenever I visited desperately poor countries in Africa or Asia. Big foreign aid programs that distribute dollars by the millions or food by the ton are fine and good. They are essential. But what these countries also need is human commitment – aid workers and volunteers who come to their communities and live among their people as they teach them how to read and write, how to organize schools and health clinics, and how to inform themselves about birth control and the care of infants. These "boots on the ground" teach villagers to adopt agricultural practices that will increase their crop yields and show them ways they can protect their environment. This on-the-ground assistance was what I tried to provide when I volunteered in developing countries. It is why I was in Afghanistan.

I could not do it alone. Although I was able to spend part of each year in Afghanistan, I needed someone to look after things when I was not there, someone based in Bamyan who could oversee our projects, deal with the local authorities, and maintain our contacts with other NGOs in the region. I put out an appeal through Ottawa's large Hazara community. One day in 2002, Abdullah Barat knocked on my apartment door. Born in Bamyan Town in 1961 and raised there during a period of relative calm, Abdullah fled his country to escape from the Taliban. Arriving in Canada as a refugee in 1995, he built a career managing ten Pizza Pizza outlets in Eastern Ontario. He had just received his landed immigrant status when he appeared at my door in 2002. I knew within minutes that he was the person I needed, a person I could trust.

Although he was initially reluctant to give up his job and the comforts of Canada for the risks and hardships of his homeland, Abdullah soon agreed to return to Afghanistan. He became the first and only employee of Future Generations Canada. With a small office in Bamyan Town, a computer, and a Toyota pickup truck donated by a sponsor in Canada, he launched new projects and took control of existing ones. He was brave in the face of danger; in 2001, the year before he started, Taliban fighters had invaded the mountainous territory where he would be working to blow up the famous "Bamyan Buddha," the oldest statue of Buddha in the world. A born networker, Abdullah was enterprising in finding ways around bureaucratic and political obstacles. He gave us immediate credibility with the people of Bamyan. He was persuasive. In even the most sensitive situations, such as discussing birth control with villagers, Abdullah was able to convince conservative Afghans to adopt new ways of dealing with traditional issues.

He organized a soccer team to direct young men away from drugs. He created jobs for three youths by helping them to start two small retail businesses, one to sell parts and accessories for mobile phones, the other dealing in vehicle parts. In a Future Generations partnership with a much larger NGO, Norwegian Church Aid (with operations in twenty-four developing countries), he introduced a rural electrification project. Local residents, male and female, were

trained to install and to maintain solar panels in two villages. They
provided electricity for forty families.

Another project created safe employment for war widows.
Abdullah asked the Department of Women's Affairs in Bamyan to
identify twenty of the neediest widows in the town. He put them
through a restaurant management course that he had devised.
Here – unedited – is an excerpt from his request to our board for
ten thousand dollars to cover the costs of the eight-month program
(four months to train the women, four months to get the restaurant
open and running):

Problem Identification
- No income for widow women, their children weave carpet
  sixteen hours each day instead of going to school to study.
- For survival, sometime young widows become prostitute in
  order to safe their life and their children life even it would be
  another danger of getting killed for adultery.

Goal
- Create jobs for twenty widows to bring decent income for
  them. With the income they can have, they would feed themselves and their children, educate their children and would
  create self-respect to these twenty widows.

Beneficiaries
- The direct beneficiaries of this project will be twenty widows
  and their children. Also, indirect benefit would be to a lot of
  widows that give them confidence to work outside of their
  houses in order to have income.

I take particular satisfaction from the success of a quite different project: the creation of Afghanistan's first national park. The
spectacular Band-e Amir National Park comprises six deep blue
travertine-lined lakes in the Hindu Kush mountains of central
Afghanistan.[5] It is sometimes described as Afghanistan's Grand
Canyon. If the country ever finds peace and becomes safe for visitors, the park will be an amazing tourist attraction and a valuable
economic asset.

The idea for the park was born during the May 2005 road trip that
I described in the opening chapter, when we were stopped and robbed

by Taliban guerrillas, Abdullah was beaten, and I was frightened out of my wits. When we got back to Kabul, we went to the Canadian Embassy to report the ambush to Ambassador Chris Alexander.[6] We also told him about the national park. Chris was immediately enthusiastic. The Afghan government, he told me, had just appointed an independent commissioner of environmental protection – officially Director-General of Afghanistan's National Environmental Protection Agency (NEPA). "And, Flora, you must know him. It's Mustafa – Mustafa Zahir."

Indeed, I did know Mustafa. In one of those serendipitous coincidences that occurred throughout my life, the powerful Afghan official who could make Band-e Amir National Park a reality had been a student at Queen's University when I worked there. He lived just down the street from me in Kingston and his favourite professor was my boss in the political studies department, John Meisel. I got to know Mustafa and his family story. He was the grandson of Afghanistan's last king, Mohammad Zahir. Deposed in 1973, Mohammad lived in exile in Italy while the Taliban ruled in Kabul. In 2002, he returned to Afghanistan and was given the title "Father of the Nation."

Chris called Mustafa at the palace where he was living with his grandfather. When Chris put me on the line, Mustafa said, "Flora, are you calling me from Kingston?"

I replied, "No, I'm here in Kabul."

"I'm coming right over to see you," he said. As we talked about the park, he became tremendously excited and insisted, "You must come and meet the king tomorrow and tell him all about it."

I did. The ex-king was as enthusiastic as his grandson. He was full of stories, telling us he had been the first monarch ever to make the trip from Kabul to Bamyan, driving himself in his 1969 Cadillac. When he got to the outskirts of Bamyan Town, the people were so excited that the king had come to see them that they took the Cadillac, with him in it, and carried it to the main square. He thought the park was a wonderful idea. With the support of the Father of the Nation and his Canadian-educated grandson, Band-e Amir National Park opened in April 2009.

Throughout Abdullah's years as my lieutenant in Afghanistan, he and I worried about his Canadian immigration status. He was a permanent resident and he desperately wanted citizenship, not only for himself, but for his wife and their children, too. But how could he qualify when he had to spend most of every year in Afghanistan?[7]

He asked me that question at our first meeting in 2002. I did not have the answer, but I told him not worry. If he went back, I would find a way.

Easy to promise, hard to deliver – even (or maybe especially) for a former immigration minister. The bureaucracy moves with "deliberate speed" – if it wishes to move at all. It took eight years. Eight years of lawyers (largely pro bono, thank heaven) and hearings. Eight years of arguing, pleading, appealing, and lobbying before we finally prevailed, and Abdullah was approved for citizenship. On 24 June 2010, eight years and one month after Abdullah and I made our first trip together to Afghanistan, I had the honour and privilege, in my capacity as a member of the Privy Council of Canada, to swear in Abdullah Barat as a citizen of Canada. It was a very special moment for both of us.

––––––––––––––––––

Over the years, I made ten extended trips to Afghanistan from the high central mountain provinces of Bamyan, Parwan, and Oruzgan to the more central provinces of Ghazni and Paktia. I was not a tourist or a visiting celebrity. I went to see, not to be seen. I was a volunteer who came to villages to help in any way I could. I got to know the local people. I travelled with them, met their families, played with their young children, shared their meals and slept in their mud-brick huts.

This long, close relationship leads me to several observations. The Afghan people are hard-working and ingenious, but they need education and jobs. They need help to rebuild their nation. Progress is being made, if not uniformly throughout the country. A form of local governance is emerging, although not necessarily a form consistent with western models. Rebuilding the Afghan military to contain and ultimately defeat the Taliban is going to take a long time. Rebuilding the nation politically, economically, and socially will take longer. To meet these challenges, the Afghan people must be able to count on the security of international support.

In the broad sweep of history, Afghanistan has been around for a long time. It has suffered attacks, defeats, and partial occupation, but it has never been conquered. It is still a country caught between two potential futures – a fragile democracy that moves forward, or a failed state. I wish I could be definitive, but, as I write this, I can only say the jury is still out.

POSTSCRIPT

The dangers in Afghanistan kept escalating. In 2008 alone, thirty-four aid workers were reported killed and ninety others abducted. We moved Abdullah's family to the safety of India. Abdullah carried on in Bamyan even though his office was vandalized and his computer stolen. But when he started getting serious death threats, the board of directors of Future Generations Canada decided, in 2011, to bring him home. Worried that I might be murdered or kidnapped for ransom, the board, over my strenuous objections, voted to withdraw from Afghanistan. Future Generations Canada was dissolved in May 2012.

I am not a quitter. I have to ask: Were my efforts wasted? I cannot believe they were. I pray that the seeds I and many others have planted will one day produce blooms in a democratic Afghanistan – a peaceful state where war fades to a distant memory. I hope it will be an open, generous society that accepts women as the equals of men in all walks of life. If such be my legacy, I would embrace it proudly.

Memories and Tributes

Flora MacDonald inspired a generation of Canadian women and became a role model to their daughters. She was recognized for her public service and humanitarian work at home and abroad. During her lifetime, she was named Companion of the Order of Canada, a member of the Orders of Ontario and Nova Scotia, and Toronto Scot of the Year; in India, she was awarded the Padma Shri; in Canada, the Pearson Medal of Peace, the World Federalist Peace Award, and the Eve Award from Equal Voice; plus at least eighteen honorary degrees from Canadian and American universities.

The city of Kingston named its four hundred-boat harbour in front of City Hall the "Flora MacDonald Confederation Basin," and the city of Ottawa built a $12 million footbridge over the Rideau Canal, where she loved to skate. "Flora Footbridge" opened after her death. The governor of Bamyan province in Afghanistan paid tribute to her humanitarian work in his country, and he accepted a memorial plaque, to be installed at Band-e Amir National Park in the Hindu Kush mountains in recognition of Flora's role in the creation of Band-e Amir, Afghanistan's first national park.

When she died, memories and tributes poured in. Here are portions of some of them:

Tahir Zohair, governor of Bamyan province
Flora MacDonald took a keen interest in Afghanistan – particularly the appalling situation of women under the Taliban. Flora travelled to Bamyan many times at great personal risk to develop schools for girls and promote women's local leadership. She is remembered as the embodiment of Canada's commitment to the rights of women and girls.

Humanitarian Daniel Taylor, president of Future Generations (USA)
Flora was inspirational, a force of nature, one of those people who
changed the course of history, made us want to take another level of
risk, and found fun in serious work.

Former Prime Minister Joe Clark, from his eulogy
It was my privilege to work with the irrepressible, irreplaceable
Flora MacDonald for more than fifty years. I knew her as a friend,
as so many of us across the world and country felt ourselves to
be "Flora's friend." Many people who had never actually met her
sensed that if they were in need, and if she knew, she would be
at their side. As a colleague, she was a parliamentarian who profoundly respected both the institution and the citizens she served,
and a minister of uncommon curiosity and courage and accomplishment. And as a force in our society and world, she was a champion who not only espoused important changes, but was regularly
among those who made them happen. She was a contagious example of how much good an active, committed individual can accomplish and inspire.

Prime Minister Justin Trudeau
Flora MacDonald was a great Canadian whose leadership and compassion will be sorely missed.

Former Governor General David Johnston
She was a dear friend, a remarkable politician, and a compassionate humanitarian. Many of us benefitted from her counsel, and our
communities and our world have been enriched by her compassion.

Cape Breton Post
There's something to be envied about anyone who is capable of
responding to an international emergency such as the Iranian hostage
crisis of 1979 and who can also hold their own during a Cape Breton
ceilidh. It's her strength of personality and her self-confidence that
seems to have resonated most with anyone who met her. Her life
story is a great tale to share with those who are too young to remember this trail-blazing and strong-willed woman who once called
Cape Breton home.

Senator Donna Dasko, co-founder, Equal Voice
Flora MacDonald captured the imagination of women across the country when she ran for the leadership of her party in 1976. Flora was the true, essential trailblazer for the women of her era.

Ed Broadbent, former NDP leader and Flora's MP in Ottawa
Flora was the real McCoy – warm, spontaneous, and gutsy. She was instinctively progressive but not at all dogmatic. In our post-parliamentary lives, when we worked together on certain projects, I was lucky to find a partner who simultaneously loved the world in all its diversity, and yet strived to make it more just. She was a gem.

Former Conservative cabinet minister Lisa Raitt
[She] demonstrated that any career was possible – even for a girl like me from Whitney Pier, Nova Scotia. She cleared our path, and I am grateful.

Ian Burchett, retired Canadian diplomat, from his eulogy
As a young west coast Canadian at Queen's University in Kingston, I became a student volunteer in her constituency office and then Flora's local driver. Believe me that was no easy task! To this day, I still have many agonizing memories of late-night drives between Kingston and Ottawa. Flora always doubted my caution, when despite her insistence, I would not pass a truck on a double line at the crest of a hill. In all these years, I seemed to have been drawn back to Flora, as many of us were. She was energetic, a role model, adventuresome, and of course, hard working. Volunteers in the constituency, staffers on the hill, colleagues in the party, partners in the NGO community and later as neighbours, close friends, companions and care givers, we were in fact, Flora's family – Flora Fanatics!

Phat Nguyen, president, Toronto Vietnamese Association
Minister MacDonald was instrumental in saving tens of thousands of South Vietnamese by developing a federal matching program together with the generous Canadian public to sponsor and rescue "boat people" from inhumane refugee camps across South-East Asia. We are forever grateful for her immeasurable compassion and humanitarian support.

Carolyn McAskie, a retired diplomat and one of the Silk Road Seven
In Tibet, we saw Flora's strengths of perseverance, single minded-ness, and ability and desire to lead (to say nothing of her love of Scottish walking songs). It was not easy to get close to her; she was very much a self-made woman, but later we saw her soft side. It was a time to treasure.

London Daily Telegraph
She proved her mettle at the August 1979 Commonwealth confer-ence in Lusaka when she declined to go shopping with ministers' wives and drove out to spend five hours in a Zimbabwean refugee camp deep in the bush. She was also intensely involved as a leader in the global response to the crisis of the Vietnamese boat people. As a result, more than sixty thousand Vietnamese refugees were allowed to enter Canada.

Former Green Party leader Elizabeth May
Canada has lost a great humanitarian, an exemplary parliamentar-ian, and wonderful leader.

Feminist Maureen McTeer
I never heard Flora describe herself as a feminist, as if the term was too narrow for her world view. She believed firmly that the individ-ual could and must make a difference, and she spent her life doing just that. Flora lived as if each day were her last. This alone is a worthy legacy.

Michel de Salaberry, retired Canadian Ambassador to Iran, Egypt and Jordan
On a February 2004 visit to Cairo, she came back to my home about three hours late, after nightfall, alone, after her driver had come back with Anne Stanfield, both of them in despair for having lost Flora in the throngs of a built-up area not far from the Saqqara pyr-amids. Flora never understood why we would have worried. She had wandered out to explore a street market, at some point had realized that the car had left, and had simply hitched a ride back home. She was as delighted by the people who had helped her as they were of their new Canadian acquaintance. She was then seventy-eight.

Senator Lowell Murray, from his eulogy

Nine years ago, we celebrated her eightieth birthday. No expensive tribute dinner in a five-star hotel for Flora; rather "Flora's Picnic" on Parliament Hill, open to all, who came by the hundreds on a sunny Sunday afternoon in June. Flora was really glad to be back among those friends and political colleagues; however, she was most deeply touched by the presence of so many who worked, as she did, for such causes as the Canadian Council for Refugees, CARE Canada, UNICEF, and Future Generations Canada. They were "Flora's people" and she cherished them. When it came to doing God's work on earth, Flora walked the talk.

Richard Stursberg, former CBC executive vice-president

I used to skate to work along the Rideau Canal to my job at the Department of Communications. One day, Flora and I discussed the United Way campaign and how to encourage employees to give generously. She challenged me to race the length of the canal. "Everyone can bet on it," she said. I was in my late thirties and she was in her early sixties. She could see what I was thinking – "Come on, Richard. I don't care who wins or loses. It's for a good cause." I soon discovered how sly, funny, and competitive she was. When we arrived at the canal, she was carrying skates with two-foot-long blades. "Oh," she said, innocently, "did I forget to tell you that I was the Nova Scotia women's speed skating champion?"

Anne Stanfield, widow of Robert Stanfield

Shortly after Bob died, I received a phone call from Michel de Salaberry, who was an old friend and then our ambassador to Egypt, with an invitation to visit him in Cairo. It was just the distraction I needed and happily accepted. When Flora learned of the planned trip, she asked if she could come with me. I was delighted. Flora would be a good travel companion; she was adventuresome and fearless – at times a danger-ous combination. One day we decided to visit the pyramids and the great sphinx. At one point I realized I had lost Flora. I turned back and found her sitting cross legged on the ground in a circle of camel drivers. She was negotiating the price of two camels to take us into the desert. Another day Flora proposed that we should extend our adven-tures to Egypt's Western Desert region of the Sahara. I can still see Flora seated atop a huge sand dune with her arms wrapped around her knees. She was taking in every minute of the beauty around her. That is the Flora I cannot forget.

Acknowledgments

Flora MacDonald would insist I begin by expressing her deep appreciation and gratitude to her family – parents Mollie and Fred MacDonald, her sisters Jean (Grearson), Helen (Moffitt), Sheila (Muttart) and Lorna (Hogan), and her brother Ron (MacDonald) – for their love and unstinting support at every step of her life journey. Readers will have met them in chapter 3. She would also wish to pay tribute to three men whom she called mentors at crucial stages of her life: her father Fred, who taught her never to let her gender be a barrier because she was as good as any male (and probably better than most); Robert Stanfield, one of nature's gentlemen, a leader who set the standard for decency, moderation and respect for others in the honourable pursuit of politics; and Professor John Meisel, who (as noted in chapter 9) brought her to Queen's University at a turning point in her life and gave her an opportunity to grow into the leader she became.

Flora would want to acknowledge the support of special people during her years in politics: friends and allies Hugh Hanson, Lowell Murray, Richard Hatfield, David MacDonald, Gordon Fairweather, Joe Clark, Dalton Camp, Finlay MacDonald, Eddie Goodman, Ron Atkey, Terry O'Connor, George Perlin, Michael Vaughan, Murray Coolican, David Elder and Michel de Salaberry. All are introduced in the book. Jean Perlin was Flora's closest female comrade; she fought in her campaigns in Kingston and ran her office in Ottawa; accompanied her on trips to third world refugee camps; and hiked the Silk Road with her. Margit Herrmann, Flora's personal secretary (executive assistant in today's workplace), somehow kept her boss's hectic life in order.

The book experienced an uncommonly long gestation, as noted in the introduction. At each stage, we were fortunate to have supporters to nudge it along. Our agent, Linda McKnight, enthusiastic from the outset, continued to provide wise counsel following her retirement from Westwood Creative Artists. Doug Gibson, a fine editor, immediately recognized the significance of Flora's story. Michel Wyczynski and the other good people at Library and Archives Canada were extraordinarily helpful, setting aside a room where Flora and I could review the records – tens of thousands of pages – of her years in Parliament and government and photocopying whatever we needed. Historian Jack Granatstein at York University gave permission to use his 1967 oral history interviews with Flora and Camp for chapter 6, the Diefenbaker chapter.

The Canadian book publishing industry has been struggling for years. When publishers cannot afford to underwrite the costs of research, travel and other expenses, authors are left to their own devices. Transcribing sixty-plus hours of taped interviews with Flora was the biggest single expense. Fortunately, Robert Hoshowsky, a colleague from my days at *Maclean's*, took on the chore at a modest hourly rate, and he did it well. I am indebted to my good friends Hugh Winsor and Christina Cameron for giving me keys to their home to use whenever I came to Ottawa to meet Flora; I was there often enough that they took to calling their guest room the "Flora MacDonald Suite." Special thanks as well to the wonderful Thomas Kierans, investment banker, philanthropist and Flora fan. When there was no money for research, Tom quietly provided the wherewithal for Ravi Amarnath, then at Queen's University, to assist by assembling details of Flora's humanitarian work in India, Tibet and Afghanistan.

Several people read all or parts of the manuscript and offered helpful advice: Bronwyn Drainie and Yves Gionet in Toronto, Ernest Hillen in Cambridge and Jean Perlin, living in retirement in Australia. Jean also shared her personal knowledge of Flora's complicated relationship with Brian Mulroney (discussed in chapter 14), and she supplied a colourful account of the trek of the Silk Road Seven in chapter 15.

Jean also hunted down photographs for Linda Grearson, Flora's niece, who tackled the task of finding pictures for the book. Filmmaker Peter Raymont – who captured the drama of Flora's leadership bid in his documentary *Flora: Scenes from a Leadership Convention* – and Alexandra Hubert of the National Film Board helped Linda to secure still photos from the film. Her photo quest was also aided by Joe Clark and his executive assistant Roseline MacAngus; by Kelly Ferguson and Nancy Fay at Library and Archives Canada; Ken Hernden and Heather Home, archivists at Queen's University; Carina Duclos and Kimberley Asiri at the Ottawa city archives; and Ian Thompson, former associate publisher, Halifax *Chronicle Herald*. Anik Grearson used her computer skill to enhance the quality of older images, magically transforming the unusable into the publishable.

Others helped in the manuscript's final stages. Kathy Kruivitsky, Flora's accountant and a director of Future Generations Canada, explained how FGC was funded and operated. Abdullah Barat, Future Generations country manager for Afghanistan, described the projects he and Flora initiated in that country. Ann Jansen was notable among the industry insiders who offered advice on the perils of publishing in Canada. My friend Patrick Martin, who had been a player on Flora's leadership team, contributed the toboggan story in chapter 11, while Ron MacDonald, Flora's brother, came up with the St Andrew's Day anecdote in chapter 8.

The book you have just read would not have been possible without the wholehearted support of Philip Cercone, editorial director, his assistant Joanne Pisano, and their crew at McGill-Queen's University Press. Managing Editor Kathleen Fraser was a pleasure to deal with, as was Neil Erickson, who managed the production of *Flora!* through his firm Sayre Street Books. Louise Piper did a superb job as copy editor. My thanks as well to the publicity and marketing folks at MQUP for their hard work to make *Flora!* a great success. And, not least, thanks to lawyer Warren Sheffer for his advice and patience in assisting with the book contract.

Unfortunately, Flora's final years were not easy. As her health declined, she became increasingly dependent on friends and caregivers. I know she would want me to express her profound thanks to Elizabeth Davies, André LeBlanc, Cathy Doolan and Cecilia Falcone Germano for everything they did for her as the end neared.

Geoffrey Stevens

Notes

1 A literal translation of samawat would probably be "refuge" in English.

CHAPTER TWO

1 Brittany, in northwestern France, is the traditional homeland of the Breton people. It is still sometimes called Lesser or Little Britain.

2 The words of Samuel Johnson are quoted on a plaque honouring Flora MacDonald at Fort Edward Blockhouse in Windsor, Nova Scotia. There are also memorials to this gallant woman in Inverness, Skye and Uist in Scotland. – G.S.

3 My father being the fourth of four boys, I think they ran out of good Scottish names. He was named George Frederick MacDonald after the long-serving premier of Nova Scotia, George Frederick Murray. It may seem strange that my grandfather, a proud Tory, would give his son the name of a Liberal premier, but they were friends. Murray invited my grandfather to go to Halifax as his guest at the opening of the Nova Scotia Legislature each year.

4 Some literary sleuths believe the Treasure Island in Robert Louis Stevenson's tale was his fictional representation of Norman Island, a deserted key in the British Virgin Islands. – G.S.

CHAPTER THREE

1 My elder sister Jean recalls our parents telling her about the principal's advice. I was not aware of it at the time.

2 Owned and operated by the Newfoundland Railway, the ss *Caribou* made the Newfoundland-Nova Scotia crossing three times a week with a naval escort during the war. Of its 237 passengers and crew, 137 perished on that fateful day, 13 October 1942.

3 Meaning: "wonderful to relate."

4 "Then Agrippa said unto Paul, 'Thou art permitted to speak for thyself.' Then Paul stretched forth the hand, and answered for himself."
Acts 26:1-32, King James Version.

5 The Campbells behaved themselves. Fred MacDonald lived to be eighty-eight. Mollie MacDonald was three weeks shy of 102 when she died.

CHAPTER FOUR

1 The English finally did correct a historic wrong by returning the Stone of Destiny. On St Andrew's Day, 30 November 1996, Prince Andrew, representing his mother, Queen Elizabeth II, formally presented the stone to Michael Forsythe, the secretary of state for Scotland. It may be seen today in Edinburgh Castle.

2 My loathing for "Butcher" Cumberland persists. Years later, in the summer of 1989, I was invited to address a conference at which the formation of an organization known as the Commonwealth Human Rights Initiative was discussed. I ended up chairing that group for a number of years. The meeting was held in a lecture room in Cumberland House, an estate on the grounds of Windsor Castle. I was appalled to discover that I would be speaking under a large oil portrait of "Butcher." Before beginning, I climbed on a chair and turned the dreaded duke to the wall. My listeners were stunned. Whether they were intrigued or horrified, I could not tell.

3 Selfridges is the retailer that coined the slogan, "The customer is always right."

4 For all the time I was away, I made a point of writing a detailed "Dear Folks" letter home every week or so. When I had access to a typewriter, I would type the letter and send it to my parents with carbon copies for my siblings. When I was traveling, I would write in longhand and send the letter to my father who would type it with copies for everyone. It was an efficient way to keep in touch. It also amounted to a lot of words. A typical letter might fill four to six single-spaced legal-sized sheets. The

letters – something over a hundred thousand words – are now in are now in Library and Archives Canada in Ottawa.

5 There are, as I learned, nine gallons to a firkin and two pins to a firkin.

6 Beverley Baxter (1891–1964) was a piano salesman in Toronto before he went overseas to serve in the First World War. After the war, he stayed in Britain where he became one of that country's best-known journalists as editor of the *Daily Express* and a political commentator for the *Sunday Times* group. His "Letter from London" in *Maclean's* was "must" reading in thousands of Canadian households during the Second World War.

7 The hospital, which traces its origins to 1215, is where Florence Nightingale started her famous nursing school in 1859.

8 Now part of the University of Westminster, London Polytechnic was founded as Regent Street Polytechnic in 1881. It was the first institution in the United Kingdom to offer a full university education to working-class people. The curriculum includes tailored professional programs, short courses, and night, as well as day, classes. There are currently about twenty-four thousand students.

9 Dorothy and I managed to see the Queen once more before we left London for the summer. Two of our male friends, Peter Goodman, a South African, and a New Zealander, George Turner, escorted us to the Epsom Derby. The Queen and Duke of Edinburgh were in the Royal Box and the rumour among the common folk was that, on account of the coronation, the race had been fixed in favour of her horse, Aureole. However, Aureole, was beaten by four lengths by Pinza, ridden by Sir Gordon Richards.

10 The Dodgers would break the hearts of Brooklyn fans by moving to Los Angeles. The Braves started in Boston, paused in Milwaukee and moved on to Atlanta. – G.S.

11 Intellect, liberalism, and idealism went only so far in the United States of the 1950s. Adlai Stevenson was crushed by Republican Dwight Eisenhower in the 1956 election, as he had been on his first attempt four years earlier. Defeated by John F. Kennedy for the Democratic Party nomination in 1960, Stevenson later served as United States ambassador to the United Nations.

12 The Nova Scotian Leonard Jones is not be confused with another Leonard Jones, a one-time mayor of Moncton, New Brunswick, whom Robert Stanfield refused to accept as a Progressive Conservative candidate in the 1974 federal election because of his virulent opposition to bilingualism. Jones, however, won the Moncton seat as an independent.

CHAPTER FIVE

1 Despite his distrust of Fleming, Diefenbaker made him minister of Finance. Another leadership rival, Davie Fulton, became minister of Justice.

2 Camp and his advertising associates created two powerful ads that became the centerpiece of the Tories' $200,000 advertising campaign in the 1957 election. One listed our endorsements and declared, "It's Time for a Diefenbaker Government." The other used a *Globe and Mail* cartoon by James Reidford that depicted the Peace Tower as a guillotine. It carried the headline, "Black Friday," a reference to the day when the Liberals used closure to cut off debate on the pipeline bill.

3 Sidney Smith was re-elected in the 1958 general election, but his tenure as secretary of state for External Affairs was brief. He died unexpectedly in March 1959 and was succeeded at External by Howard Green.

4 The governor general has two official residences, Rideau Hall in Ottawa and the Citadel in Quebec City. On this occasion, Governor General Vincent Massey was in residence at the Citadel.

5 In the end, I did vote Conservative, reluctantly.

CHAPTER SIX

1 Diefenbaker still holds the record of the largest majority in Canadian history. His 209 seats represented 79 per cent of the 265 seats then in the Commons. Brian Mulroney is the runner-up, with 211, or 75 per cent, of the 282 seats in an expanded House in 1984.

2 Dalton Camp and I were both interviewed, separately and at length, about the Diefenbaker years as part of an oral history project conducted by Professor Jack Granatstein and his colleagues at York University in the late 1960s. Transcripts of those interviews are in the university archives.

3 I acquired quite a reputation myself for late-night telephoning. When Bob Stanfield retired as national Conservative leader, he told people there was one thing he was really looking forward to: no more phone calls at midnight from Flora MacDonald.

4 Hatfield was right. The Landry family had originally come from New Brunswick.

5 The subject of interference surfaced later, during the 1962 election campaign, when the new American ambassador, Walton Butterworth, held briefings for Canadian journalists at his residence in Ottawa. Diefenbaker interpreted the briefings as an attempt to influence the election. The Americans saw them as an effort to correct some of Diefenbaker's public

misrepresentations of policy on Canada. I agreed with Diefenbaker, but I blamed our journalists for letting themselves be used more than I blamed the State Department for using them. In any event, I do not think the episode had any effect on the election outcome.

6 In fact, Robarts, who understood the mood of Ontario, took virtually no part in the election after that first appearance.

7 My intuition proved correct. Canada eventually did accept nuclear warheads. But it was too late for Diefenbaker. By then, several cabinet ministers had resigned, his minority government had been defeated in Parliament, and it had lost the April 1963 election.

CHAPTER SEVEN

1 Egan Chambers ran in Montreal's St Lawrence-St George riding. He was crushed by Liberal John Turner, the future party leader and prime minister.

2 Rupert Brooke was commissioned in the Royal Navy at the outset of the First World War and joined the Dardanelles expedition. He never saw enemy action. He died of septicemia as a result of a mosquito bite – or possibly of food poisoning – on a hospital ship off Skyros in 1915. I had long been enamoured of his famous poem, "The Soldier" –

> *If I should die, think only this of me:*
> *That there's some corner of a foreign field*
> *That is forever England.*

3 Camp did try privately to persuade Diefenbaker to compromise on the flag – to no avail.

4 That campaign raised about $40,000, which was not too bad under the circumstances.

5 Lucien Rivard, a minor underworld figure with purported connections to the Liberal Party, was sought by United States authorities on narcotic charges. He was arrested in Montreal. There were allegations that an aide to a Liberal cabinet minister had offered a bribe to the lawyer representing the government not to oppose bail for Rivard. While fighting extradition, Rivard escaped from Bordeaux jail after he borrowed a garden hose to flood the skating rink, even though the temperature was above freezing. He used the hose to climb the jail wall. A royal commission criticized Liberal Justice Minister Guy Favreau's handling of the affair. Favreau resigned. Rivard was eventually recaptured and sentenced to twenty years in prison. – G.S.

6 With the second question – "Should the leader resign?" – deleted from
   the questionnaire, members of the national executive voted on the first
   question, whether to hold a leadership convention. The exact tally was
   never announced, but the vote was heavily against calling a convention.

7 George Hogan also sought election in Toronto. He was crushed by Liberal
   Robert Winters in York West. Depressed by his defeat and beset by
   personal and business problems, Hogan committed suicide in early 1966.

8 Prior to his appointment as national director, James Johnston owned the
   Aurora Banner. He sold that paper to the *Toronto Star* and purchased the
   Sentinel Star in Cobourg and the *Evening Guide* in Port Hope. He died
   in 1988.

CHAPTER EIGHT

1 Camp was not the only one left out of the loop. Diefenbaker also did not
   discuss Johnston's appointment with Gordon Churchill, the Winnipeg MP
   and former cabinet minister, who had been the conduit between the Hill –
   the leader's office and the caucus – and national headquarters. In the
   absence of a national director, Churchill was the person to whom I
   reported. He told me he knew nothing about Johnston's appointment
   until he read about it in the newspapers. The circle of people in whom
   Diefenbaker confided was growing ever smaller.

2 Don Jamieson won that by-election easily. Appointed to Pierre Trudeau's
   cabinet in 1968, he served in a variety of portfolios, including Foreign
   Affairs, until 1979. After he left politics, he was named Canadian high
   commissioner in London.

3 Camp deliberately did not mention Diefenbaker by name at the Albany
   Club or any time in the months leading to the party's annual meeting in
   November. If he referred to the leader at all, he would call him "Charlie."

4 Dalton Camp, oral history interview with J.L. Granatstein, 14 December
   1967.

5 *The Night of the Knives* was published in 1969. A frequent critic of Joe
   Clark's leadership, Bob Coates continued in Parliament for another
   nineteen years. In 1984, Brian Mulroney appointed him minister of
   National Defence. Coates resigned from the cabinet less than a year later,
   following a minor scandal involving a visit he made to a strip club while
   he was in Germany on government business. He died in 2016.

6 Camp's concerns were well founded. Hees placed second on the first
   ballot, behind Bob Stanfield but ahead of Duff Roblin, the eventual
   runner-up.

CHAPTER NINE

1   Tom Axworthy is the brother of Lloyd Axworthy, who held a number of federal cabinet posts, including foreign minister. John Rae's younger brother, Bob, became premier of Ontario as a New Democrat and later served as interim leader of the federal Liberal Party.

2   Reform does not come quickly to the correctional service. Despite some physical improvements at P4W over the years, in 1970 the Royal Commission on the Status for Women also recommended that the prison be closed. It took another thirty years, but it finally happened in 2000.

3   Ironically, it was Brian Mulroney's Conservative government, of which I was a member, that scrapped FIRA, replacing it with Investment Canada, a federal agency with a mandate to encourage, not to limit, foreign investment.

4   The National Defence College fell victim to federal budget cuts in the 1990s when the government decided to scrap the program. I thought that was a shame.

CHAPTER TEN

1   Sauvé and Monique Bégin became ministers in the Trudeau government and Sauvé later became speaker of the House and then governor general. Albanie Morin died during her second term in 1976. The New Democrat, Grace MacInnis, represented Vancouver-Kingsway from 1965 to 1974. She was the daughter of J.S. Woodsworth, the first leader of the Coopérative Commonwealth Federation, forerunner of the NDP.

2   Progress came slowly. Although five more women were elected as Liberal MPs in the 1974 election, I remained the only woman MP in the Progressive Conservative caucus until Jean Pigott was elected in a by-election in 1976 in Ottawa-Carleton.

3   Ian Green, who had been an active member of the Young Progressive Conservatives, later served as an assistant to Bob Stanfield, then joined the federal public service where he rose to become a deputy minister. He was very bright.

4   Of the 710 people who have been executed in Canada, 697 were men and 13 were women.

5   Having campaigned against wage and price controls in 1974, the Trudeau government reversed itself in 1975, implementing an anti-inflation program that included wage and price controls. The program remained in effect until 1978.

6 Although the death penalty was deleted from the Criminal Code in 1976, it actually survived (although it was not used) in the National Defence Act until 1998 as punishment for such crimes as cowardice, desertion, unlawful surrender, treason, and mutiny.

7 In 1967, Mary Walker Sawka, a nuisance candidate, had polled two votes at the Tory leadership convention. In 1975, Rosemary Brown ran second to Ed Broadbent for the national leadership of the New Democratic Party.

CHAPTER ELEVEN

1 Michael Vaughan went on to become a parliamentary reporter with CBC Television. Murray Coolican became a deputy minister in the Ontario government and married Bob Stanfield's youngest daughter, Mimi. Michel de Salaberry became a Middle East specialist and Canadian ambassador to Jordan, Iran and Egypt. Patrick Martin was co-host (with Bronwyn Drainie) of CBC Radio's "Sunday Morning" program, then joined *The Globe and Mail*, where he has been the paper's Middle East correspondent and Comment editor. Terry O'Connor became a judge. Ron Atkey regained his seat and became a cabinet minister. Joe Clark won the leadership and became prime minister.

2 By 1976, Indira Gandhi had been prime minister of India for 10 years, Sirimavo Bandaranaike was in her second term as prime minister of Sri Lanka, and Golda Meir, known as the "Iron Lady" of Israeli politics, had already served for five years as prime minister of her country (1969–1974). Another "Iron Lady," Margaret Thatcher, had been chosen leader of Britain's opposition Conservative party in 1975. In Canada, by the end of the 1970s the New Democrats were the only federal party that had come close to choosing a woman to lead them; Rosemary Brown, a Black activist from Vancouver, placed second to Ed Broadbent at their leadership convention in 1975.

3 At the leadership convention in February 1976, Claude Wagner led for the first three ballots, only to be beaten by Joe Clark on the fourth.

4 "Questions About the Hopeful," *The Globe and Mail*, Oct. 7, 1975

5 Three other candidates who stayed on for the second ballot were embarrassed. Paul Hellyer's total dropped by 113, John Fraser's by ninety-three and Pat Nowlan's by forty-four.

6 The "Flora Syndrome" does not affect women candidates alone. The syndrome surfaced again at the next Tory convention, in 1983, when Michael Wilson, a former cabinet minister, received only 144 first-ballot votes, about one-half of the number he was sure he would get.

CHAPTER TWELVE

1 Two years later, Pierre Trudeau appointed Wagner to the Senate. The appointment could be interpreted either as a humanitarian gesture, as Wagner was in failing health, or as a cynical bid to capture his seat, which the Liberals did in the ensuing by-election. Wagner died just a few weeks after the 1979 election.

2 Neither of these proposals came to fruition. Equalization arrangements continue to be a nettlesome issue in the dialogue between Ottawa and the provinces. Premiers are still talking about the need for restraints on federal spending power. Some things never change. – G.S.

3 Jean Pigott's arrival in Parliament meant I was no longer the only woman in the Tory caucus. Unfortunately, she was there for only three years. She lost to Liberal Jean-Luc Pepin in the 1979 general election.

4 Although the Progressive Conservatives won a plurality of the seats, the Liberals with their massive vote in Quebec led in the popular vote nation-wide with 40 per cent to our 36 per cent. We carried the popular vote in seven provinces, all except New Brunswick, Newfoundland, and, of course, Quebec. Quebec was a huge disappointment; we took only two of the province's seventy-five seats. An equally large disappointment was the failure to elect significant numbers of women. Of 195 women candidates for all parties in the 1979 election, only ten were elected and only two were Tories – Diane Stratas from Scarborough, Ontario, and me.

CHAPTER THIRTEEN

1 It was one of the great exoduses of human history. The United Nations High Commissioner for Refugees estimated that over a period of several years no fewer than 929,000 refugees from Vietnam and later Cambodia managed to reach asylum while another 250,000 died at sea, either drowned or murdered by pursuers or pirates.

2 Diefenbaker's final train ride attracted crowds in every town it passed through. There was massive media coverage. Most news organizations assigned someone from their Ottawa bureau to travel on the funeral train. The *Globe and Mail*, however, sent its celebrated medical reporter, Joan Hollobon, from its Toronto office. When asked why, the paper's managing editor explained, "We wanted her to make sure the old bastard was truly dead."

3 The Jewish vote was of particular concern to Atkey. His riding, Toronto

St Paul's, was a swing seat and 23 per cent of its voters identified themselves as Jewish.

4 Joe had a tendency to become stubborn when crossed. The same trait
caused him to insist that John Crosbie's budget be put to a confidence vote
in December 1979. We could have delayed the vote for a few days until
our absent members, including me, were present, but the vote went ahead.
We lost it – and, with it, the government.

5 Stanfield also produced a final report in which he recommended the
Canadian government offer support for a Palestinian homeland. By then it
was February 1980 and none of us cared. We were locked in an election
campaign that we were doomed to lose.

6 John Crosbie brimmed with overconfidence. In his 1997 memoir,
No Holds Barred, Crosbie wrote: "I approached the election campaign
with gusto, confident that the Canadian people would vindicate us. I
thought we'd hand the Liberals the defeat of the century. This view was
widely held among Conservatives, and it was not until the results of
polling, both private and public, started to come in during January that
we realized we were likely to be defeated."

7 Pelletier gave his account of the hostage crisis and the dogged reporting
that led him to the story in *The Canadian Caper*, a book he co-authored
with Claude Adams, published by Macmillan of Canada, in 1981.

8 In his book, Pelletier quoted Roger Lucy's outburst: "Jesus Christ, goddam
incredible! ... They screwed up a goddam entry date in this visa. The CIA
screwed up. Can you beat that? Those assholes fucked up."

9 These were not the final words on the "Canadian Caper." A 2012
Hollywood film, *Argo*, directed by Ben Affleck, angered Canadians who
remembered the hostage crisis. The film portrayed the exfiltration of the six
Americans as a CIA-inspired, CIA-controlled operation, minimizing
Canada's role. When former President Jimmy Carter was invited to come to
Kingston to accept an honorary degree from Queen's University later in
2012, he agreed – on condition that Flora and Ken Taylor be invited to
attend so that he could thank them personally for saving the six Americans.
In his convocation address Carter termed *Argo* "a distortion," adding that
the Canadian scheme was "one of the most remarkable rescue operations in
history." From Kingston, he went to Ottawa to thank Joe Clark. – G.S.

CHAPTER FOURTEEN

1 I found myself in a similarly awkward situation when canvassing with
Rod Black for the vote of another elderly man in Halifax during the

1963 federal election. A different election, a different old man – it is in Chapter 7.

2 Brian Mulroney, *Memoirs 1930–1993* (Toronto: McClelland & Stewart, 2007), 53.

3 In 2004, Rosie Abella, born in a displaced persons camp in Germany after the Second World War, was elevated to the Supreme Court of Canada by Prime Minister Paul Martin, making her the first Jewish woman to serve on the nation's highest court.

4 Michael Sabia was appointed deputy minister of Finance in December 2020. – G.S.

5 Mulroney, *Memoirs*, 494–97.

6 In a diary entry for 16 September 1984, the day before the Mulroney cabinet was to be sworn in, Gotlieb wrote that he feared the Americans would be disappointed by the Conservatives. "[Mulroney's] team is inexperienced. His party is full of red conservatives (Clark, MacDonald). The bureaucracy will have great influence." – Allan Gotlieb, *The Washington Diaries 1981–1989* (Toronto: McClelland & Stewart, 2006), 248.

7 Gotlieb, *The Washington Diaries,* 11.

8 *Ottawa Citizen,* 29 November 2006.

9 Mulroney, *Memoirs,* 115.

CHAPTER FIFTEEN

1 One involvement led inexorably to others. My post-politics career has included membership on the board of directors or advisory council for the Canadian Council for Refugees, CARE Canada, Future Generations Canada, Commonwealth Human Rights Initiative (Patron); Friends of the Library and National Archives Canada; Partnership Africa-Canada; and United Nations Development Fund for Women (UNIFEM) Canada. In addition to IDRC, I have served as chair of HelpAge International, Shastri Indo-Canada Advisory Council, Partnership Africa-Canada, and Future Generations International.

2 To put this figure in perspective, the estimated number of casualties in Rwanda genocide is greater than the combined loss of lives of Canadian and American soldiers during the Second World War.

3 While some have been critical of General Dallaire's efforts to curb the violence during the genocide, it has been well documented since 1994 how underfunded the mission was and how little chance General Dallaire's troops had to control violence. After returning to Canada, General

Dallaire suffered from post-traumatic stress disorder, and attempted to take his own life. He has managed to cope with the disorder, and from 2005 to 2014 he served as a member of the Canadian Senate. His experiences before, during and after the Rwandan genocide are masterfully articulated in his book, *Shake Hands With The Devil*.

4   When I became involved with the work of the Carnegie Commission on Preventing Deadly Conflict, which was established in 1994, I appealed to the United Nations secretary general of the day, Boutros Boutros-Ghali, to set up an office to assemble and coordinate information from NGOs around the world, especially in emergency situations. The idea was never followed through.

5   The country was known as Zaire from October 1971 to May 1997, during the reign of Mobutu Sese Seko. Following the ousting of Mobutu, new leader Laurent-Desire Kabila changed the country's name to the Democratic Republic of the Congo.

6   Lucie, a graduate of the Kennedy School of Government at Harvard University, spent nearly two decades representing Canada at the United Nations and a number of other international bodies. In 2009, following her retirement from the civil service, she was awarded the Department of Foreign Affairs' Lifetime Achievement Award of Excellence.

7   Smillie, an architect of the Kimberley Process, ultimately lost faith in its effectiveness and resigned from the process in 2009.

8   The Second Congo War claimed thirty-eight million lives between 1998 and 2003.

9   An author and social activist, John Trent went on to become a professor and chair of the department of political science at the University of Ottawa where he is a fellow of the university's Centre on Governance.

10   Kerala is known for its large Christian community, its literacy rate (the highest in India), and its excellent educational institutions. Many highly trained young women from Kerala come to Canada where they work in our hospitals in x-ray departments and other specialized jobs.

11   According to the late Canadian diplomat Geoffrey Pearson, who appointed me chairperson of the Shastri Institute, the organization arose out of discussions between former Indian Prime Minister Jawaharlal Nehru and Geoff Pearson's father, former Prime Minister Pearson, over how India could repay Canada for its shipments of grain in the 1960s. They decided that funding Canadians academics to study in India would be sufficient payment.

12   The official language of the state is Assamese, an Indo-Aryan language that is also spoken in parts of Arunachal Pradesh and Bhutan.

13 The maximum number of seats that can be occupied in the Lok Sabha is
    552, made up by an election of up to 530 members to represent India's
    twenty-eight states, up to twenty members to represent India's seven
    Union territories and no more than two members of the Anglo-Indian
    community.

14 In 1961, according to the Census of India, no fewer than 1,652 different
    languages were spoken in the subcontinent. The 2001 census reported that
    twenty-nine languages each had more than one million native speakers.

15 The highest civilian award in India is the Padma Bhushan, followed by the
    Padma Vibhushan, the Bharat Ratna, and then the Padma Shri. In 2008,
    a second Canadian, Dr Joseph Hulse, a biochemist and former
    vice-president of the International Development Research Centre, was
    awarded the Padma Shri.

16 The majority of my work in India was in its northern states; particularly
    the north-eastern states, which are quite unique and are largely ignored by
    other NGOs.

17 In Hindi, Gaon means "village," while Bura means "the head or leader or
    elder."

18 By the time I joined Daniel Taylor, an estimated 80 per cent of Tibet's vast
    forests had been destroyed by human activity. Deforestation caused the
    soil erosion that produced massive deposits of silt, which raised riverbeds,
    contributing to devastating floods and landslides downstream. Daniel and
    I travelled to mountain villages throughout the Tibetan Plateau – "The
    Roof of the World," as it is often called – to enlist local people as partners
    in our Future Generations campaign of conservation and reforestation.

19 At the high altitudes (4,000–4,500 metres) where we worked, the temper-
    ature in winter was generally below freezing during the day, while dropping
    at night to minus 20-25 degrees Celsius and, on occasion, to minus 40.

20 That spectacular photo of Mount Everest hung on a wall in my Ottawa
    apartment for many years.

21 No one on the Canadian team made it to the summit of Everest without
    oxygen that year. It was not until 24 May 2010 that Laval St Germain, a
    Calgary pilot and father of four, accomplished the feat. St Germain was
    quite an adventurer. On New Year's Eve, 2018, he reached the top of
    Antarctica's Mount Vinson and thereby added the "Seven Summits" to his
    resume, having climbed the highest peak on every continent. – G.S.

22 The Gama Valley is one of the few valleys in the Himalayas without a
    village. According to Tibetans, this valley was opened to them in the 8th
    century by Guru Rinpoche, the "Precious Master," who founded Tibetan
    Buddhism.

23 This pass was actually higher than either of the base camps on Mount
   Everest. The south base camp, in Nepal, was at 5,360 metres; the north
   one, in Tibet, was at 5,545 metres.
24 Seth is most famous for his 1,474-page novel, *A Suitable Boy*, which was
   awarded the Commonwealth Writers Prize 1994.
25 Guru Rinpoche is said to have brought Vajrayana Buddhism – a system of
   Buddhist thought and practice – to Bhutan and Tibet in the 8th Century.
   Some of his followers regard him as a second coming of Buddha.
26 The members of the Silk Road Seven, in addition to Jean Perlin and me,
   were: Alex Volkoff, who was posted with CIDA in Beijing; Carolyn
   McAskie, former Canadian High Commissioner in Sri Lanka; Sylvia
   Spring, freelance journalist and film maker and Carolyn's partner; Dianne
   Kennedy, one of my political supporters in Kingston who worked as a
   volunteer in villages in Nepal and India; and Jenny Raper, a British hiking
   friend from Geneva where Jean was posted with CIDA.
27 Tashi deLek translates roughly as "blessings and good luck."

CHAPTER SIXTEEN

1 The Shahidan valley is in western Bamyan province, about 260 km
   northwest of Kabul.
2 Shura is an Arabic word for "consultation," or the process of
   decision-making by consultation and deliberation. The term is
   mentioned in the Quran and is a word that is sometimes used when
   referring to the parliaments in Muslim-majority countries.
3 Bamyan Town lies northwest of Kabul, Afghanistan's capital, in the
   Bamyan valley at an elevation of 2,590 metres. Bamyan is first mentioned
   in fifth century-AD Chinese records. It was visited by the Buddhist monks
   and travellers Fa-hsien around AD 400 and Hsüan-tsang in AD 630.
4 Resistance to females in government is not confined to the so called
   "less developed" or "developing" world. As foreign minister in Clark's
   cabinet in 1979 – at that time I was the only female foreign minister in
   the world – I often had people at conferences look oddly at me and ask
   "What are you doing here?" or worse, "Would you please fetch me a
   cup of coffee?" I have never been the coffee-fetching kind.
5 The American historian Nancy Dupree wrote in her 1970 book,
   An Historical Guide to Afghanistan, that a full description of Band-e Amir
   would "rob the uninitiated of the wonder and amazement it produces on
   all who gaze upon it."

6 Christopher Alexander was Canada's first resident ambassador in Afghanistan. He left the diplomatic service and was elected to Parliament in 2011. He served as Minister of Citizenship and Immigration from 2013 to 2015 when he lost his seat. He ran unsuccessfully for the leadership of the Conservative Party of Canada in 2017. – G.S.

7 To become a Canadian citizen, an adult must have lived in Canada for at least three years (1,095 days) over the course of the previous four years before applying.

Index